The Columbus Conspiracy

A 16th-century allegorical woodcut that
might be entitled "the ship of discovery"
navigating through the night of Europe's
geographical ignorance. The cross-like
objects are not religious tokens but are
backstaffs, a primitive ancestor of the
astrolabe and sextant.

Anonymous woodcut, frontispiece from Chamisso's
Reise um die Welt ed. Leipzig 1842.

An Investigation into the Secret History
of Christopher Columbus

The Columbus Conspiracy

Michael Bradley

HOUNSLOW

The Columbus Conspiracy
Copyright © 1991 by Michael Bradley
All Rights Reserved.
ISBN 0-88882-131-X

Second Printing, October 1991

Publisher: Anthony Hawke
Editor: Dennis Mills
Designer: Gerard Williams
Typography: Attic Typesetting Inc.
Printer: Gagné Printing Ltd.
Front Cover Woodcut: Courtesy New York Public Library

Publication was assisted by
the Canada Council and
the Ontario Arts Council

Hounslow Press
A Division of Anthony R. Hawke Limited
124 Parkview Avenue
Willowdale, Ontario, Canada. M2N 3Y5

Printed and bound in Canada

For those who offered assistance and encouragement:
my friend, John Ross Matheson,
Susan Savage, Rob Iveson, Deanna Theilmann-Bean;
and for my son, Jason.

But mostly for Jacques de Molay, René d'Anjou,
Esclarmonde de Foix, Christopher Columbus,
Henry Sinclair and all the other heroes and
heroines who struggled to preserve a secret
treasure. The world knows it vaguely only by the
troubadour code words "Holy Grail," but it may well
have been, and may remain, the living reality
behind human progress in the West.

Contents

Foreword

by Dr. W.A. Douglas Jackson

We know that it is extremely unlikely that Columbus could have been the son of humble wool-carders. He acquired too much (unexplained) education to have sprung from such origins in the Middle Ages. From his arrival in Portugal it is evident that he wielded some mysterious power, prestige and even wealth. This suggests to a number of modern experts that he could only have been the scion of some royal or noble family, a family just as mysteriously obscure as Columbus himself. But his rank allowed him to marry quickly into Portuguese aristocracy when he took Felipa Perestrello as his wife, and, when she died, his rank allowed him to court several noble and wealthy women of Spain as mistresses. He was the favored friend of Spanish dukes and the Portuguese king and queen—not to mention Isabella herself. He hobnobbed with the richest men in Spain on an easy and familiar basis, and these men actually financed his voyage. In class-conscious medieval Europe, these cannot have been the accomplishments of a wool-carder's son who was supposedly only a merchant skipper from Genoa.

Then, as Bradley points out in a very subtle analysis of the documents of agreement between Spain and Columbus (the "Capitulo" and the "Titulo"), Columbus possessed some power that extracted truly preposterous concessions from the Spanish monarchs. Not only that, but the Church advisors of Ferdinand and Isabella—and perhaps the Vatican itself—somehow feared Columbus or his voyage would not have taken place. Then, in some strange fashion still hidden from history, Columbus's successful negotiations with Spain seem to have had some connection with the bloodless surrender of Granada, which ended the "Moorish Problem" for Spain and the Church. On his return from the New World in 1493, Columbus

1

did not return directly to Spain, which had hired him, but to Portugal, the rival of Spain. These facts are inexplicable, the correlations highly suggestive. It is clear that much less than the whole truth has ever been available to "conventional history."

The Columbus Conspiracy is one of the most thought-provoking and controversial books it has been my pleasure to read—just as thought-provoking and controversial as *Holy Grail Across The Atlantic*, which first kindled my interest in Michael Bradley's work. And, in many respects, *The Columbus Conspiracy* is a natural continuation of *Holy Grail Across The Atlantic*, not exactly a sequel but obviously inspired by following the same body of data and some of the same clues. Having met Michael Bradley and having enjoyed many fascinating hours of discussion with him, I know two things about him: he is a serious and conscientious researcher who seeks all the facts he can find and shies away from none of them (as historians so often do); he has an adventurous mind and is unafraid to speculate about constructing a pattern that will accommodate all the facts, however shocking and unfamiliar the resulting pattern may be!

The Columbus Conspiracy is certainly shocking and unfamiliar, but is Bradley's revision of history closer to historical truth than the conventional view of Columbus? I cannot say and even Michael Bradley is cautious about making any such claim. Each reader must judge this exciting new construct on an individual basis. What can be said is that this new look at Columbus not only (for once) accommodates all the facts, but also provides a plausible correlation between religious, economic, military and exploratory events, and forces of Columbus's time. Bradley's revision may not be the "truth" about history, or may not be the whole truth—but it may well be closer to the mark than the conventional picture of Christopher Columbus "of Genoa."

And, indeed, even conservative and conventional historians are now being forced to admit that the traditional picture of Christopher Columbus is one on which the paint has seriously begun to flake and peel. We no longer have a coherent view of Christopher Columbus, but it's something like a jigsaw puzzle: the canvas of history often shows through without any hint or color of the "real" Christopher Columbus. As Bradley points out, we do not even know for certain where Columbus was born, let alone where he was buried. We do not know who he was at all—a merchant sailor from Genoa (the traditional view), a French pirate, a Mallorcan navigator? All of these are possibilities, and the last two offer more historical documentation than "Genoa."

In *The Columbus Conspiracy*, Michael Bradley offers a speculative reconstruction of history, which gives Columbus a satisfactory identity, explains his power and motivations, plausibly correlates other events with the Columbus project, and gives a new perspective on the discovery of America. Whereas this reconstruction seems to embrace all the known facts and strange correlations, it may still not be the truth. But even if it is not the historical truth, no reader will be cheated!—because Bradley plausibly weaves Christopher Columbus into one of the most heroic, romantic and evocative themes of Western culture. For Bradley, Columbus emerges as a central actor in the long saga of the Holy Grail, a man with a secret and noble mission. Even as fiction, *The Columbus Conspiracy* is an exciting and readable story.

But what if it is the truth. . . ?

Dr. W.A. Douglas Jackson
Department of Geography
University of Washington
Seattle, Washington

Author's Forewarning

This book challenges the familiar, traditional story of Christopher Columbus. This unorthodox interpretation of the life of the great discoverer will doubtless anger and disturb some readers who may find it too controversial and too provocative for their taste. Others, however, may find it a refreshing, closer approximation to historical truth—a truth which has always been whispered since the time of the earliest Columbus scholars, a truth daily becoming more insistently audible as new data come to light.

Strangely enough, however, *The Columbus Conspiracy* is not primarily based upon new research and new facts. It is based on a re-examination and re-interpretation of many facts long known to specialists in the study of history and navigation. The problem with these facts has always been that, although they were known by scholars, they could not be made to fit into a coherent and consistent story of the man's life. These facts seemed anomalous because they did not harmonize with the major themes of Columbus's life, career and magnificent achievement. They dangled senselessly. Like unanswerable question marks. Like unspeakable doubts. And so these facts about Columbus were orphaned by almost all biographers. They were simply ignored.

The most familiar American biographer of Columbus, Samuel Eliot Morison (*Admiral of the Ocean Sea*, 1942), mentioned some few of these orphaned facts in a non-sequitur way but made no attempt to insert these awkwardly shaped bits of data into the jigsaw puzzle of Columbus's life. Morison seemed almost defiantly determined that there should be no puzzle, no doubts. For him, Columbus's story was a straightforward one: a Genoese navigator had the novel idea of sailing west to reach the East and, after many frustrations overcome by his own indomitable will, succeeded in "discovering" the New World as a fully orthodox champion of Roman Catholic Spain.

A more recent biographer of the great explorer, the Italian historian, Gianni Granzotto (*Christopher Columbus: The Dream and the Obsession*, 1984), courageously faced the awkward facts but he could not make them conform to any definite and coherent pattern. Granzotto was unable to present a "New Columbus" for our consideration, one as solid as Morison's myth but different. Granzotto was able only to show that the Columbus of Morison and our schoolbooks was as insubstantial and as meaningless as some ephemeral image suggested fleetingly by a summer cloud. The Italian historian ends his book by making the somewhat pathetic point that we do not even know for certain where Christopher Columbus is buried.

More important, perhaps, we do not even know who he was. There is no strong evidence, much less proof, that he was born in Genoa. There are facts suggesting that the man who "discovered" the New World was French, not Italian; that he was a pirate, not a merchant captain; that he was Jewish or a Cathar heretic, not an orthodox Roman Catholic. And finally, there's a great deal of evidence supporting the notion that he sailed on behalf of Jews, Cathar heretics and Moors against the interests of Catholic Spain.

All of this, and more, is strongly suggested by the many awkward and orphaned facts that have been swept beneath the carpet of historical study by scholars.

The Columbus Conspiracy will retrieve these data from under the rug and dust them off well. The awkward facts about Columbus's life will be correlated with the accepted ones. A pattern will emerge that makes sense within the context of the religious and political conflicts of Columbus's time. I do not claim that this pattern is *true*. I claim only that it makes sense and accommodates all the known facts, not just comfortably selected ones. But, because it accommodates the ignored facts along with the accepted ones, the new vision of Columbus offered in the following pages may well deserve serious consideration.

If this new vision of Columbus seems to have some merit, then we are inevitably forced to consider the possibility that Christopher

Columbus was part of a great conspiracy, a conspiracy that was hoary with age even in 1492. Indeed, the evidence for this possibility cannot easily be dismissed.

And if this evidence cannot easily be dismissed, then we are compelled to leave our mental doors ajar to accept a view of European history, and of our own present and future, that is at odds with the purely materialist-economic perspective of civilization's development that has come to dominate the scholarship of our time. If the evidence presented in *The Columbus Conspiracy* is accepted even as a mere possibility, then we must concede that much of our history may have been molded and shaped by an elite, clandestine group working toward some goal we can but dimly perceive.

Further, although Columbus's epic voyage of 1492 happened five hundred years ago, it will become obvious that the conspiracy of which he may have been a part is apparently still going on. Christopher Columbus propelled world history into a new phase, and yet he seems to have been only another worker in an ongoing effort that began centuries before he himself was born.

If this is truly the case, forces beyond our understanding may still be actively forming our present and future beneath the thin veneer of materialistic political economics we like to call reality. Just as The Great Conspiracy apparently originated before Columbus's birth, so it may well have endured long after his death. There are intriguing facts supporting an argument that both earlier and later explorers, colonizers and leaders of the Americas were often secret participants in the same ancient covenant. Their secret purpose seems not to have been wholly submerged beneath the oblivious strivings and jostlings of modern, mass society.

The case for *The Columbus Conspiracy* cannot be proved absolutely. Absolute proof will elude us simply because much of the crucial evidence has been withheld from us by Christopher Columbus himself, and by his supporters and opponents alike, for reasons that become clear as the argument of this book unfolds. But even though the case for *The Columbus Conspiracy* cannot be definitively proven by the data that survives, a vast amount of circumstantial and related evidence is strongly suggestive. Perhaps readers will judge it to be at least as persuasive as evidence for our comfortable schooldays myth.

It may be that the cultural development of humanity has never been what it seems to contemporary scholars and informed laymen. It may be that conventional history is a tragically flawed lens through which we viewed our upward struggle toward civilization with great distortion.

Michael Bradley
Toronto, Canada
January 1991

"It must also be said that Columbus, with his impenetrable silences and the general ambiguousness surrounding most of his life, does nothing at all to help clear the doubts that he leaves in his wake."

Gianni Granzotto, *Christopher Columbus: The Dream and the Obsession* (1984).

"Only puny secrets need protection. Big secrets are protected by public incredulity."

Marshall McLuhan

Chapter One

Landfall

The night of Thursday–Friday, October 11–12, 1492 was, in the words of Samuel Eliot Morison, "the night most fraught with coming events that has ever been lived, on any ship and on any sea."[1]

It was the 33rd day outbound from the Canaries of Columbus's epic first voyage. The tradewinds had returned in strength a few days before, after being fickle for a week or so, and generated an enormous ground swell. Columbus reported in his log that the swells of the last days were the largest he had ever encountered. The surface waves atop the swells were, thankfully, modest. The three ships of Columbus's little fleet rode the huge swells safely, being carried up smoothly to the great height of the crests, and then slipping down into the troughs just as gently. As an experienced navigator, Columbus might well have suspected that land lay not too far ahead simply because of the size of the ground-swell. The gentle rollers of the wind-driven North Equatorial Current were encountering the barrier of the New World's continental shelf. All mariners knew that large swells formed when ocean currents began to encounter offshore shallows.

There were other indications of land. For the past few nights, flights of birds had passed above the fleet, and always the flocks had been on a southwest course. A few days previously the helmsmen on the three vessels had been instructed to alter their own steering so as to follow the birds. So, because of these indications of land, expectation and anticipation were almost as palpable aboard the ships as the bulwarks themselves. Land was ahead.

Nonetheless, the Admiral of the Fleet, Christopher Columbus, allowed the ships to run west-southwest under full sail, and they were making up to 10 knots in the boisterous trades, an exceptional speed for ships of the time. But Columbus had also ordered extra lookouts during the past few days, and on the night of 11–12 October the Admiral himself lingered on the high poop deck of his flagship, the *Santa Maria*, with the west in his eyes.

At about ten o'clock on Thursday night, Columbus thought he saw from the crest of a swell a faint flicker of light to the southwest. . . ."It was like a little wax candle whose flame went up and down, something which very few would have thought to be evidence of land." Not trusting his own eyes alone, Columbus called Pedro Gutiérrez to the high poop deck of the *Santa Maria*. Did Gutiérrez see the flicker? Yes, he too could make out the dim little light. But Rodrigo Sánchez, when he was summoned to the sterncastle of the flagship, peered to the southwest and saw nothing. Lacking this confirmation, Columbus did not signal to the other ships but bided his time.

Four hours later, about 2:00 A.M. on Friday, October 12, Rodrigo de Triana of the *Pinta* sang out the long-awaited "Tierra!" "Land ho!" from the crow's nest. This time there was no doubt. First, Martín Alonso Pinzón, captain of the *Pinta* confirmed the sighting and then all hands aboard the three ships could make out the indisputable solid shadow on the western horizon. Columbus estimated the land to be about six miles distant. Since there might well be offshore reefs and rocks obscured by the giant swells, he prudently ordered the little fleet to heave-to until dawn.

Sunrise revealed an island, the first land since leaving the Canaries a little over a month before, ". . . the most landlike land of all the land that any sailor has ever seen."[2]

There was no safe anchorage on the windward and seaward side of the island where the groundswell tripped on the bottom to tumble over itself in a heavy surf, so Columbus was obliged to order the fleet to sail around the island into the lee of the land. The island was not very large and this manoeuver required about seven hours. A little after noon the ships dropped anchor in five fathoms of crystal clear water to a firm sand bottom about midway along the island's leeward shore. One boat was lowered from each ship, and Columbus stepped onto the beach flanked by his two captains, Martin Alonso Pinzón of the *Pinta* and Vincente Yáñez Pinzón, commander of the *Niña*. With them on the beach were a number of ships' officers and functionaries representing the monarchs of Spain. Rodrigo de Escobedo, a lawyer, was present to record every word of Columbus's declaration of formal possession. This was not long in coming. Columbus named the island San Salvador ("Holy Savior"), and claimed it for Ferdinand and Isabella of Spain.

Rodrigo de Escobedo wrote as Columbus spoke. All those present on the beach signed the document as witnesses as soon as the parchment was dry.

Local Indians peeked from the palmetto underbrush and from behind the trunks of scattered palm trees, bemused by the strange antics of the strange men on their beach. We cannot know what they thought, or conjectured, for at that frozen instant in time there was no possible communication between the Spaniards and the Caribbean Indians. Later Spanish accounts stated that these Indians believed that Columbus had performed a magical rite of some kind, but that was after the Indians had learned of the Spanish lust for gold, after some had been kidnapped to perform as translators, after at least one of their women had been brutally raped. Perhaps, when communication of a basic sort became possible, they sought to appease the Spaniards in their naive way by attributing to Columbus magical powers which had value in their own society, but which unknowingly damned them as pagans to be exploited further. Bartolomé de Las Casas recorded their actions on the beach for posterity:

> The Indians, of whom there was a large number, gazed dumbstruck at the Christians, looking with wonder at their beards, their clothes and the whiteness of their skins. They directed their attentions toward the men with beards, but especially toward the admiral, who they realized was the most important person of the group, either from his imposing physical appearance or from his scarlet clothing. They touched the mens' beards with their fingers and carefully examined the paleness of their hands and faces. Seeing they were innocent, the admiral and his men did not resist their actions.[3]

This meeting between befuddled Caribbean Indians and self-possessed Spaniards proved to be the most fateful and momentous encounter in reliably recorded human history. It changed the world, and very rapidly, too. Within forty years most native Amerindian cultures and civilizations were completely halted in their natural development; within four hundred years native Americans had been all but completely exterminated. At the same time, and just as rapidly, Europe was flooded with new wealth and new vitality. New World gold financed the Renaissance and, two hundred years later, New World products like cotton and rum formed the basis for the Industrial Revolution. Europe itself, all but stalled in a religious and economic miasma in 1492, discovered the vitality (goaded by greed) to found colonies across the Atlantic which have, in some ways, superceded the political, economic, social and intellectual structures of their European parent cultures.

Repercussions of the 1492 voyage were not, of course, limited to effects on Europe and America. The entire world was changed, uprooted, and catapulted out of life-patterns that had endured for thousands of years. Columbus's discovery was the curtain-raiser of a drama that the world is still acting out.

And Columbus's discovery has been grossly misunderstood. What *did* Christopher Columbus actually discover that precipitated such a dramatic impact on the world?

Chapter Two

Key to Discovery,
Key of Bondage

Columbus did not "discover" America or the New World. Europeans have a conveniently egocentric view of the world and, as Thor Heyerdahl, among others, has pointed out, when Columbus waded ashore on San Salvador's beach there were people there to meet him. Anthropologists are generally agreed that humanity did not evolve separately on the American continents, and so the puzzled Indians of San Salvador must have migrated there somehow. *Their* ancestors really discovered America and most ethnologists are agreed that they did it by crossing the Bering Land Bridge from Asia during, or before, the last Ice Age.

But if we mean, in European Man's egocentric perspective, that "discovery" is properly defined *as discovery by Europeans*, then Columbus can still not be credited with discovering the American continents in this way.

It is now well beyond dispute that Norsemen visited the North American continent from about 980 A.D. until perhaps the 14th century. The more conservative historians are willing to accept that Vikings occupied the L'Anse aux Meadows site in northern Newfoundland, but most historians now believe from the *sagas* that an extensive stretch of the Atlantic seaboard from Nova Scotia to Chesapeake was also known to the medieval Scandinavians.

Less universally, at least some scholars are ready to concede that Irish seafaring monks reached America earlier than the Vikings. An adventurous handful of experts support the idea that America was reached even earlier because obscure lines hint that some western land was well known to several Classical writers of the Ancient World. We need only to quote two of them who offer rather circumstantial accounts of the Punic-Iberian discovery, descriptions of this new continent, and what became of this early European presence in the Americas. First, Aristotle in Section 84 of *On Marvellous Things Heard*, wrote in the 4th century before Christ:

> In the sea outside the Pillars of Hercules they say that an island was found by Carthagenians, a wilderness having wood of all kinds and navigable rivers, remarkable for various kinds of fruits, and many days' sailing distance away. When the Carthagenians, who were masters of the western ocean, observed that many traders and other men, attracted by the fertility of the soil and the pleasant climate, frequented it because of its richness, and some resided there, they feared that knowledge of this land would reach other nations, and that a great concourse to it of men from various lands of the earth would follow. Therefore, lest the Carthagenian Empire itself should suffer injury, and the dominion of the sea be wrested from their hands, the Senate of Carthage issued a decree that no one, under penalty of death, should thereafter sail thither, and they massacred all who resided there.[1]

About three hundred years later, Diodorus of Sicily wrote in a similar vein:

> Over against Africa lies a very great island in the vast ocean many days' sail from Libya westwards. The soil there is very fruitful, a great part whereof is mountainous, but much likewise a plain, which is the most sweet and pleasant part, for it is watered with several navigable rivers... The mountainous part of the country is clothed with very large woods, and all manner of fruit trees and springs of fresh water... There you may have game enough in hunting all sorts of wild beasts... This island seems rather to be the residence of some of the gods, than of men.
>
> Anciently, by reason of its remote location it was altogether unknown, but afterwards discovered on this occasion: The Phoenicians in ancient times undertook frequent voyages by sea, in way of traffic as merchants, so that they planted many colonies in Africa and in these western parts of Europe. These merchants succeeded in their undertaking and thereupon growing very rich, passed at length beyond the Pillars of Hercules,

into the sea called the Ocean. At first they built a city called
Gades [the site of modern Cadiz, Spain—Author's note]. The
Phoenicians, having found out the coasts beyond the Pillars,
and sailing along by the shore of Africa, were on a sudden
driven by a furious storm off into the main ocean, and after
they had lain under this violent tempest for many days, they at
length arrived at this island, and so they were the first that
discovered it.[2]

Seneca, the Roman writer, also spoke of a true continent across
the Atlantic that actually bounded and "contained" the real ocean[3].
Our word "continent" derives, of course, from the concept of a land
barrier or dyke that contained the true ocean beyond the Pillars of
Hercules. Men of the Mediterranean were fully aware that their
little sea was but a pond compared to the Ocean that lay westward
from Gibraltar.

These accounts are admittedly both vague and somewhat
generic in description, yet we cannot doubt that the writers possessed fairly detailed knowledge of a Carthagenian-Phoenician discovery across the Atlantic even if the geography of the "very great
island" was hazy.

The tendency of 20th-century scholars has been to debunk early
claims of the discovery and colonization of the New World. They
have argued, instead, that the Carthagenians, Phoenicians and the
Iberian Celtic mariners they recruited or enslaved merely discovered
the Canary Islands, and possibly the Cape Verde Islands, off the
coast of Africa but did not actually cross the Atlantic to the
Americas. It is becoming increasingly clear, however, that it is
modern scholarship that needs debunking. There's no doubt that
the Carthagenians and Phoenicians did sail southward along the
coast of Africa and planted numerous colonies on the way. The
ruins of Lixus in present day Morocco demonstrate the scope of this
ancient Punic undertaking because the city of Lixus, judging from
its ruins, seems to have been larger than Carthage itself. Yet we
know absolutely nothing about Lixus because the ruins have never
been excavated. The crumbling remains of the huge Atlantic seaport
continue to disintegrate beneath an inexorable overgrowth of man-
grove swamp and papyrus reed. The sheer size of the Lixus ruins
mocks both our knowledge and our ignorance about what may have

been accomplished on the Atlantic when Rome was but a collection of huts.[4]

Modern scholarship is correct on one point: Carthagenians and Phoenicians *also* discovered the Canary Islands, and very probably the Cape Verde Islands too. There is absolute proof that Carthagenians reached the Azores. In 1753 an ancient earthenware pot full of Carthagenian coins was found, after a severe storm, within previously unknown stone ruins on the beach of Corvo, one of the Azores Islands. These coins dated from the decade 330–320 B.C. and were so numerous that they comprised almost a full set of Carthagenian coinage from that particular decade. Numismatists have determined that it would have been impossible, in the early 1750s, for anyone to have gathered such a complete set of Carthagenian coins and so there can be no question of hoax or fraud regarding this find. As for the ruins in which the pot was found? While scholars bickered about the authenticity of the coins, another storm buried the ruins in sand again, and the exact location has been lost and forgotten.[5]

The center of the Canary Islands group lies about 250 miles out into the Atlantic off the coasts of Morocco and the Spanish Sahara. The center of the Cape Verde Islands is five hundred miles west of Senegal and Mauritania. Both island groups are well within the influence of the Northeast Trades and the North Equatorial Current. If mariners frequented these island groups in Carthagenian and Phoenician times, it is simply inevitable that, sooner or later, several ships would have been caught in storms and sent far enough westward to be entrapped in the westward-flowing currents and wind zones, with no hope of return. Assuming that such ships could remain afloat, their next landfall could only be the West Indies. Indeed, for these very reasons of winds and currents, Columbus chose the Canary Islands as his point of departure in 1492. There is every reason to believe that some Carthagenian and Phoenician mariners made the same crossing inadvertently two thousand years before.

The Azores Islands are another matter. This group lies one thousand miles due west of Lisbon, almost in mid-Atlantic and also in the trade wind zone. Anyone who reached the Azores, and we know the Carthagenians did because of the coins on Corvo, was already well across the Atlantic. If shipwrecked Carthagenian mariners on Corvo managed to repair their vessel, they could not have returned to the Pillars of Hercules against the grip of the trades and currents. They, too, would have been sent to America on the wind-and-current conveyor belt, and yet from the Azores their voyage to America was already almost half completed.

There is nothing inherently unlikely about the fact that Carthagenian, Phoenician and Celtiberian ships may have discovered the American continents sometime around 800–300 B.C. Objectively, such a discovery seems rather probable.

Probability tends toward certainty when the evidence of archeology is added to the persuasion of prevailing winds and currents. In South America, an early 20th-century linguist, Bernardo da Silva Ramos, published (1931) a two-volume work containing over 2,800 apparently Carthagenian-Phoenician-Celtiberian inscriptions which he discovered and photographed in the Amazon basin.[6]

From North America comes the same sort of evidence. Professor Barry Fell of Harvard has brought to public and popular attention the numerous ancient European ruins and inscriptions in New England (*Saga America*, *America B.C.*, etc.). A research organization called NEARA (New England Antiquities Research Association) has pinpointed over three hundred pre-Columbian European sites in the Northeastern United States. Salvatore Michael Trento (*The Search for Lost America*) has documented evidence for very early European visitors and colonists south of New England in the New York–New Jersey area and also as far west as Pennsylvania.

Dr. Gérard Leduc of Montreal's Concordia University challenged conventional Canadian archeology with his discovery of 42 stone cairns and other stonework, on the border of Quebec and Vermont. Undoubted European artifacts, including a metal chisel, have been found which carbon-date to about 500 A.D. or earlier.[7]

These finds have been denied and ignored by established, conventional historians and archeologists in the United States and Canada. Yet, of course, they cannot be denied and ignored forever. There is simply too much evidence accumulating on an almost daily basis, and it is demanding to be heard. "America" was discovered long before even the founding of Rome by Europeans, and long, long before Columbus.

Carthagenians, Phoenicians and Celtiberians were not alone in discovering the New World. Some Celtiberians migrated to the British Isles, bringing their knowledge of western land with them. Irish monks called *papar*, fleeing sin and seeking pure solitude, sailed out into the Atlantic between about 500–700 A.D. and also, apparently, reached America.[8] When the Northmen began to raid Ireland about 750 A.D. they, too, learned of the land to the west. After the Vikings had established themselves on Iceland and Greenland, they sailed to the New World. Lief, son of Eric the Red, made one voyage, probably to southern New England, and established a house. Lief's half-sister, Freydis, borrowed Lief's house as a headquarters and, in company with the Icelandic brothers Helgi and Finnbogi, explored the coast in two ships. A few years later, probably between 1018–1021 A.D., a friend of Lief's, Thorfinn Karlsefni, mounted a major expedition to the New World comprising three ships which explored the coast from the Gulf of Maine to Chesapeake Bay. After Karlsefni came Thorall the Huntsman. It is recorded also that one Icelandic merchant, Ari Marson, was blown by storm to the New World and baptised there. Marson had the opportunity to be repatriated by a later Viking expedition, but elected to remain on the western side of the Atlantic because he was held in such high esteem by the people. All this, and much more, is solemnly recorded in the four major "saga" sources: *The Flateyjarbók*, *The Hauksbók*, *The Lándnamabók* and *Eriks Saga Rauda*. The basic facts can no longer be reasonably doubted.

Europeans in the northeast of North America are confirmed by the Indian traditions of the region. According to the legends related by the Mohawk chief, Joseph Brant (*The Life of Joseph Brant, Thayendanega*, page 484), the white men who anciently lived among the Indians were so numerous and so established in metal-working that the Indians feared their power. All were massacred—a legend curiously resonant of the Carthagenian massacre reported by Aristotle.

So, we have more than ample evidence that Columbus did not "discover America." It had been discovered many times previously by various seafaring peoples. Before returning to Columbus and deciding what he really did discover, one other episode of transatlantic voyaging needs to be mentioned if only to redress long-held prejudices.

Before the European "Age of Discovery" there were very advanced cultures, and even true civilizations, in Africa. In West Africa the empires of Ghana, Kanem-Bornu, Mali and Songhay existed more or less concurrently, but also succeeded one another as dominant political entities of the region. In East Africa, along the Indian Ocean coast, an entirely black African civilization called "Zanj" raised many beautiful cities of stone that have only recently come to light from the overgrowth of thick coastal vegetation. Both West African and East African polities boasted a material culture, and social development, that not only rivalled Europe but often overshadowed contemporary Europe. This is simply a fact, but one that has not yet percolated down into our history books. Archeology in Africa has only recently begun, in many respects, and the data have not yet entered the realm of popular Western knowledge. The high cultures and civilizations of Africa have never been suspected by Europeans, until modern archeology, for a very simple reason: no known European travelled south of the Sahara in medieval times; and no known European penetrated into the East African Indian ocean region in medieval times. The reason for this is equally simple: both regions were Arabic spheres of influence that were hostile to Europeans.[9]

Africa can truly be called a "dark continent" from one point of view. It is largely dark to Europeans because of European ignorance, not dark because of African inadequacies. Therefore, it is from Arabic sources only that we can gain a glimpse of the medieval African civilizations that have perished. Two such sources are an exceedingly obscure North American manuscript entitled *Masalik-al-absad* by Omari, and travel snippets composed by an Arab globe-trotter named Ibn Batuta. Batuta, besides describing multi-storied houses and buildings in the capital of Mali, has the following to say about Malian society, law and order:

> They are seldom unjust and have a greater abhorrence of injustice than any other people. Their sultan shows no mercy to anyone who is found guilty of the least act of it. There is complete security in the country. Neither traveler nor inhabitant in it has anything to fear from robbers or men of violence. They do not confiscate the property of any white man who dies in their country, even if it be uncounted wealth. On the

contrary, they give it, into the charge of some trustworthy person among the whites, if such can be found, until the rightful heir takes possession of it.[10]

At the time that Ibn Batuta wrote this, sometime around the year 1300 A.D., the capital of Mali had a population of about thirty thousand, roughly the size of medieval Paris. Not only was the capital a city of multi-storied houses and effective law, but it was a city inhabited by far-from-shy women. As a good Arab who had travelled throughout the Arab-dominated world of his time, Ibn Batuta was more than a little shocked:

> Their men show no sign of jealousy whatsoever. No one claims descent from his father, but on the contrary from his mother's brother. A person's heirs are his sister's sons, not his own sons. This is a thing which I have seen nowhere in the world except among the Indians of Malabar. But *those* are heathens; *these* people are Muslims, punctilious in observing the hours of prayer, studying books of law, and in memorizing the Koran. Yet their women show no bashfulness before men and do not veil themselves, though they are assiduous in attending prayer.[11]

Turning, perhaps thankfully, from the behavior of Malian women to military matters, Batuta noted that the Emperor of Mali was "master of a power that is formidable" and could put 200,000 mail-clad cavalry in the field. In reading between the lines of the tragic little that survives about medieval West African culture, we can conclude at least the following: The Emperor of Mali was very much more powerful, militarily, than any European monarch of 1300 A.D. This fact explains the curious circumstance that while Europe itself *was more than half occupied by Arabic invaders in the year 1300 A.D.*, the Islamic *jihad* had been stopped by black, mail-clad warriors south of the Sahara. The Malians accepted some aspects of Arabic culture, but remained, as more than half of Europe did not, politically and socially independent of the Arabs and of Islam. We can also discern that Malian culture was fully equal to medieval European culture, and that Malian law and status-of-women were more evolved than in contemporary Europe.

The important point for our purposes is, however, that these medieval Malians were seafarers. It is recorded by Omari in his *Masalik-al-absad* that one Emperor of Mali named Kankan Musa, as a young man, had participated in an Atlantic exploration. Sometime around the year 1350 A.D., Ibn Amir Hajib asked Kankan Musa about this voyage and received the following reply:

> The monarch who preceded me would not believe that it was impossible to discover the limits of the neighboring sea. He wished to know. He persisted in his plan. He caused the equipping of two hundred ships and filled them with men, and of another such number that were filled with gold. He said to the commanders: Do not return until you have reached the end of the ocean, or when you have exhausted your food and water.
>
> They went away and their absence was long: none came back and their absence continued. Then my single ship returned . . . we sailed for a long while until we met with what seemed to be a river with a strong current flowing in the open sea. My ship was last. The others sailed on, but as each of them came to that place they did not come back, nor did they reappear; and I do not know what became of them. As for me, I turned where I was and did not enter the current.

We can only speculate, but perhaps the young Kankan Musa refused to enter the current, not out of cowardice, but because he was the heir to the Malian throne and had the duty of returning to his people, if at all possible, rather than perishing vainly. There are two points of extreme importance about this account: first, the voyage must have taken place sometime around 1300–1325 because Kankan Musa was an old man when he related this story; second, the story is true because the North Equatorial Current is correctly described as "a river with a strong current flowing in the open sea," a description which could only come from an eyewitness of the phenomenon.

This Malian voyage of 1300–1325 may well have some relevance to Columbus's own success less than two hundred years later, as we shall see. Surprising relevance.

But the reason for covering Malian culture and seafaring in some detail is to demonstrate that black Africans, too, discovered America before Columbus. The specific voyage of 1300–1325 may not have reached the New World. Perhaps all the ships perished. Nonetheless, there can be no doubt at all that black West Africans did reach the Americas at a very early date. Long before the Spanish. The Africans reached America early enough to influence, and become a part of, some native American cultures. Black warriors are depicted in a temple at Chichen Itza dated to about 900–1000 A.D. Huge stone facial sculptures of black warriors are a distinctive feature of Olmec art, and this means that black Africans must have reached Yucatan and the Gulf of Honduras sometime between 500 B.C. and 500 A.D.

It seems that black Africans must have penetrated the Amazon basin even earlier. Cultivated plants of African origin, such as the plantain, the bottle gourd, the peanut and 13-(small) chromosome cotton were well established in South America as early as 1000 B.C. Cotton-wrapped mummies found at Arica, Chile, radiocarbon-date to the era 1000–750 B.C. and African plantain leaves are found in the same graves.[13] Obviously, there was a long and rather continuous contact between West Africa and the New World from a very early time. I do not think we can reasonably suppose that most of these black African voyages resulted from purposeful transatlantic navigation, just as most of the early Carthagenian-Phoenician-Celtiberian voyages could not have been purposefully planned. In both cases, the voyages were probably inadvertent. Hapless storm-driven mariners entered the current-and-trade-wind conveyor belt and found themselves castaways in the Americas. The survivors melded into existing native cultures and civilizations as best as they could.

No, Christopher Columbus did not discover America. Indeed, it seems that almost all the seafaring people bordering the Atlantic discovered America long before him.

Nonetheless, we must face the fact that it was Columbus's voyage and not earlier ones, that immediately changed the world. The reason for this lies in the importance of what Columbus really discovered. If scholars and ordinary people have suffered from misconceptions about what Columbus discovered, Christopher Columbus himself was not at all confused. He discovered how to use the ocean, and he knew it. He wrote of himself as the recipient of a divine gift of insight: .

> Of the barriers of the Ocean sea, which were closed with such mighty chains, He gave thee the keys.[14]

Columbus intuited how the wind-and-current systems of the Atlantic worked. He deduced that the system was a clockwise,

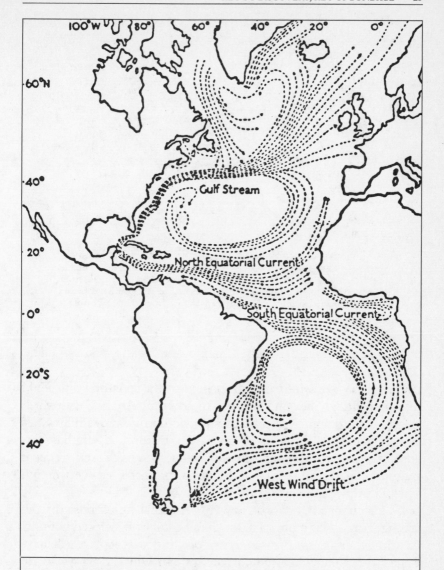

Columbus's "Key to the Barrier of the Ocean Sea," his correct deduction that winds and currents of the Atlantic form a circular clockwise-flowing system in the northern hemisphere. Ships could reach America near the equator and be blown back to Europe by prevailing westerlies creating the Gulf Stream.

Courtesy: Harper & Brothers, New York. From *Conquest by Man* by Paul Hermann.

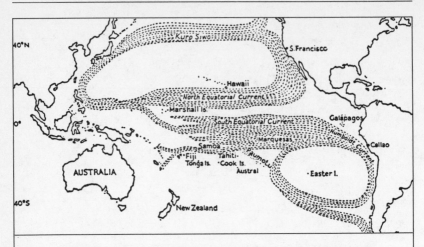

Columbus's key worked in the Pacific, too, where a huge clock-wise-flowing system of winds and currents in the northern hemisphere allow Pacific crossings in both directions. Mariners soon learned that Columbus's key even worked in the southern hemisphere in all oceans although the system flowed in a counter-clockwise direction.

Courtesy: Harper & Brothers, New York. From *Conquest by Man* by Paul Hermann.

circular system of winds and currents. Near the equator a ship could find prevailing winds and currents to cross the Atlantic westward; going north to higher latitudes, a ship would find prevailing winds and currents to enable it to return to Europe. Columbus was absolutely correct. He discovered the key to reliable and frequent transatlantic navigation. The Atlantic has been crossed every month since 1494.[15]

What changed the world, however, was that Columbus's discovery, his "key", was more valuable than he knew. It worked not only on the Atlantic, *but also on every ocean in the world*. All have basically circular wind-and-current systems which flow westward near the equator and eastward nearer each pole. The only complication, and one rapidly grasped by mariners, was that the system is clockwise in the northern hemisphere and counter-clockwise in the southern hemisphere. Once that fact was realized, which took only a few short years, the entire world lay open to European exploration and exploitation. Columbus's landfall was not simply a landfall on a small West Indian island, it was a key or a passport, to any landfall Europeans cared to make anywhere in the world. That is why Columbus's voyage changed the world and had almost immediate repercussions that went far beyond the association of Europe and the New World.

Africa was devastated.

King Alfonso IV of Portugal (1325–57) seems to have been the first Iberian monarch to have sent out purposeful voyages of discovery to the south and west.[16] The Canary Islands seems to have been "re-discovered" by the Portuguese during Alfonso's reign. Prince Henry "The Navigator" of Portugal (1394–1460) continued this exploratory tradition with a great deal more efficiency and enthusiasm. The Portuguese goal was never "to reach the east by sailing west," but to reach the Spice Islands in the vague east by sailing around Africa, then across the Indian Ocean to present-day Indonesia. In early 15th century Portugal, there were two main schools of thought regarding Africa among geographical experts, such as they were. One faction inclined toward the belief that, towards the south, Africa began to curve eastward across the Indian Ocean and that the southern extremity of Africa actually connected with the spice realms, or was separated by a narrow strait from the hazily imaged islands. This faction of geographers held the Indian Ocean to be a large inland sea bounded on the south by a curving African coast and the "spice lands" or "spice islands," wherever they might be, in the far unknown east. This curious belief about the curvature of Africa towards the east derived from the experience of Alexander the Great of Macedon.

In 327 B.C., Alexander succeeded in reaching the Indus River from Bokhara in his bid to conquer the known world. His army, however, wanted only to return to the Mediterranean and was on the verge of mutiny. The last straw was the terrible experience of some soldiers in the Indus River. After their hot and thirsty forced march from Bokhara, some men threw themselves into the cold, clear inviting water of the Indus. Their refreshment was short-lived, unfortunately, because a very large number of them were immediately attacked, killed and eaten by crocodiles. Crocodiles! All men of the Mediterranean knew that crocodiles were found only in the Nile River and nowhere else. Consequently, the belief among

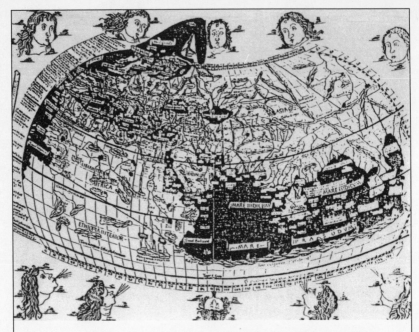

Johan Schnitzer's world map of about 1437 reflects the European notion that Africa curved toward the east, making the Indian Ocean an inland sea.

Alexander's scientific corps, or "Bematists," became a notion that somehow the Nile and the Indus must be joined by tributary rivers or marshes allowing crocodiles to infest both large rivers. For this to be possible, Africa had to curve toward the east somewhere in the unknown southern hemisphere. This belief endured, at least among some geographers, to warp the Europeans' world view.[17]

The second faction of geographers, however, believed that Africa did come to a termination somewhere far to the south of the equator. Indeed, there existed a chart in Portugal in the early 1400s that actually showed this final cape of the African continent, and which clearly showed that the Indian Ocean was not an inland sea. This chart had been drawn by a cosmographer called Fra Mauro, and he drew a termination to Africa because of reports that an Indian Ocean Zanj captain had actually doubled Africa's southernmost cape in 1420. News of this feat somehow reached Iberia, and was considered reliable. We cannot hope ever to know the name of this unsung Zanj sea captain who discovered the Cape of Good Hope about 65 years before this great achievement was unfairly attributed to Bartolomeo Diaz, nor can we hope to know precisely how news of his voyage managed to reach Portugal. All we know is that it happened, that a chart was prepared by Fra Mauro based on this priceless information, and that this same chart guided Diaz on his long-awaited, successful voyage to reach the same cape in 1487–1488.[18]

Based on the discovery of this unknown Zanj captain, Portugal began sending exploratory probes down the West African coast as early as 1425–1430. Portuguese progress was painfully slow, almost inching down the African shore, with each voyage going only a small distance beyond the previous one. By 1444 the Portuguese had reached Cape Vérde at 19 degrees north of the equator and only about two thousand miles south from Lisbon. This was not a very creditable performance for twenty years of effort, but the discovery of Cape Verde by the Portuguese was fraught with far-reaching and tragic implications. It was at Cape Verde that the Portuguese directly confronted black Africa for the first time. A very small number of negro captives and slaves had always been known in the Mediterranean world since, probably, the earliest Egyptian dynasties of about 3200 B.C., just as a very small number of whites were slaves and captives of Malian nobles. In both cases, though, the rare people of "strange" color were regarded as valuable curiosities, precious "collectables" sometimes offered for sale by Arabs. But the European world was separated from direct contact with the black African world by the pitiless barrier of the Sahara.

That barrier was outflanked by the Portuguese voyage of 1443–1444 and Europeans clashed with black African culture for the first time. The encounter took place either in the estuary of the Senegal River which flanks Cape Verde to the north, or in the estuary of the Gambia River to the south. It was an unguarded outpost of black Africa, or the encounter might have gone very differently. Portuguese swords and primitive firearms made the skirmish a rout, and many prisoners were taken. These black Africans were unloaded on the quays of Lisbon in 1444 and the slave trade can be said to date from that time. Again, though, these directly obtained, black African slaves were regarded mainly as curiosities. Even 50 years later, at the time of Columbus's first voyage, there was merely a handful of black African slaves in Iberia and they were regarded as valuable rarities.

It was only when the Spanish began to exploit the New World seriously that the economic potential of black Africans was suddenly realized. Spanish forced-labor and brutality quickly exterminated the native Americans around the Caribbean. Modern anthropologist Claude Levi-Strauss related what happened to the Caribbean Indians in his *Tristes Tropiques*:

> In what used to be called Hispaniola (today Haiti and Santo Domingo), the native population numbered about one hundred thousand in 1492, but had dropped to about 200 a century later, since people died of horror and disgust at European civilization even more than of smallpox and physical ill-treatment.[19]

What happened on Hispaniola was duplicated throughout the region until the Spanish found themselves facing a serious labor shortage in the gold and silver mines and on their cotton and sugarcane plantations.

The answer was to replace the decimated Amerindians with a constant flow of black Africans. Cohesive African empires, like that of Mali, existed mostly in the interior of West Africa, thankfully for the Portuguese and other slavers, and the coastal predators never had to face the 200,000 mail-clad cavalry of Mali, which was no more "medieval" than the Europeans of the time. True, the Europeans had primitive firearms—but so did the black Africans, arms acquired in trade from the Arabs. If the Europeans had had to confront the power of Mali directly in pitched battles, as the Arabs themselves had done, there would have been small doubt as to the outcome. Europeans would have been mauled just as the Almorovids had been defeated in the Sahelia.

But the slavers confined their attention to the weaker political states of the coasts with their isolated and largely undefended villages. Most European seafaring nations quickly realized the profits to be made in sending African slaves to the Caribbean, and such was the Spanish need for slaves that they allowed even their hated and heretical rivals, the English, to supply slaves to the West Indian islands and the so-called Spanish Main.

Slaving quickly grew to incredible proportions and, indeed, the prospect of slave-trading inspired the Portuguese to speed up their cautious inching along the African coast. It has been estimated that "one million three hundred and eighty-nine thousand slaves were taken from the coast of Angola alone in the years between 1486 and 1641."[20] Anti-Spanish England found slaving profitable: "Liverpool records show that in the eleven years of 1783 to 1793, about nine hundred Liverpool voyages were made for slaving and carried over three hundred thousand slaves."[21]

The coastal states of West Africa were utterly destroyed and the population was decimated. Hordes of terrified survivors fled inland, a disparate flood of refugees of various languages, cultures, religions and previous tribal-political affiliation; haunted, homeless people made brutal by the appalling European brutality they had witnessed. The flood of disorganized and desperate refugees inundated the inland empires like Mali, Kanem-Bornu and Songhay, destroying their social and political cohesion.

And, as the final, fateful tragic stroke, the Arabs entered the slaving arena on something approaching European proportions. Burdened by hordes of brutalized survivors fleeing inland, and now attacked by Arab armies from across the Sahara, the once-proud and civilized West African empires collapsed beneath the double blows from Europe and Islam. The last pitched battle between a cohesive African army and the Arabic invaders occurred in 1591 A.D. when the forces of El Mansur of Morocco defeated the outnumbered cavalry of Songhay's Askia Ishak.[22] This battle took place somewhere northwest of Lake Chad, a decisive battle completely unknown to Europeans and one fought in the almost complete silence of unhearing, unheeding "History"— the final, vain defiance of enlightened Africa. Shattered people succumbed to barbarism in the unfair struggle for survival. We have read Ibn Batuta's description of Mali before slaving began. Four hundred years later, when the first European explorers pushed inland, they found only terrified, superstitious and brutally cruel bands of savages, and it was too easy to believe that black Africans had always been that way. Britain's Commander Bacon described Benin when his troops reached the inland city in 1897:

Truly has Benin been called a city of blood. Its history is one long record of savagery of the most debased kind...Blood was everywhere... On the right was a crucifixion tree with a double crucifiction on it, the two poor wretches stretched out facing west, with their arms bound together in the middle...At the base were skulls and bones, literally strewn about, the debris of former sacrifices, and down every main road were two or more human sacrifices.[23]

What happened to West Africa was duplicated once the Europeans reached the Indian Ocean and the East African coastal cities of the Zanj. African historian, Britain's Basil Davidson, writes of the coming of Vasco de Gama and the Portuguese to East Africa:

They cut savagely across all those many complex strands of commerce which centuries had woven between these myriad ports and peoples of the east; and they wrecked the whole fabric of that trade, leaving behind them, when their force was spent, little but ruin and disruption.

Schooled in the bitter rivalries of Europe, they fell upon these tolerant and easy-going civilizations of the Indian Ocean with a ferocity and violence that were like nothing seen here through many centuries.[24]

The Far East was almost immediately, like Africa, affected by Columbus's key to the barriers of the Ocean Sea. Just as soon as the Spanish under Cortez had conquered Mexico, and the Spanish under Pizarro had conquered the Incan Empire of Andean South America, they pushed out into the Pacific with the knowledge of circular wind-and-current systems.[25] Using Acapulco as their primary base, the Spanish began regular crossings to the Philippines, once Alvaro de Mendaña had proven that Columbus's key worked in the North Pacific as well as in the North Atlantic.

The Far East immediately lost its isolation and, like the Africans, was threatened on two fronts at once. Portuguese approached the Orient from across the Indian Ocean while Spain encroached upon the Orient from across the Pacific. When the force of Portuguese and Spaniard was spent in the first confrontation of East and West, the wind-and-current key remained and other European seafaring nations used it: English, Dutch and French. All of the Far East was colonized except China and Japan. Indonesia went to the

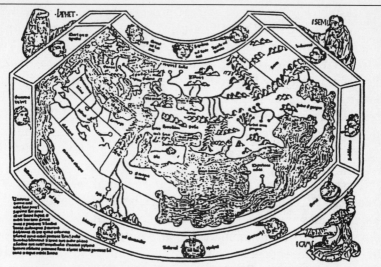

Another map from the 15th century which appeared in Hartman Schedel's *World Chronicle* of 1477. This map is based largely upon Ptolemy's geography of the 2nd century A.D. Note again that Africa is shown to connect with the Orient, leaving the Indian Ocean as an inland sea. The large island in this inland ocean is not Australia, but "Taprobane" (Ceylon, the modern Sri Lanka) and its much-exaggerated size reflects the immense wealth it was thought to possess, not its actual modest geographical extent.

Dutch, India and Burma to the British, Southeast Asia to the French. China was simply too big to be colonized by any one European power, so it was partitioned among many and stripped of any real independence or power. Only Japan remained uncolonized, relatively unbowed and reasonably independent.

It is, indeed, interesting to view more recent events like World War II from the long perspective of San Salvador's beach in 1492. For, from that perspective and using any reasonable and objective criteria, Japan won World War II and not the Allies. Consider the matter from the Japanese point of view. Meeting the onslaught of European seaborne powers bent on colonialism required that Japan, if it was to remain independent alone of all Oriental peoples, adopt European technology as rapidly as possible. Japan did this between 1850 and 1905 with astonishing speed but not without great disruption to its traditional culture. An objective historian might say that

Japan established her independence by defeating the Russians, to the Western world's shock and dismay, in 1905. But what about the long-term preservation of that independence? A Japanese strategist, viewing the nearby world of 1930, could not fail to note that all the easily obtainable raw materials required by modern technology and modern warfare were in European hands. Columbus's key had given the British Burma's rubber, had given the Dutch Indonesia's oil, had given the French Southeast Asia's rubber, oil and metal.

From the point of view of the Japanese strategist of 1930, the future looked grim. The strategic raw materials necessary for modern warfare, and thus independence, were in European hands, not Asian ones. Lacking strategic raw materials, Japan's ability to wage modern war would inevitably decline compared to the European colonial powers surrounding it. Japan's only chance of long-term, continued independence was grimly obvious in 1930. Japan had to make war upon the European colonial powers while Japan yet possessed the ability to wage modern war. The objective, win or lose, must be to destroy European colonialism in the Far East. Indeed, if that could be accomplished, even defeat could not be tragic in the long view. After some period of occupation, the Asian strategic raw materials would become available for Asians *if only European colonialism could be ended*, and the dominant technological nation in the aftermath could only be Japan, at least for a half-century or so until China developed significantly.

It is obvious that, even in defeat, Japan achieved its all-important goal: destruction of European colonialism. Japan won World War II by any objective assessment, and the last act of that war has just recently been played out in Vietnam where French and American colonialism was finally defeated.

Europe, the Americas, Africa and the Far East were dramatically affected by Columbus's five-hundred-year-old landfall and the invaluable key it represented, and we are still living out some of these repercussions today.

But, for the sake of completeness, it has to be noted that the Middle East was affected no less than the rest of the world.

On the morning of May 29, 1453, Columbus was about two years old and an event of devastating magnitude had just happened to Europe. Adults would hear about it, and talk about it, and worry about it just as soon as ships arrived with the news. Constantinople had fallen to the Arabs. Europe was cut off from world trade because now the Arabs absolutely controlled all the trade routes to and from the Far East where silk and spices originated. Henceforth, Europeans could only obtain these coveted commodities from the Arabs, who would be sure to charge even more exorbitant prices than the merchant-thieves of Byzantium.

It was, indeed, the capture of Constantinople and the commercial isolation of Europe that inspired a more rapid tempo to seaborne exploration from Portugal and Spain. With the land routes to eastern riches now firmly in Arabic hands, the only hope was to outflank the Arab economic blockade by sea. With hindsight it seems inevitable, but at the time it seemed highly improbable, that this would be done. Yet it was, in spite of geographical ignorance and in spite of inadequate ships. The Portuguese broke the blockade first, but only by slogging the long route around Africa without the benefit of prevailing winds and currents for most of the passage. It was Columbus's key that truly broke the blockade first for the Spanish, and then the English, French and Dutch were able to outflank the Arabic blockade too.

Although it is difficult, if not truly impossible, for Westerners of the late 20th century to appreciate the gut-fear that was a reality during all of Columbus's life, it is simply a fact that Arabic power dominated, controlled, threatened and over-shadowed all of Europe during the time from the fall of Constantinople in 1453 until the battle of Lepanto in 1571 when the Turkish fleet was almost totally destroyed by the forces of the Holy League. During the 118 nervous years between the fall of Constantinople and the sea-battle of Lepanto, years which encompassed the lives of Columbus and his contemporaries, all of the Middle East, Greece, the Balkans and much of modern Hungary, Spain and Czechoslovakia lay under the Arab yoke. Europe struggled constantly against total inundation. At one point in Columbus's life, Turkish territory began just 20 miles west of Vienna; during Columbus's middle years, just before he undertook his 1492 voyage, the Arabs still controlled much of Spain.

Columbus's key reversed this situation, although it took two or three generations to do it. Not only were the Europeans able to outflank the Arab economic blockade and reach the Far East by sea, but they were able to outflank the Arabs militarily too. In the late 1400s and early 1500s Portuguese ships on the Indian Ocean took the Arab empires by surprise, striking right at the heart of Arab power, by attacking the Arabian peninsula itself. Many smaller Arabic sultanates were captured from the sea, including the fairy-tale kingdom of Oman, which no European had previously visited except as a slave. From across the Pacific came the Spanish who broke the Arab commercial and naval dominance of the China Seas. Within a century of 1492, the entire Indian Ocean and the China Seas, which had formerly been the undisputed playground of Sind-bad the Sailor, were under the guns of European caravels and galleons. No Arab dhow, baggala or sambuk dared to show its romantic crescent-shaped lateen sails on the high seas of the East. Arab sea-power declined to modest, nervous coastal voyages and subsistence fishing, just as Arab culture and dominance steadily declined with the seal of historical fate stamped firmly upon it by the victory of Lepanto in the Mediterranean itself. Turco-Arabic cul-ture, supremely dominant in the world in Columbus's lifetime, shriveled so that by 1900 Turkey was called "the sick man of Europe," and other Arabic states descended into the disorganization and bickering we witness today.

One of the minor mysteries of history must be Arab failure to respond to Europe's initially feeble efforts to become a sea power. Nowadays we don't think of Arabs as a maritime people, but up until the 16th century they definitely were. Omani ships regularly sailed across the Indian Ocean to Canton at a time when European voyages were short coastal passages.[26] In terms of pure maritime technology, the Arabs had developed ships that could sail effectively to windward when Europe's caravels and galleons could sail only with a wind astern. The Arabs possessed shipboard firearms and cannons, better steel, and could have matched European progress in weaponry.

But they did not. Can it be that entire cultures possess a curious and mysterious life-span of their own which is only partly depen-dent on outside influences? Civilizations seem to arise, flourish and decline according to some "cultural clock" that seems to have little to do with material factors. The 16th century seemed to be Europe's time to arise, and the Arabs' time to decline, regardless of the fact that most cultural, economic and military advantages lay definitely with the Arab world.

I have dealt with the effect of Columbus's key on the Middle East last in terms of world regions because, during Columbus's time, cultural dominance centered in the Middle East, and Turco-Arabic power was *the* direct and relevant challenge and threat to Western Europe.

Yet. . .

Beneath the visible conflict of soldier, merchant, sailor, diplomat, sultan and king, something else also centered in the Middle East which was not hostile to Western Europe. On the contrary, this secret something had the power to bind the Jewish, Christian and Islamic intelligentsia together in what might be called a *new* Western religion, or, less cautiously, *the* true Western religion. This faith was based on a secret which was not "new" at all, even back in 1492, but which had been known to an inquiring elite for perhaps thirty-five hundred years. It seems that this secret had been long shared by the more intelligent and less dogmatized Jews and Arabs, which is why Judaism was not only tolerated, but actually flourished, under the Arabs. Certain Christians had always known the secret, too, but discovered its dramatic relevance and potential only when Europeans in significant numbers reached the Holy Land because of the Crusades. And there, beneath the highly visible conflict of Frank and Saracen, a few Christian kings, princes and clerics formed a bond in common with their Jewish and Islamic colleagues who had also known and protected the secret. On one level they may have been compelled to fight against each other by social, cultural and primitive religious forces beyond their control, but on another level they shared a bond of great strength which could not be revealed to the mass of their own people. The reason is simple: few could believe the secret because of their parochial cultural and religious indoctrination, whether Christian, Jew or Moslem; and therefore ignorance and fanaticism had always been the greatest enemy of those who knew the secret.

There can be no doubt that *belief* in such a secret existed among many Christian, Jewish and Moslem intellectuals, which included some clerics of all three faiths, and some kings, princes and nobles because only such classes has access to education. It does not matter whether this secret was, and is, a true one. What matters is that some highly-placed people *believed it to be true*, and some still do.

Was Columbus an initiate into this secret doctrine that transcended orthodox Judaism, Islam and Christianity? He was not a cleric or a noble, yet he was an educated man. One might say that because of his profession, which suddenly became of crucial importance to Europe, he was one of the first representatives of the modern, secular "middle class." He was a navigator, cartographer and bookseller and, as such, was one of a new class of people to be educated outside the Church and the nobility. And further, as someone who officially represented neither Church nor State, he was ideally placed to be initiated into a secret that cut across the dogmas and politics demanded by orthodox Judaism, Islam and Roman Catholicism.

Columbus may have been ideally placed to have been initiated into the secret doctrine, but was he?

Let's take a closer look at that group gathered on the Caribbean beach on Friday, October 12, 1492. There was the admiral, Christopher Columbus himself, and his two associate captains, the Pinzón brothers. There was Rodrigo de Escobedo, the lawyer. There were a number of Spanish soldiers and adventurers who later wrote their own accounts of the landfall and the Conquest.

There was one functionary conspicuous by his absence. *There was no Roman Catholic priest present at that historic landfall to sanctify the achievement as a pious undertaking for the glory of God.* Had the expedition's priest died during the month-long voyage? No. As strange as it may seem, since the voyage was made on behalf of their "most Catholic Majesties," Ferdinand and Isabella of Spain, *no priest sailed with Columbus's fleet of three ships and 90 crewmen.*[27]

Is this not curious, anomalous, or almost an impossibility?

And is it mere coincidence that Columbus's fleet weighed anchor at sunrise, August 3, 1492, and set sail for the Canaries en route to that most historic of landfalls? That date, August 3, was the deadline for all Jews to leave Spain. Columbus's fleet left on the same tide as vessels carrying fleeing Jews, and sailed in company with these refugee vessels for many miles.

School children are still taught the myth that Isabella pawned her jewels to finance Columbus's voyage. Yet scholars know that the money was provided by Luis de Santangel, Alonso de Harana, Alonso de Carvajal and Diego de Harana. *Is it mere coincidence that all four of these financial moguls were "conversos," or Jews who had supposedly become good Roman Catholics?*

Is it mere coincidence that one of Columbus's pilots, a long-time friend and colleague in navigation was a Moor? And can it be only coincidence that Granada, the last and redoubtable Moorish fortress in Spain, agreed to a bloodless "surrender" the day before Columbus finally signed his agreement with Ferdinand and Isabella?

These are just a few of the orphaned facts and anomalous coincidences that swirl around the life of the man history calls Christopher Columbus. There are many, many more. They fit into a pattern, but it is a pattern that few will want to believe.

What were Columbus's motivations for undertaking the 1492 voyage? What were his secret thoughts when he waded ashore on the beach of San Salvador?

We can, of course, never know. We can only rely upon what Columbus wrote, and very little of that survives in indisputable original copies. Yet some does, and we know that Columbus was obsessed with finding gold. This is a motivation that we moderns can understand, and the temptation is to leave it at that. Columbus wanted to get rich, and become a noble in class-conscious Spain, and gambled a daring voyage to do it. It is simple. Too simple. Columbus also wrote that he did not require gold for its own sake. He wanted gold to finance another crusade . . . one that would bring glory to Ferdinand and Isabella of Spain.

But this makes no sense, and Columbus above all men would have known that it made no sense, even if it flattered the egos of the two Spanish monarchs and lulled their suspicions. Spain had just barely solved the "Moorish problem" herself, and required the negotiated surrender of the largest Arab stronghold to do it. There were not enough knights and soldiers in Spain to take Granada by force. How, then, could Spain even dream of making an assault on the Holy Land? All the gold in the world would not have made a new European crusade either possible or successful. Everyone in Europe, except perhaps vanity-ridden Ferdinand and Isabella, knew that well enough.

There's evidence that Columbus's dream of a new crusade was in the nature of a code-phrase and a suspicion-lulling profession of orthodoxy. His actions and legal agreements, not his written flattery to Ferdinand and Isabella, provide a hint of his true motivation and his real obsession.

The legal agreement that Columbus signed with Ferdinand and Isabella on April 17, 1492, reveals something of his innermost motivations and single-minded obsession. His voyage *was* a crusade and, if it was successful, it would establish a New Jerusalem in a New World, not provide gold to re-take the old Jerusalem in the Holy Land. That much seems obvious simply from the conditions he extracted from recalcitrant Spanish monarchs.

In order to understand what Columbus meant by a crusade, we must take a look at the previous crusades in the Holy Land. The popular idea of them is a Christian attempt to wrest the Holy Lands from Arab and Islamic hands, and most of the crusaders were recruited by this religious propaganda. But, for the leaders of the crusades, there was another goal entirely, one that has never come to popular attention, one that concealed their belief in a momentous secret. The clandestine goal of the leaders of the crusades was to re-establish a unique blood-line on its rightful throne: Jerusalem. As unlikely as it may seem, many Jews and Moslems actually supported this plan because the human lineage in question physically bonded together the three great religions of the Western World.

The First Crusade was successful in that it did re-establish this ancient human bloodline on the throne of Jerusalem. But the success was short-lived. The Christian Kingdom of Jerusalem, which was not quite Christian at all, survived for less than a century. Fanatic and parochial Roman Catholics, Moslems and Jews did not want the founding of a new faith that would overshadow orthodoxy, and the common soldiers on both sides could not understand this new faith or believe its secret. Columbus's voyage was another attempt to establish a New Jerusalem.

But the world that actually resulted from his discovery was not the world that Columbus himself envisioned when he stepped ashore on San Salvador. His dream was betrayed by the greed of Spanish royalty and nobility, by the fanaticism of the Church of Rome, by the cruelty of the Inquisition and by the ubiquitous brutality of his time. His magnificent vision was thwarted, just as the real purpose of the crusades was thwarted. Before we can hope to grasp the totality of Columbus's dream, we must backtrack into history. Before we can concede the possible existence of the ancient, courageous conspiracy of which he seems to have been a part, we must understand what the crusades were really all about.

Chapter 3

Blood Royal

Three hundred and ninety-three years before Columbus's world-changing voyage of 1492, in the year 1099 A.D., Christian warriors of the First Crusade succeeded in capturing the city of Jerusalem and some of Palestine from the Islamic Saracens. An obscure French nobleman, Godfroi de Bouillon, was one of the leaders of this three-year struggle, which began in 1096. Godfroi took part in the final desperate battle in the streets of Jerusalem and it is worth noting here, because it has considerable relevance later, that Henri de Saint-Clair of Scotland fought beside Godfroi in the final storming of Jerusalem. Perhaps it is also worth noting that 33 years earlier, in 1066, no less than six Saint-Clairs had fought at Hastings for William Plantagenet, later called William the Conqueror, and these Saint-Clairs played no small part in the ultimate, difficult—almost impossible—breaking of King Harold's ring of axe-wielding House Carls.

Why the Saint-Clairs fought so valiantly for the man who styled himself after the *planta genesta* in 1066, and repeated the perform-ance in 1099 for Godfroi de Bouillon in Jerusalem, conceals a saga of family loyalty, courage and nobility that has seldom been equalled in world history. Indeed, the Saint-Clair family story is much like an iceberg: nine-tenths of their motivation has been concealed beneath the surface of historical complacency, while conventional historians remain content to note only the obvious visible tip: names and dates. Someday, someone should write the entire Saint-Clair saga for an unbelieving world.[1]

In a kind of election which still puzzles historians, obscure Godfroi de Bouillon was chosen to be King of Jerusalem "by an anonymous conclave of clerics and secular leaders."[2] But there is an element of curious mystery about this fundamental act of the Christians in the Holy Land, just as much more mystery was to come later. Although Godfroi de Bouillon was made King of Jerusalem for all practical purposes, and is accepted as that by historians, it does not appear that he actually accepted the title of king. Godfroi styled himself "Defender of the Holy Sepulchre." A sepulchre is a tomb, and the Holy Sepulchre is the cave in which Jesus Christ was buried outside the walls of Jerusalem. The fact is that although Godfroi was a formidable warrior, after the capture of Jerusalem in 1099 A.D. de Bouillon seems to have transformed himself into a kind of spiritual leader, a sort of mystical "king of kings."

His most notable official act as *de facto* King of Jerusalem was to found the "Order of Sion (Zion)," but to this day conventional historians have no inkling of the purpose of this Order, what sort of Order it was (knighthood? priesthood? scholars?), who was in it, or what became of it.[3] It is only known for certain that this "Order of Sion" surfaced again on July 20, 1956, when it was listed in France's *Journal Officiel* claiming a membership of 9,841 persons organized into ranks ranging from "Knights" to "Constables." It should be mentioned here that all social and political groups in France are required to declare themselves by registration and publication in the *Journal Officiel*, and it is a criminal offence to give a false description of the group's purpose or to give false information about the address of the group's headquarters, etc. Notwithstanding this legal obligation, the address given for the Order of Sion's headquarters did not exist. The leader of the Order was, however, listed accurately. He was, and is, Pierre Plantard *de Saint-Clair*. No legal action was taken against the Order of Sion for publishing a non-existent address.[4]

Godfroi de Bouillon's elevation to the throne of Jerusalem may be puzzling to contemporary scholars, but it bothered no one at the time. Godfroi himself apparently knew what would happen before he left on the crusade, assuming always that the crusade would prove successful, because he relinquished all of his French titles and land.

He committed himself completely, and the future of his lineage, to the gamble of conquering the Holy Land.

Events became a bit more straightforward with the accession of Baudoin, Godfroi's younger brother, to the throne of Jerusalem. . . but only marginally more straightforward. In the year 1118, Baudoin created the "Order of the Knights of the Temple," better known to history as the "Knights Templar," which was headquartered in the ancient Temple of Solomon "from which it is supposed that the fledgling Order derived its name."[5] At about the same time, Baudoin also created the "Order of the Knights of St. John of Jerusalem." The Knights Templar and the Knights of St. John were destined to have remarkably differing historical fates. The Knights Templar were the overt and obvious sword-arm of the de Bouillon dynasty and shared that bloodline's heroic and tragic fate. The Knights of St. John, on the other hand, were overtly committed to hospital work in addition to military duties, and they did not participate in the final hopeless defence of the de Bouillons. Instead, they stayed in the Holy Land until the Arabs gradually retook it from the Christians. The Knights of St. John then retreated to a succession of island fortresses out of direct reach of Arab power: first the island of Rhodes, and later the island of Malta. They are best known to history as the "Knights of Malta" and, as such, had a curiously powerful part to play in world affairs and world exploration up until the days of Champlain and his discoveries in Canada and the United States, a mysteriously potent influence that has relevance to later chapters. On a highly visible level, the Knights of St. John ("Knights of Malta") still exist today, still performing first-aid and hospital work under the guise of the St. John's Ambulance organization whose first-aid manuals and ambulance vehicles still bear the distinctive Maltese Cross.

But it was the Knights Templar that quickly captivated the imagination of European nobility and attracted the flower of European chivalry. Rules of conduct for the Order were drafted by no less a personage than St. Bernard, and these rules involved a demanding daily schedule of prayer, weapons training, military drill, manual work and meditation. An initiate into the Order had to relinquish all of his personal wealth, land, titles and coat-of-arms, and take the vows of poverty, chastity and celibacy. Knights Templar had but one insignia: a red "cross pattée" emblazoned on their white

surcoats and white shields. In spite of the tough entrance requirements and demanding daily rules of the Order, the Knights Templar
never had to organize a recruiting drive. The Order was swamped
with volunteers, of which only a small number were accepted.
Knights of the Order swore obedience only to the de Bouillon
dynasty and to Christ. A papal decree made them totally independent of any other secular authority and, in theory, the Knights
Templar and the de Bouillons were answerable only to the pope (on
earth) and only to God above.[6] In spite of its obscure origins in the
Pyrenees region of southern France, the de Bouillon lineage of
Jerusalem was accounted equal to the most illustrious of European
royalty and their Knights Templar rapidly gained the reputation for
being the Western World's elite military organization.

It is said that the Knights Templar never retreated and never
surrendered. On the battlefield they gave no quarter and asked for
none, though they were generous to fallen and disabled foes. Myths
and legends grew around them so rapidly that a handful of Knights
Templar could rout a much larger force of Saracen cavalry by both
superior warrior skill and psychology: their supposed prowess was
such that most of their foes felt beaten before any battle actually
started. Likewise, there are stories that just one Templar could
prevent the retreat of a mauled Christian force and transform
demoralized knights and soldiers into courageous warriors. They
quickly became the terror of Islam in the Holy Land and, at the
same time, compelled almost awed military respect for the de
Bouillon bloodline among European nobles and royalty.

The Templars were involved in naval warfare, too, and had a
fleet of ships based at La Rochelle in France. This fleet has much
relevance to later events involving transatlantic voyages, just as the
ships of the eventually island-bound Knights of Malta came to have
similar or even greater relevance.

Although individual Templars took vows of poverty, the Order
itself almost immediately became immensely wealthy. Some people
conjectured that this almost instant wealth derived from some
treasure discovered in the Temple of Solomon since, as was well
known from the Bible, King Solomon had undertaken a number of
lucrative voyages southward to the fabled "Land of Ophir," his
mariners bringing back shiploads of gems and gold.[7] More likely,

however, Templar wealth resulted from donations of money and land by initiates into the Order.

Indeed, Templar wealth excited awe and envy among European nobility just as their military prowess excited awe and fear. The Order quickly put its money to work in a way that no other organization of the time could. Being independent of all secular authority by papal decree, and being "international" in composition as a matter of course, Templars set up safe warehouses all over Europe. These were intended to assist merchants and craftsmen to greater productivity. At the same time, Templars undertook to protect merchant caravans on the appalling and dangerous European roads of the time. Naturally, given their reputation, no casual band of ill-armed robbers would dare attack a Templar-guarded pack-train. Additionally, because of their wealth and rapidly established Priories all over Europe, Templars were able to issue letters of credit based on monetary deposit to merchants in one place, which would be honoured by a Templar Priory anywhere in Europe. In short, Templars re-invented banking and became the bankers of their age, offering what would be called in modern terms "checking accounts." Merchants no longer had to carry bulky and tempting amounts of coinage around with them. This was a financial refinement that had not been seen on any large scale in Europe since the heyday of the Roman Empire, and it immediately stimulated trade and commerce.

Their fiscal pursuits place the Templars in an ironic position. On the one hand they indisputably represented the apex of knighthood and chivalry in feudal Europe; but on the other hand they engaged in mercantile activity which stimulated the rise of a merchant, middle class that would eventually undermine feudalism and chivalry itself. Templar warehousing, banking and pack-train guarding could not really be considered proper knightly activities in the 12th and 13th centuries and suspicion about Templar motives began to grow among increasingly disgruntled European nobility. Able to operate independently of all secular authority meant that Templars could set up their warehouses and banks anywhere they wished in Europe, even in cities and domains supposedly belonging to the local duke, count, baron, prince or king—or abbot, for that matter. Not only did the fees charged for warehouse space and honoring letters of credit go into Templar coffers and not into the strongboxes of the regional noble or "prince of the Church," but these Templar mercantile services encouraged the development of a merchant class, which had slim loyalty to the prevailing feudal system and perhaps less to the prevailing corrupt Roman Catholic Church. The Templars played a significant part in the social and economic evolution of Europe toward a more modern profile, and they were increasingly unappreciated by medieval vested interests.[8]

It seems that Templars were also behind the short-lived phenomenon of Gothic-styled cathedral-building. All of the great Gothic "Notre Dames" were constructed only during the 194 years of Templar ascendancy in Europe. This may be only a coincidence, but it is nonetheless a fact. True Gothic architecture, except for mock-antique revivals, seems to be associated with Templars. It has been noted by a number of scholars of architecture that the Gothic cathedral conforms to an exact and unvarying canon of design, a design which apparently derived from the plan of the Temple of Solomon in the Holy Land, headquarters of the Templars. But the Temple of Solomon, in turn, was supposedly based on the design of certain Egyptian temples and King Solomon employed Egyptian architects and masons to build his temple. According to some architectural authorities, the original Egyptian design, or canon, actually represented a reclining human female figure constructed, symbolically, of stone. After the temple rites, worshippers passed through the symbolic pubis of the female figure and were thus "reborn" in a state of greater purity.[9]

Gothic cathedrals apparently preserved this ancient Egyptian canon of architecture, and worshippers in all the "Notre Dames" were likewise reborn. All medieval Gothic cathedrals were originally designated as "'Notre Dame'-of-some city"—"Our Lady of Salisbury," for example. The "Lady" in question is popularly believed, of course, to be the Virgin Mary, mother of Jesus. But there are some indications that another Mary was actually being honored, in secrecy, in all the Templar-associated Gothic cathedrals.

Aside from the architectural canon, the financing of these cathedrals is believed to have been made possible by Templar money. We find that a Templar Priory was located very near to every "Notre Dame" ever built, sometimes within the shadow of the spires. One of the major mysteries about the sudden spate of cathedral-building is how, at the time, towns could afford to raise them. The cost of Salisbury Cathedral, as just one example, was far beyond the fiscal resources of medieval Salisbury's small population. The money, and the organization of master masons, must have come from some outside source. It seems that the Gothic "Notre Dames" all over Europe, in cities and smaller towns alike, were raised by a travelling corps of master masons and architects employed to construct a concealed message in stone and paid by Templar money. The message may have been concealed from the viewpoint of the average, oblivious worshipper of the 12th and 13th centuries, just as today's worshippers (or tourists) in the same cathedrals suspect nothing unorthodox—but the message, and secret, is supposedly known to some people.

In addition to their immense wealth and their military power, the Knights Templar enjoyed a very special prestige because of their important duty: *Templars, above all, were an elite force established in order to guard the Holy Grail.* "Everyone" in Europe knew this during the early 13th century because the poetical compositions of (mostly) southern French troubadours emphasized it. These romances captivated the intelligentsia of Europe, such as it was, and were avidly read by all who were literate. Even those who couldn't read, such as the less refined lords, ladies and rough knights in backwater courts and castles, heard these romances recited by travelling minstrels. All of these poetical compositions were woven around King Arthur and the Holy Grail. And, although the poetry stressed that King Arthur had lived long ago, the Holy Grail itself still existed and was presently, in the 13th century, guarded by Knights Templar. We moderns may regard this as a medieval fancy, and modern literary experts regard this troubadour literature as romance and nothing more, *but the Holy Grail was simply considered to be a fact at the time.* Indeed, even its location was common knowledge. The Holy Grail was guarded by Templars in the castle of Munsalvaesch, which modern scholars accept as the southern French citadel of Montségur.[10]

The Holy Grail.

What was this thing that has inspired so much European literature, legend and speculation?

Most people throughout the centuries since it first emerged in the poetry of the troubadours have thought of the Holy Grail as some sort of cup, vessel or platter. The most popular explanation has been that it was the Cup of the Last Supper, the same cup which was held aloft by Joseph of Arimathaea to catch the blood of Christ when Jesus' side was pierced by the spear of Caius Longinius, the Roman Centurion. As another variant, some people have considered it the platter upon which Salome bore the head of John the Baptiste. These are popular beliefs as to what the Holy Grail might have been, or be, but it did not take modern scholars long to muddle the issue with irrelevant pedantries. Since the Holy Grail was associated in the romances with King Arthur, and since Arthur ("Arthyr") was himself a Celtic hero, experts in Celtic literature and myth pointed out that the Holy Grail possessed legendary magical properties very similar to those of Carridwen's Cauldron. According to some of the troubadours, the Holy Grail was something that could perpetuate itself and from which flowed spiritual and physical sustenance. Carridwen's Cauldron of ancient Celtic myth seemed to be roughly similar: pieces of a dead person placed in the cauldron for a year and a day would emerge alive and correctly assembled; the cauldron could perpetuate people. Further, Carridwen's brew that accomplished this miracle also contained wisdom.

A Welsh tale about one of Carridwen's regeneration operations informs us that rather than stir her brew for the required year and a day herself, she hired a local boy named Gwion to perform this irksome task. He did this day after day faithfully enough until one fateful day a drop of the bubbling brew splashed out of the Cauldron onto Gwion's finger, blistering it. Gwion immediately popped the burned finger into his mouth in order to cool it and soothe the pain. He immediately acquired wisdom which, among other things, informed him that Carridwen planned to kill him as soon as he'd finished the dreary job of stirring the Cauldron. Rather than await his fate, Gwion sensibly abandoned his job and put as much distance between himself and Carridwen as possible. He changed his name to Taliesin ("Shining Brow") and, with his wisdom, became the most famous bard, or *ollave*, of Celtic history. Taliesin/Gwion was smart enough to propose a riddle to the 26 learned bards who served King

Maelgwn Gwynedd of North Wales. The bards couldn't guess the answer to the riddle.

In short, this Holy Grail seemed very similar to Carridwen's Cauldron and therefore some modern Celtic scholars take the position that the Holy Grail derived from the dawn of Celtic myth, . that the concept was picked up by Norman-French invaders of 1066, and that eventually troubadours refined the idea by creating the cycle of Grail Romances around the vague personage of King Arthur. This might be called the "establishment" or "conventional" explanation of the Holy Grail, and the entire convoluted argument is covered in *The Search for Arthur's Britain*, edited by the well-known British Arthurian author, Geoffrey Ashe. This book also relates how modern scholarship equates King Arthur with other mythical and legendary Celtic sun-kings and seasonal kings like Llew Llaw Griffes.[11]

There is, thankfully, a more straightforward explanation for the Holy Grail which derives from an analysis of linguistics. Provençal was the language of the southern French troubadours of the Pyrenees region, and almost all the Grail Romances were originally composed in this almost-extinct tongue. It was a language comprising almost equal parts of medieval French, medieval Spanish and Arabic. For the troubadours writing in the Provençal language, "Holy Grail" was rendered as *San Graal*. French historian and linguist, Jean-Marie Angebert, has shown that this *Graal* is actually an artificial and concocted word that never occurred in the Provençal language before 1188 A.D. and appears for the first time in *Le Roman de Perceval, ou Le Conte del Graal ("The Romance of Perceval, or the Tale of the Grail")* by Chrétien de Troyes. The word *Graal* seems to have been coined from three other words: the native Provençal word *grasale*, which means a vase or vessel of some sort; the Latin word *gradual*, which means a prayer book; and the Arabic *al gor'al*, which means "something inscribed upon."[12]

In actual pronunciation, however, the troubadours' *San Graal* approximates closely the medieval and modern French "Sang Réal." This means "Blood Royal" and a bit more. The French word *réal* has the same meaning as the English word "real," but more strongly. Real means "genuine," the "real thing," and the French word has that same meaning with much more emphasis. "Real" blood was "royal" blood of the elite that represented genuine, worthwhile humanity. The reason that this "royal" blood was more valuable, more "genuine" and held greater potential for fully human progress or evolution was that "royalty" had been created by divine dispensation, divine guidance, divine choice and even by divine intervention. Another meaning of "Sang Réal" could be *Holy Blood*, not just "blood royal," because of the divine nature of its creation.

We modern people of a democratic age may not be able to muster much sympathy for such a view, but it was a strong belief of the times. True royalty derived from divine dispensation, or intervention, and this represented the best or most genuine human genetic stock.

With all this in mind, we come to the conclusion that the Holy Grail not only *held* the "blood royal" or "Holy Blood," but that it *was* the blood royal or Holy Blood. What can this mean?

It really seems rather simple. The Holy Grail was not any sort of metallic, wooden or ceramic cup or vessel that held Holy Blood or any other liquid. The Holy Grail was a lineage, or bloodline, *of people* in whose veins flowed the Holy Blood, or blood royal, and who were the living vessel in which this blood was preserved and by which it could be perpetuated.

San Graal was a pun, a troubadour-concocted code phrase whose purpose was to disguise a monstrous heresy from the Roman Catholic Church.

But who was the Holy Blood?

Two things made identification obvious. First, Templars were believed to be the guardians of the Holy Grail and the Templars had been created by the de Bouillon dynasty of Jerusalem. Second, the Christians under the de Bouillon kings lost Jerusalem in the year 1187 A.D. The first Grail Romance emerged into European literature just one year after this defeat, 1188, with the work of Chrétien de Troyes. The obscure bloodline of Godfroi de Bouillon was the Holy Blood, which was why he had been elevated to the throne of Jerusalem. But, in losing the kingdom the de Bouillon dynasty also lost both its geopolitical power base and its special sanctity, which protected it from those, high up in Church and nobility, who would much rather destroy the lineage and let the world forget about it.

Because of the defeat of the dynasty in 1187, the bloodline of Godfroi de Bouillon also faced extinction at the hands of European rivals both secular and religious. Those in possession of the incredible de Bouillon secret knew very well that the bloodline was unlikely to survive the converging forces of orthodox retribution. A history, or eulogy, of the Holy Blood was therefore necessary to preserve the truth for humanity. The first "Tale of the Grail" therefore appeared only one year after the de Bouillon dynasty's defeat in the Holy Land.

Retreating from the Middle East, the de Bouillon family, its supporters and their Templars fell back to southern France and the Pyrenees region from which the de Bouillons had sprung. And, almost immediately, troubadours *from that very region* began to compose the eulogy. And it was necessary.

Southern France and the loyal supporters of the de Bouillons there enjoyed only a brief and nervous respite of 22 years before the powers of orthodoxy co-operated to crush them. In 1209 A.D. the pope called for a crusade against southern France, and the heretics it contained. Northern French armies, and papal forces, invaded Provence and Languedoc. The object was not to defeat and conquer, but to exterminate. Heretical supporters of the de Bouillon dynasty, and the dynasty itself, were to be utterly wiped out if at all possible. One of the most merciless religious wars the world has ever known raged in southern France for a third of a century. During all of this time, Grail Romances were composed and sung by Provençal knight-poets. They travelled all over Europe reciting their works so that the story of the Holy Blood would not perish even if the human representatives of it did. The last heretical stronghold, the citadel of Montségur, haven of the Holy Grail, fell to the invaders on March 16, 1244.

People in southern France believed that the de Bouillon dynasty was the Holy Blood and the "Holy Grail." What was the foundation for this belief? What were the proofs of it, if any? We may smile at such a naive-seeming belief, but we should bear in mind that thousands of courageous men and women died for it during the 35-year war in the Pyrenees.

Why was the de Bouillon lineage considered to be supremely "holy" or "royal"?

Offering an answer to this question will lead us to the heart of the *alleged* momentous, ancient secret truth that inspired the heresy known as Catharism.

But before we listen to these whispers from humanity's most remote past as monotheistic beings, and before attempting to assess whether these incredible rumours and beliefs may hold a grain of truth, we must conclude that there has always been a popular misconception about the real nature of the crusades.

The First Crusade, the one led by Godfroi de Bouillon, was not only or even mostly an attempt to wrest the Holy Land from Islamic hands. It was mostly an attempt to re-establish a lineage of people who may have had a legitimate claim to the city of Jerusalem, a blood-line that uniquely contained within itself the possibility of reconciling Jew, Christian and Moslem within one harmonious world community. That possibility, and that dream, was betrayed and opposed by vested interests of Jewish, Christian and Islamic orthodoxy which had no desire to be supplanted and which inspired ignorant followers to fanatical denial of the crusade's objectives. Godfroi de Bouillon wanted to create a "New Jerusalem" in the Holy Land where the three great faiths of the West could be reconciled. He failed, but this sort of crusade is what apparently motivated Christopher Columbus and his supporters and financial backers. His voyage may have been a crusade to establish a "New Jerusalem in a New World" and, I think, this is the light in which we should view his motivations. It is also a perspective and a light that will permit some insight into the anomalous facts and unlikely coincidences of his life. He seems to have been a part of an ancient, noble conspiracy to create a world of religious toleration between Jew, Christian and Moslem. A New Jerusalem. That, I think, was Columbus's concept of a crusade, and the only worthwhile kind of crusade.[13]

Later crusades, it is true, those inspired by the Roman Church after the initial concept had been obscured and all but obliterated, were simply a geopolitical struggle to take Palestine from the Moslems. But the First Crusade was qualitatively different, and even in failure left echoes of worthy motivation that could inspire men like Columbus.

Chapter 4

Echoes of Ancient Truth?

Europe today bears little social or political similarity with Europe in the 13th century. Eight hundred years ago, Europe, like most of the world, presented a patch-work quilt of distinctive regional enclaves that fragmented the sub-continent. These regional enclaves represented the historical detritus of the many migrations, invasions, amalgamations and refugees that European peoples had experienced over countless centuries. Each small geographical region boasted its own characteristic culture, language and, sometimes, even its own genotype of "sub-racial" population which was fairly distinct from its neighbors. Most of these distinctive cultural and linguistic regions have long since been submerged, and amalgamated, in the evolution of European nation-states that appear on maps today. But as late as the time of Queen Elizabeth I of England, for example, the local cultures of Yorkshire and Somerset were completely different in character and the languages of the two places were all but unintelligible to each other. Linguistics were a very real problem in early English parliaments, and it was a problem not really solved until the Shakespearian plays created a common English vocabulary of about 20,000 words.

One unsubmerged European enclave still exists in a highly visible form in today's Europe: the Basque provinces of southern France and northern Spain straddling the Pyrenees mountains. Basques preserve their distinctive language, which does not appear to belong to any other family of Indo-European tongues, and they preserve their equally unique culture. Indeed, the Basque language, culture and physical appearance is so different from their Spanish and French neighbors that there is a strong and determined "Basque independence movement" punctuated by occasional violence in the form of riots and bombings directed against their French and Spanish overlords.

Some anthropologists have concluded that the Basques are a remnant of Europe's oldest "modern man" population, survivors of a cultural/linguistic group and genotype that inhabited Europe during glacial times, and that their language may be the oldest surviving one in the world. Perhaps, according to some experts, the Basque language is a lingering example of the speech of cave-dwellers, even though it has naturally evolved over time. When the glaciers began to retreat about 15,000 years ago, inviting a large number of immigrants to enter Europe from Africa and eastern Eurasia, the Basque-like people then living all over Europe were either mostly exterminated or absorbed by the newcomers except for a substantial group that found refuge in the Pyrenees. There, they have remained to this day, while the larger tides of European history and migrations swirled around the foothills of their mountain fastness. And so the ancient Basque culture and language survives vitally into the late 20th century.[1]

One might say that conditions in 13th-century Europe were more "Basque-like" than the reality of today. Roads were almost non-existent and long-distance trade routes were exceedingly tenuous. Mountains, forests and marshes represented very real barriers to travel, communication and cultural exchange over most of Europe.

Only in Eastern Europe was there an encroaching tongue of Asian steppeland, the plains of Hungary and East Prussia south of the Friches Haff, presenting a convenient corridor for a succession of rapid invasions and rapid cultural changes. Just west of this corridor, however, the steppes and plains gave way to marshes and dense forests and rugged mountains. Peoples coming through this corridor tended to become slowed down immediately in their westward migration, so that on these Hungarian plains there was a succession of incoming cultures more or less stacked on top of one another at the bottleneck. Perhaps the first distinctive people to arrive was the so-called "battle-axe" culture which eventually wended its way through German forests to Denmark and Scandinavia. Then came steppe Cimmerians, later to be called Cymry, who finally ended up in Wales; then other Celtic-speakers who found enclaves in various parts of Europe, like the Goidels who settled in Ireland; then "Goths" who became Germans; then strange Caucasian people from the depths of Asia whom history knows as "Huns"; then steppe herdsmen from southern Russia called Khazars, who had been converted to Judaism (of all things!) and who later spread all over Eastern Europe as the "Ashkenazim" who were decimated during Hitler's Holocaust; Mongols came on the heels of the Khazars and effected their dispersion as "Ashkenazim"; Tamerlane led a mixed group of Caucasian-Oriental horsemen through the Hungarian steppe-gate, but turned around and went back to Asia when Europe didn't seem worth conquering; then Ottoman Turks surged through Hungary and stayed long enough to instill a lasting fear of Arabic domination in Columbus's day; and finally the Nazi juggernaut rumbled on Panzer treads through the gate in the opposite direction, towards Russia and the wider steppes, just as Gustavus Adolphus of Sweden and Napoleon Bonaparte of France had previously done, and just as briefly, before the Red Army came surging back through the steppe corridor in 1944–45 to give Nazi Germany its death blow.

Hungarian culture, above all, is indelibly stamped with the culture and characteristics of all these disparate peoples who have passed through the steppe-gate and who have found their momentum abruptly halted by the marshes, mountains and forests immediately ahead. Like confused and milling passengers stranded in some storm-bound airport awaiting infrequent and delayed planes to take a trickle of their number, too slowly, to their intended destinations, these disparate peoples finally formed an eclectic and vital association of immense intellectual stimulation. Perhaps that is why, considering its relatively small population, Hungary has given an inordinate number of writers, scientists, artists and musicians to the world; and why Hungarians seem adaptable enough to flourish in every country of the Western World.

But most of the migrants passing through the Hungarian Gate did finally move on to find havens where they settled. Just as the western Pyrenees on the Atlantic coast provides a refuge for the ancient

Basques, the eastern Pyrenees also became a chosen haven for people who arrived much later. These people were mainly of Celtic stock, but not wholly so. After the fall of the fortress of Masada in 70 A.D., Jews fleeing Roman persecution arrived in significant numbers in the same eastern Pyrenees region and were accommodated by the Celts already there. The two peoples blended, despite differences in culture, language and religion. Still later, during the 11th century, Moorish-Arabic refugees streamed into the eastern Pyrenees fleeing from the victories of Ruy Diaz, Count of Bivar, better known to history as "El Cid" (from the Arabic *sayyid*, "lord") who began the conquest, or "re-conquest," of Spain for Christianity. These Arabic-speaking, culturally Moorish immigrants were also accommodated, very possibly because of the large number of Jews that accompanied them. Some of these Jews had arrived in Spain in the Diaspora following the fall of Masada, but most had arrived in Spain with the army of Tariq ibn Zayid, the Berber chieftain who invaded Spain in 711 A.D. Again, it was probably the Jews among the Moors fleeing from El Cid who eased the acceptance of this new influx of refugees. Jews had blended with the Pyrenees Celts before, and Jews accompanying refugee Moors probably helped the Celts to accept these Arabic-speakers with a minimum of friction. A unique mountain civilization evolved from the melding of Celt, Jew and Moor, and the geographical extent of this civilization needs delineating.

The Pyrenees chain extends to the Alps of western Switzerland and to the so-called "Maritime Alps" of northwestern Italy, Liguria, whose largest town was, and is, Genoa, the supposed birthplace of Christopher Columbus. From the geologist's point of view, this is all one mountain system and it is broken only by the valley of the Rhône River. The term I've used, "eastern Pyrenees," really has no geological or geographic relevance, but serves to emphasize that while the Basques firmly controlled the western, Atlantic, end of the mountain chain, the mixed civilization of Celt, Jew and Moor just as firmly established itself in the eastern part of the mountains, including parts of Switzerland and northwestern Italy. This civilization had no name in the 13th century because people there, as elsewhere in Europe, thought of themselves as members of fiefs held by local dukes, counts, princes and rather petty kings. People did not usually think of themselves as being members of any larger cultural, geographic or political entity.

Nonetheless, without too much over-simplification we can call this civilization "Provençal" because of the common language it evolved and which was spoken from the Basque-speaking frontier in the west to Italy and Switzerland in the east. As was mentioned before, this language was a meld of Frankish, Visigothic and Arabic in about equal proportions and written in the Roman script. It also contained a fair number of Hebrew loan words which were transliterated into the Roman script.

There seems little room for doubt that Jewish culture was the cement between the Celts and Moors of this unlikely civilization, and this is indicated by both personal names and place-names of the region. To cite just a few examples, we have the towns of Sion and Levi in southern France, while Miron "Le Levite" was a 6th-century count of the region and King Clothair II's brother was named Samson. Scholars have traced the area's early Salic Law back to Judaic Law.

This Provençal civilization differed greatly from the rest of Europe. Secular literature was being created in these southern mountains when most of Europe was illiterate. This southern realm was wealthy because of trade contacts with the Arab world. Its material culture boasted luxury goods that were rare in the remainder of Europe, or non-existent save for envious whispers: ivory that came from Arab merchants, and which did not originate from the elephants of Africa, as one might expect, but from fossil mammoth tusks obtained in Siberia; silk from China; rubies and emeralds from the half-legendary island of Taprobane (Ceylon); spices from Indonesia; books and musical instruments from the Middle East and Moorish Spain; and constant visits from scholars, writers, artists, "scientists" and philosophers from the cream of Jewish, Arabic and Christian cultures.

Aside from intellectual development and wealth, Provençal culture differed from the rest of Europe in at least two other respects. First, the status of women was much higher in this southern realm than anywhere else in 13th-century Europe. During the 1200s a number of fiefs were owned and held by women in the Pyrenees and there were even acknowledged women military leaders like Esclarmonde de Foix, commander of Montségur castle. Women also had access to secular education and there were a number of women troubadours.[2] It was in this southern realm that a novel attitude toward women evolved—novel at least in medieval Europe for nothing similar had been seen since the fall of Rome: the idea that women could be respected and cherished as individuals rather than be regarded as inferior creatures useful only for rape and reproduction. *Amor courtoise* was invented in these southern mountains, the theme of countless troubadour ballads. Nowadays this is always translated as "courtly love," which is the literal translation, and has come to be regarded as exaggerated romanticism. But I think that the words are better rendered as "gentle love" since, if one reads troubadour poetry, and particularly the work of women poets, romanticism is not exaggerated at all. Much healthy and uninhibited sexuality is described, and also obviously condoned by the troubadours' culture. The vast difference from male/female relations in the rest of Europe, though, was that this sexuality was not for the purpose of rather impersonal reproduction, the only kind of sexual expression condoned by the Roman Catholic Church, and consequently it did not tend toward brutality. *Amor courtoise* encouraged a view of women as complete human beings and natural sexual relations between men and women included respect, love, restraint and also a good deal of intellectual interchange.

From *amor courtoise* came a corollary that affected knighthood and warfare: the idea of chivalry. This was the novel notion that a true knight was not simply a loutish and lethal fighting man for his overlord, but had a higher obligation to protect the powerless as well as to be a valiant warlord. Indeed, the greater the knight's prowess as a fighting man, the more he was expected to exercise that power in defence of women and other non-combatants and to extend mercy to fallen foes. The "European" ideal of chivalry was created in the Provençal civilization and codified by the troubadour knight-poets of southern France.

Another non-material way in which this southern civilization differed from the rest of Europe was religions. Its major religion was not Roman Catholic Christianity at all, but a "heresy" known as Catharism or Albigensianism (after the town of Albi, a center of this unorthodox faith).

It is difficult, if not truly impossible after the lapse of eight hundred years, to recover the truth about what Catharism really was as a religion. We cannot securely grasp its actual tenets and beliefs. There is a contemporary "Cathar revival" of significant force in France and Europe today, but the rites and teachings of these self-proclaimed neo-Cathars may be just as bogus as the mumbo-jumbo uttered by Druidiots at Britain's Stonehenge on midsummer morn.

At the grass-roots level of participation affecting the "peasant-in-the-field," Catharism seems to have presented a vaguely Christian profile. There were Cathar churches operating in competition with Roman Catholic ones. Cathar churches boasted much larger congregations than the Catholic churches because the Roman clergy of the times was blatantly corrupt. There were Catholic churches in "Provence" in which a Mass had not been celebrated for generations.[3] In these churches, Cathar religious services incorporated readings from the Bible and utilized Christian parables, but some experts think that this was done merely to offer simple peasants something similar to the Christianity they'd known for centuries.

At higher levels of initiation it has been questioned whether Cathars were Christian at all. Steven Runciman, a respected historian of the crusades, believes that they were "western Budhists."[4] Idries Shah, a Middle-Eastern expert and author presently living in Britain, has argued that the Cathars closely resembled a European version of an Islamic mystical sect known as *Sufis*.[5] This word comes from the Arabic *suf*, meaning "blue," and it does seem to be true that 13th century Cathars did wear blue robes while modern neo-Cathars favor this color as well. Still other experts associate Cathars with the so-called "Bogomil Sect,"[6] of which little is known except that adherents of it migrated from Bulgaria into the Pyrenees region during the 11th and 12th centuries A.D. Walter Birks and R.A. Gilbert, co-authors of *The Treasure of Montségur*, are of the opinion that the Cathars were fully Christian alright, but were a sect that either preserved or somehow recreated the simple tenets of early Christianity that existed before being submerged beneath the pretentions accretions of Rome and pope. According to Birks and Gilbert, genuinely Cathar-like congregations still exist in the mountains of Turkey near Lake Van.[7]

It is known that the Cathars believed in living love and revered Jesus as a teacher of it. They rejected the cross as a proper symbol upon which to focus meditation, for they believed that Christ's legacy of living love had not ended on Calvary but still existed in vital form. Cathars also rejected the concept of priests. Instead, they had "spiritual leaders" or "gurus" (there's really no other word) called, in Latin, *perfecti* or "perfected ones," and known as *parfaits* in the Provençal language of the time. These "perfects" seem not to have been officially ordained in any way, but seem to have been people who were recognized as having achieved a certain level of spirituality. *Perfecti* took vows of poverty, celibacy and, apparently, vegetarianism.

In another departure from Roman Catholic Christianity, *perfecti* could be both men or women. In the early 13th century there were more women *perfecti* than men. These *parfaits* gave the sermons, such as they were, in Cathar churches. Before the pope called for a crusade against these people, St. Bernard was sent to preach among them in an attempt to convert them to orthodoxy. But he seems to have been impressed with the Cathars instead. He wrote:

> No sermons are more Christian than theirs, and their morals are pure.[8]

There are some who suspect that St. Bernard became a Cathar in secret and was initiated into their great secret doctrine. This is the same St. Bernard who drafted the rules for the Knights Templar.

Although they rejected the cross, Cathars had their own symbols. They venerated the dove as a symbol of peace and God's grace. They also venerated the dragon, the "serpent" in the Garden of Eden, as the entity which brought knowledge to mankind. Apparently, the Cathars believed that it was impossible to attain truth, and impossible to practice "living love," without certain knowledge. Because of this, the Cathars are classed as "gnostics" (from the Greek *gnosis* = knowledge) by the few students of comparative religion who have bothered to study them.

One more thing is important to know about the Cathars, at least for our limited purposes: they were believed to possess the Holy Grail. As was mentioned before, the actual geographical location of the Holy Grail was more or less common knowledge in 13th-century

Europe. It was guarded by Templars in the Cathar citadel of Montségur, a five-sided fortress built atop a peak in the Pyrenees, a castle commanded by Esclarmonde de Foix. But by "possession" it was meant that the Cathars not only guarded the Holy Grail in one of their castles, but owned it in the sense of understanding what it was.

We have already concluded that the Holy Grail must have been the bloodline of Godfroi de Bouillon which, in fact, originated within the Provençal civilization and Cathar territory. De Bouillon's line had come from the Dukes of Razès centered on a town called Rhédae in medieval times, the modern hamlet in the Pyrenees called Rennes-le-Chateau.

Why was the lineage of the de Bouillons considered holy?

The answer to that question uncovers one of the most incredible and momentous secret beliefs in human history. It was the belief that nurtured Catharism. It was a belief that the Roman Church eradicated so thoroughly that only echoes of it remain to be heard dimly by historical experts, while the average, educated Westerner has been able to hear nothing at all.

Until recently. The story of how this ancient secret belief has again come into the light of some understanding is almost as incredible as the secret itself. In this case, truth is definitely stranger than the wildest fiction, because the truth is that the secret was revealed by a series of documents deposited anonymously in France's Bibliothèque Nationale during the 1950s and 1960s. These documents included, but were not limited to, genealogical charts that traced the bloodline of Godfroi de Bouillon back to Jesus Christ. Other documents fleshed out the complex associations existing between this lineage and Cathars, Templars, Knights of Malta—and modern organizations and individuals who apparently wield mysterious power today.[9]

The entire affair has been something of a *cause célèbre* in the intellectual and popular press of Europe for about 40 years. Dozens of books and magazine articles have been written about the de Bouillon ancestry and the genealogies that purport to prove it and, naturally, most of these were written and published in France. The story did not really break for the Anglo-Saxon world at large until the 1982 publication of *The Holy Blood and The Holy Grail*, although I had referred to it four years earlier in 1978 in *The Iceman*

Inheritance, which was published only in Canada. In the intervening years there have also been three British Broadcasting Corporation documentaries about the incredible French revelation, but these have never been televised to North American audiences. Since 1982 there have been other English-language books about the de Bouillon secret, notably *The Messianic Legacy* and *The Temple and The Lodge* by the authors of *The Holy Blood and The Holy Grail*, and my own *Holy Grail Across The Atlantic*.

It remains true, however, that the vast majority of North American readers are totally unfamiliar with this entire story. It must be sketched in, at least, if the argument of this book is to carry any weight. However, I will try to outline the beliefs about the lineage of Godfroi de Bouillon as briefly as possible while hopefully offering enough evidence to make the secret seem plausible. Readers who are interested in the almost unimaginable wealth of detail concerning this momentous secret are referred to the English-language books mentioned above as well as to the original French-language books listed in the bibliography.

It is important to bear in mind, while reading the following brief account of the "Secret of the Holy Grail," that it may not be true. Indeed, the account will contradict so many of our most dearly held beliefs, opinions and dogmas that few people will probably *want* it to be true, or accept it as true. In fact, it will probably seem preposterous.

That isn't really important, however. What is important is the fact, and it is an undoubted fact, that many people in the 13th century *believed it to be true*. Their belief molded their faith, lives and motivations in a way that was completely unorthodox according to the tenets of the dominant Roman Catholic Church.

Here is the story.

Christ's legacy of love did not end with the Crucifixion, of course, but lived on in His teachings recounted in the New Testament. But Cathars believed something more. They believed that His genetic legacy had not ended, either, and that descendants of Jesus had survived and escaped from Palestine. According to the Cathars, Jesus and Mary Magdalene had been married. And, according to Cathar belief, this crucial fact of Christ's life was later purposefully obscured by patriarchal and anti-feminist editors of the New Testament. Further, according to this belief, Mary had not only been the wife of Jesus, but his most devoted and favored disciple, a fact which inspired jealousy in the male Apostles and contributed to the distortion of history.

After the Crucifixion, a number of Christ's relatives managed to escape from Palestine, including at least: Mary the Virgin, mother of Jesus; Joseph of Arimathaea, who was either Jesus's uncle or his father-in-law; Mary of Bethany; and Mary Magdalene, who either then had living children by Jesus or a baby in the womb. There is some disagreement as to how this group left Palestine, some believing that they embarked of their own accord but in secrecy, and some believing that they were put into a boat without food or water and cast adrift by Pharisees. In any event, whether by conscious design or through the agency of a miracle, the group survived to reach Marseilles. It is interesting to note that an independent and non-Christian legend supports this version of events, because the Gypsies recount that Black Sara, a local Gypsy queen, swam out to meet the boat and guide its passengers into the Rhône estuary. It is also at least suggestive that there is a shrine of "Les Saintes Maries" near Marseilles where one Mary is supposed to have died and where her purported relics have been venerated since the earliest times.[10]

It is likely, however, that if any Mary died near Marseilles it would most probably have been the Virgin Mary since she was an older woman. Marseilles would not have been a safe place to stay. It was a major seaport of the Roman Empire with frequent communication with Rome because of vessels sailing back and forth. Survivors of the group made their way up the Rhône River northward along an established trade route and then crossed over to either the Seine or Rhine valleys.[11] Using one of these two rivers they reached the Channel and crossed over to Britain. They then made their way to Glastonbury where they settled.

From a purely objective point of view, this choice of a haven made excellent sense. It was within civilization, which is to say the Roman Empire, and yet it was at the very western fringe of it and as far away from Palestine as it was possible to get within the Roman world. Tradition says two things: first, that Joseph of Arimathaea stuck his thornwood staff into the ground at Glastonbury to mark the site of the church he planned to build in honor of Jesus, which would have been the first church in all of Christendom; and second, troubadour romances insist that Joseph of Arimathaea was the first guardian of the Holy Grail.

These traditions are somewhat disturbing. Although Barbara Tuchman dismisses the Glastonbury legends of Joseph of Arimathaea's presence as a "psychological need" in her *Bible and Sword*, we are faced with the botanical fact that there is a "Glastonbury Thorn" tree, which is supposed to be a descendant sprout of the original tree that grew from the staff of Joseph of Arimathaea. The normal type of thorn indigenous to Britain and northern Europe is *Crataegus oxyacantha*, but the "Glastonbury Thorn" is a specimen of *Crataegus praecox*, which is native to the eastern Mediterranean and should not be able to grown in the climate of Glastonbury but does.[12] There's no doubt that this anomalous thorn tree exists because any tourist today can view it, and photograph it, at Glastonbury Abbey as I did myself in February 1983.

Then, some of the troubadours made it clear that the Holy Grail was associated with children and the ability to perpetuate itself. This supports the linguistic contentions of Jean-Marie Angebert that the Holy Grail was a lineage of people that "held" the Holy Blood and not any sort of cup except in an allegorical sense. Now, Joseph of Arimathaea is universally agreed to have been, in legend, the first guardian of the Holy Grail during the time he lived in Britain. If it is correct that we are dealing with a bloodline of people descended from Jesus, this can only mean that Christ's widowed wife also resided in Britain under the protection of Joseph of Arimathaea, who was either her own father or her uncle.

The child of Jesus, or some of the children if there was more than one child, apparently survived to grow up and marry into the Romano-Celtic nobility and royalty of Britain. The evidence for this is slim, but suggestive. One Arthurian-age king in Wales was named Map ap Mathonwy. *Map* means "treasure" in Welsh, while *ap* means "of." What about the *Mathonwy*? I give a linguistic argument in *Holy Grail Across The Atlantic*, too detailed and ethnographic to go into here, that it is a Celtization of "Arimathaea." If this linguistic analysis is at all valid, then this Welsh king was called "Treasure of Arimathaea," which is very suggestive indeed since Joseph of Arimathaea had no treasure except the Holy Grail he guarded. If this

The famous "Glastonbury Thorn" at Glastonbury Abbey supposedly sprouted from the staff of Joseph of Arimathaea. It is a Palestinian variety of thorn and does bloom approximately at Easter. The original tree was cut down by a Puritan fanatic in the 1600s. The present tree was planted from a salvaged branch of the original one, but the present tree is not necessarily in the same location.

Photo by Michael Bradley.

Holy Grail was a bloodline descended from Jesus, and if this Welsh king married into it, the nature of the treasure becomes clear enough.

Then, we can return briefly to little Gwion who stirred the regenerative, bubbling Cauldron of Carridwen until a drop flew out and burned his finger. With the wisdom obtained from sucking the blistered finger, Gwion became Taliesin ("Shining Brow") the most knowledgeable bard in Celtic history. We will recall that Taliesin was able to propose a riddle that baffled the 26 learned *ollaves* of King Maelgwn Gwynedd of North Wales.

Now the curious thing about this Celtic "legend" is that both Taliesin and Maelgwn Gwynedd were real people who lived in the 6th century A.D. King Maelgwn Gwynedd had been an ally of King Arthur up until the Battle of Camlann, which greatly reduced the power of Arthur's Britain. Maelgwn Gwynedd saw his chance during the battle and suddenly betrayed Arthur by throwing his troops onto the side of Mordred, Arthur's son and opponent. By this treachery, Maelgwn Gwynedd won independence from the weakened Arthurian Britain. The important point, though, is that Taliesin taunted Maelgwn Gwynedd that the trifling independence he had won by treachery was nothing compared to the immortal fame he would have enjoyed in song and story if he had remained loyal to Arthur. It was dangerous to taunt kings back then, and Maelgwn Gwynedd threatened to relieve Taliesin of his head if he could not propose a riddle that the king's 26 most learned bards could not answer. As we know, Taliesin was successful and kept his head and his fame.

But what was the nature of this riddle? It is a long series of questions to which there is but one answer each. It exists today as the *Hanes Taliesin* ("Song of Taliesin") in two forms: one translated by the Lady Charlotte Guest and one translated by D.W. Nash as published in *Myvyrian Archeology*. The answer to this riddle, which has not been answered by anyone in fifteen hundred years is, I believe, simply "Holy Blood" or "Holy Grail" for the answers are all names of persons from the time of Abraham to the time of King Arthur, including Jesus. A full translation of this riddle is found in *The White Goddess* by Robert Graves. The riddle supplies part of the genealogy that comprises the Holy Blood.[13]

Taliesin and his riddle resonates fifteen hundred years later in the post-World War II world and Franklin Delano Roosevelt's personal delegates to Geneva to thrash out details of the Marshall Plan to rebuild Europe and, again, to create a "New Jerusalem." But that is an obscure fact of history to be saved for later.

Taliesin and his riddle have already brought us to the 6th century and King Arthur. If the Holy Blood/Holy Grail came to Glastonbury sometime around 33–35 A.D. it had almost five hundred years to survive, reproduce and marry into the noble and royal families of Roman-Celtic Britain. Doubtless, by the end of this time, the Holy Blood figured in most of the notable genealogies of the age. King Arthur, however, represents the culmination of the Holy Grail's career in Britain. As everyone knows, King Arthur, too, was a guardian of the Holy Grail.

In this brief outline of a long and complex story, King Arthur's precise relationship to the Grail, which is discussed in detail in *The Holy Blood and The Holy Grail* and refined and possibly corrected in *Holy Grail Across The Atlantic*, is not nearly so important as his strategic situation. Arthur's Britain was being invaded by Angles, Saxons and Jutes from across the North Sea. King Arthur attained fame by holding back this Scandinavian tide for a generation or so while his Camelot blazed defiance from the top of Cadbury Hill, but the inevitable outcome was never in doubt. Britain would be, and was, in spite of the valor of Arthur and his knights, inundated by the invaders. Facing up to this inexorable pattern of history, direct descendants of the Holy Blood were evacuated across the Channel to be handed over to a greater military power than Arthurian Britain represented and which controlled a mainland territory that could not be cut off like insular Britain.

The Holy Grail was transferred across the Channel into the hands of the Merovingian rulers of "France." After landing in Brittany, where some representatives of the Holy Bloodline stayed to settle and then to make history in 1066, the most direct descendants settled in Anjou. As had happened in Britain over the past five hundred years or so, the representatives of the Holy Blood began to marry into the Merovingian dynasty of Frankish royalty.

Perhaps this is a good time to pause and reflect on the fact that this particular time in history is called the "Dark Ages," and not without good reason. Rome had been sacked by Alaric the Visigoth in 410 A.D. and one can say that the "Ancient World" of Greece and Rome ended then. Alaric ripped the entire fabric of Western Civilization asunder, and there are some who have argued that the cloth has never been wholly mended since. Continuity in Western Civilization became a casualty of barbarian migration and invasion. Aside from the fact that hundreds of thousands of people were killed outright during the barbarian inundation of the Roman Empire, that large cities were razed to disappear entirely from history or recover to linger as small towns today, that hundreds of thousands of documents were lost or destroyed, aside from all that, the values and traditions of Greco-Roman culture were suddenly all but completely submerged beneath the oral traditions, social institutions and religions of Germanic peoples.

What happened after 410 A.D. in Rome and Italy is often very hazy for modern scholars, and what happened in the outlying provinces is even more uncertain. Secular literacy disappeared for all practical purposes, and the only records from this time derive from notes and commentaries that scattered monks and priests happened to write. This amounts to precious little, when all is said and done. Some of the surviving "chronicles," for example, make no mention at all of what happened in some years, while for some other years only the major event was chronicled. We are apt to read entries like: "571 A.D. The harvest failed and the Jutes sacked Brighton (again)." This is an imaginary quote, not a real one from a surviving chronicle, but it gives a more or less accurate idea of the documentation existing in the "Dark Ages." And we must remember that most of the chronicles were written by one or more monks cowering in just one town or monastery who could speak only of very local conditions. No one was in a position to write a history of the chaos and confusion of Europe as a whole.

How long did these "Dark Ages" last? This is, naturally, a matter of scholarly opinion and dispute. Things became a little better around the year 800 A.D. when Europe had recovered sufficient cohesion to conceive, at least, the "Holy Roman Empire" under Charlemagne, and some historians are inclined to place the boundary between the "Dark Ages" and the Medieval period here, in the year 800 A.D. Others, however, feel that historical obscurity doesn't really lift until somewhere around the year 1500 A.D. This was just after the invention of the printing press, which again made possible the creation of truly secular literature and which began to stimulate secular literacy. It was also a time when the surviving Greek and Roman literature began to reach an audience again because of their translation into regional European languages. Historical periods are artificial constructs for academic convenience, but perhaps one could say that the Renaissance or "rebirth" of Western culture was fully established by the year 1500 A.D., and that the "Dark Ages" had really ended. If one accepts this timetable, then it is interesting to note that all of Columbus's life was effectively within the "Dark Ages."

Our problem with the story of the Holy Grail is that no one would argue that it took place entirely within the "Dark Ages." In fact, viewed objectively, the story of the Holy Grail may well be the only "international history" or chronicle to survive from this period. But the frustration must be that we can place no firm dates for any of the events. King Arthur is believed to have lived in a vague "sometime" between 400 A.D. and 600 A.D. Geoffrey of Monmouth wrote in his *Historia regnum Britannae (History of the Kings of Britain)*:

> Even the renowned king Arthur himself was wounded deadly and was borne thence to the Island of Avalon for the healing of his wounds, where he gave up the crown to his kinsman, Constantine, son of Cador, in A.D. 542.[14]

We cannot trust this date absolutely, yet it gives us a rough idea of when Arthur died—say, within 50 years or so. Arthur's last battle was the Battle of Camlann, but the forces ranged against him had been coalescing for some time. If the Holy Grail was really ever in Arthur's care, and if it was truly a bloodline of people descending from Jesus, then the Holy Blood, the most direct descendants, would have been evacuated from Britain some years before the final battle when the future looked all too ominous.

Across the Channel in France, allies of Arthur, the Merovingian dynasty, fought against incursions by the same Angles, Saxons and Jutes that threatened Britain. The difference between France and Britain, of course, was that France was not an island that could be cut off and completely conquered. King Arthur could not retreat, but if necessary the Merovingians could do so toward the south of France and thus escape total defeat and total inundation. The most famous Merovingian king was Clovis, who supposedly ruled between 481 and 511 A.D. in these "Dark Ages" and who was baptised in 496 A.D. by St. Rémy.

This seems to be a fairly certain date. And, if we can trust it, it seems likely that King Arthur of Britain and King Clovis were contemporaries. The Holy Grail may have been transferred to Brittany and Anjou during the time of Clovis, or immediately before or after his time, but sometime around 500 A.D. Now, there is no proof of such a transfer, but there's an interesting circumstance that supports the possibility that it actually took place. Around the year 500 A.D. the Merovingian dynasty of France unaccountably adopted two symbols that could be related to the Holy Grail tale. First, they adopted the familiar fleur-de-lis, or "lily," of France. What most people do not know, however, is that this "lily" was a highly stylized depiction of the real flower and the "fleur-de-lis" is identical with stylized lilies depicted on Hebrew coinage from the time of King David. Readers familiar with the Bible will know that Jewish love-poetry from the time of Kings Solomon and David made frequent allusions to lilies. This flower was so prominent in Hebrew literature of the time that coins depicted it. Jesus claims descent from the House of David, and we must ask if the Merovingians adopted the identically stylized lily of David's coins as their "fleur-de-lis" because of intermarriage with the Holy Blood? It seems at least possible.[15]

Then, at the same time, the Merovingians also adopted another, stranger, symbol. Along with the "fleur-de-lis," they adorned (if that's the right word) their banners with toads or frogs. What is the meaning of this?

Merovingian legends insist that, about the year 500 A.D. if not a little before, their lineage was enhanced by union with a "sea creature" which brought knowledge and wisdom. This "sea creature" was apparently represented by the toads or frogs on merovingian flags.[16]

Now, it is merely a matter of linguistic fact that *Mary* means "of the sea." Further, there are traditions that Mary Magdalene was a descendant of Solomon and a member of the lost Benjamite Tribe of Israel. David usurped the throne from Solomon in a dynastic struggle, and Jesus claimed descent from David. A marriage between Jesus and Mary Magdalene, therefore, would have reconciled the usurped Jewish royal lineage and would have concentrated it in the offspring of Jesus and Mary. We can only speculate, but does the Merovingian adoption of the lily and the "sea creature" symbolism around the year 500 A.D. mean that this French dynasty now claimed an infusion of Holy Blood from Jesus, and an infusion of "blood royal" from both Jesus and Mary? Two symbols suddenly appearing on Merovingian banners may seem slim documentation for such a speculation, and it is, but on the other hand *any* documentation from these "Dark Ages" is rare and precious.

One thing is absolutely certain. Starting about 500 A.D., the Merovingian dynasty of France claimed to be Jewish! Which is to say that, under the politico-religious necessity, and fact, of becoming converted to Christianity by virtue of Clovis's baptism by St. Rémy, the Merovingians claimed an ancient Jewish genetic legacy. These Merovingians seem to have been a curious dynasty in some respects, and another of their peculiarities was that they practised polygamy, even under Christianity after Clovis was baptised. Assuming that the Holy Blood, or Holy Grail, intermarried into the Merovingian dynasty after being transferred from Arthur's doomed Britain, then polygamy ensured many, many children of the Holy Blood indeed. These princes and princesses, in their turn, married into noble and royal family lines of the time. This fact has prompted one respected French historian to state that the foundation of France's nobility is actually Jewish.[17]

Around the year 500 A.D. the fledgling Roman Church was in urgent need of some secular and military power that could prevent the complete inundation of Christianity by incoming pagan beliefs. The most cohesive power then existing in the shattered Roman world was the Merovingian kingship in Gaul ("France"). Clovis, a redoubtable warrior and Merovingian king, seemed just the man to save the Church after his conversion to Christianity by St. Rémy. A "perpetual pact" was made between the Merovingian dynasty and the Church of Rome: the Frankish Merovingian kings would be the secular and military power recognized and supported by Rome, while Rome would become the only spiritual and religious authority recognized and supported by the Merovingians.

It has come down to us in Church-written history of the "Dark Ages" that the Roman Church "offered" this deal to Clovis and the Merovingian dynasty, but the truth may be somewhat different. We know now that the Roman Church gleefully forged the "Donation of Constantine"[18] to give itself bogus authority, and perhaps the Church similarly fudged history concerning the deal with Clovis. The Merovingians were warriors and had no great interest in spiritual matters. Clovis was baptised only because St. Rémy promised him victory in an upcoming battle, and was canny enough not to become baptised until St. Rémy had actually delivered the goods. Clovis won and became a Christian in exchange. However, these Frankish kings were intelligent enough to know that dominion could not rest on military prowess alone but required also law, organization and some degree of written communications. Only the Church could supply these necessary aspects of rulership.

It may be then, that Clovis and the Merovingians offered the Church a deal, and not the other way around, a deal that was too good for Rome to refuse. Knowing full well that descendants of Jesus undermined the so-called "Petrine Claim" of the pope, the Merovingians may have pledged to keep their Holy Grail lineage a secret, and acknowledge the "Petrine Claim" overtly, in return for Rome's endorsement of absolute secular power in as much of Europe as the Merovingians might be able to conquer. This is a speculation unsupported by any document that survives, but it is plausible within the politico-religious realities of the 6th century. In any case, although Church-written documents sometimes exist from the "Dark Ages," they are often no more trustworthy than intelligent speculation, as the spurious "Donation of Constantine" demonstrates.

Whatever may be the truth about how the "perpetual pact" actually came about and was negotiated, it lasted in practice for only about 250–300 years. Unfortunately, after Clovis, the Merovingian fighting spirit declined. Increasingly, they manifested a lack of martial vitality that the Church so desperately needed. French history calls the later Merovingian monarchs "enfeebled kings." This was not what Christianity needed at all if it was to survive.

Starting in the year 711 A.D., very vital Islamic armies entered Spain. Within less than a generation, they threatened to pour over the Pyrenees and inundate France. Enfeebled Merovingian kings could not rise to the military challenge of the Moors. In desperation, the Church began to ignore the actual Merovingian kings and turned instead to the "Mayors of the Palace," a lineage of Merovingian vassal nobility that had come, increasingly, to manage state affairs.

It was a "Mayor of the Palace," Charles Martel, who won the Battle of Poitiers in 732 A.D. and stopped the Moorish invasion of France. From then on, the Church ignored the official Merovingian kings and placed their hope in the line of Charles Martel. Charles's son, Pepin III, was anointed King of the Franks in 754 A.D. and established the Carolingian dynasty. The Church finally betrayed its "perpetual pact" with Clovis when it anointed Charles the Great as Holy Roman Emperor in the year 800 A.D. The family of "Mayors of the Palace" would be the secular and military rulers of the Christian world, not the useless Merovingian kingship. At the same time, of course, both the Church and the supporters of Charlemagne took steps to eliminate the legitimate Merovingian bloodline.

The last Merovingian king, Dagobert II, was murdered by henchmen of Charlemagne while hunting. Dagobert's son, however, Prince Sigisbert IV, narrowly escaped death and was taken to safety by Merovingian loyalists.[19] He was spirited away to the remote Pyrenees dukedom of Razès, and so a direct descendant of the Holy Bloodline, and a direct descendant of the Merovingian "blood royal" survived. The Pyrenees sheltered this hunted lineage for 250 years until it surfaced into history again with Godfroi de Bouillon and the First Crusade. While this anciently holy and royal bloodline was in hiding, the name of "Plant-ardent" or "Plantard" was sometimes adopted for public consumption. This means "the ardently growing sprout" of the Holy Blood that Charlemagne's henchmen failed to prune.

It is worth noting that some of the Holy Blood settled in Brittany around 500 A.D. and did not enter directly into the Merovingian dynasty but maintain a low profile for half a millennium. But they never forgot who they were, and never forgot that they could claim to be the "rightful" royalty of Britain. Just as coyly as the refugee lineage in the Pyrenees, this Brittany branch of the Holy Bloodline called themselves "Planta-genesta," which means "sprout of the people." This name, however, was also a pun. *Planta genesta* was, and is, the Latin name for a very inconspicuous and low-growing variety of heather that is native to Brittany and Britain. When William the Conqueror ranged his cavalry to face King Harold's bowmen and axemen, each of his followers wore a sprig of this heather in their armor. Conventional historians believe that the dynastic name of Plantagenet derived from this token, but it was actually much more, a code-symbol denoting a sprout of the Holy Blood that had once sanctified the royalty of Romano-Celtic Britain. Within the context of this secret history of the Holy Grail, William the Conquerer was no rough adventurer determined to find a throne by invading Britain, he was a scion of ancient Romano-Celtic royalty bent on re-establishing the kingship of Arthur after a 500-year Saxon interlude. The Battle of Hastings was revenge for the Battle of Camlann.

Such is the tale of the Holy Grail up until the emergence of Godfroi de Bouillon and his successful leadership of the First Crusade. This was, supposedly, the "secret of the Cathars" and the "treasure of Montségur," guarded by Templars.

No one can state whether this story is true, or how much of it may be true. But one can say, I think, that it reads like real history. It is complicated, it is convoluted, it incorporates plausible power-struggles of individuals and of the church and state of the era. It is not always heroic or victorious. It is human. At least, that's how it strikes me.

Objectively, however, and above and beyond the personal opinions of myself or anyone else, the tale of the Holy Grail as told in greatly simplified form here provides answers to some of the puzzles of history. It explains why Godfroi de Bouillon, of all people, would have been elected to be the King of Jerusalem in the year 1099. Very obviously, some high-ranking clerics and princes knew the secret of de Bouillon's bloodline and he doubtless carried proofs of it in the form of plausible genealogies. It explains why this upstart royal dynasty of Christian Jerusalem "was accounted equal to the most illustrious of European royalty." It was equal, and more.

It also explains the Roman Church's reactions. Initially, it accepted the new rulers of Jerusalem and even honored them. St. Bernard, who had been sent to preach against the Cathar heretics, was delegated to draft the rules for Baudoin's Knights Templar. How could this be? The Vatican's own genealogists could not have been ignorant of the fact that the de Bouillons had sprung from the very center of the Cathar heresy in southern France. Godfroi de Bouillon may have done what I have conjectured that Clovis did five hundred years before. By suddenly emerging into the light of history, and by surprisingly capturing Jerusalem and being elected king, Godfroi proclaimed in no uncertain terms that the Roman Church and Charlemagne's paid murderers had failed to eradicate the Holy Blood. If Godfroi's lineage, and the proofs of it along with the bloody history, was publicly revealed then the Roman Church would be put in the position of being the oppressors of Christ's descendants. Considering the blatant corruption of Rome at this time in many other respects, many people might have been inclined to believe this. The Roman Church and the institution of the papacy might well have crumbled had Godfroi revealed his origins, or if the Church had questioned his claim to Jerusalem. An accommodation seems to have been reached simply because the Church could not repudiate the successful Christian conqueror of Jerusalem under any circumstances. The deal seems to have gone something like this. Godfroi and his successors would not reveal their secret of the Holy Blood and would profess Roman Catholic orthodoxy at least super-ficially; they would not challenge the "Petrine Claim" and the pope's right to exist. In return, the Vatican would endorse the creation of the Templars and make them independent of all other secular authority; the Cathar heretics in the south of France would be left alone; the kingdom of Jerusalem would be recognized and honored.

This was, perhaps the most dangerous time in history for the Roman Church, save only for the barbarian invasions following the fall of Rome. The conditions of the apparent "co-existence" would eventually prove fatal for the Roman Church at the cost of avoiding immediate conflict. The Cathar heresy, already very powerful, would only grow to encompass more and more of Europe; the Templars could evolve into a private, elite and numerous fighting force that could defeat any combination of European powers within a century or so; Templar fiscal activities like warehousing and banking would eventually bring to de Bouillon coffers more money than the Roman Church itself would ever be able to generate; most important, perhaps, the activities of the Templars and the Knights of St. John in both land and sea commerce would change the basic structure of feudal society so that power would shift to a commercial "middle class" and away from agrarian feudalism on which the Church depended.

The tale of the Holy Grail provides a very plausible explanation for the delicate balances and imbalances of power that emerged as historical facts, treaties and accommodations, but for which conventional interpretations cannot fully account.

The crux of the matter regarding the story of the Holy Grail is whether Jesus was married or not. The common knowledge of Christian orthodoxy is, of course, that he was not married, but the curious thing is that the Scriptures themselves do not explicitly say whether he was or not.

There is surprising evidence that Jesus was married, although this evidence is circumstantial. First of all, Jesus was a Jew and was given the title of Rabbi on more than one occasion in the New Testament. Under Jewish religious law, a Rabbi must be married:

> "The Jewish Mishnaic Law is quite explicit on the subject: 'An unmarried man may not be a teacher.'"[20]

Charles Davis, a respected contemporary theological scholar, has written:

> Granted the cultural background as witnessed...it is highly improbable that Jesus was not married well before the beginning of his public ministry. If he had insisted upon celibacy, it would have caused a stir, a reaction which would have left some trace. So, the lack of mention of Jesus's marriage in the Gospels is a strong statement not against, but for the hypothesis of marriage, because any practice or advocacy of celibacy would in Jewish context of the time have been so unusual as to have attracted much comment and attention.[21]

In fact, however, the Gospels do mention a marriage and it seems to be the marriage of Jesus himself. In John 2:9–10 is the curious incident of the wedding at Cana at which Jesus and his mother are present. Jesus's mother asks him to replenish the wine, which would be the obligation of the host and hostess, and this is the occasion of the miracle when Jesus turned water into wine. Immediately after this miracle has been accomplished, the "master of ceremonies" of the wedding "*called the bridegroom*, and saith unto him, Every man at the beginning doth set forth good wine; and when men have well drunk, that which is worse: but *thou* has kept the good wine until now."

The "master of ceremonies" is obviously speaking directly to Jesus, but also refers to him as the bridegroom in the same passage. Scholars have puzzled over this passage, but the obvious explanation is simply that Jesus was married at Cana. Mary Magdalene is the only real candidate for bride and wife. She accompanies him from the first days of his ministry and this would have been unthinkable in those times if she had not been married to him.[22] Then, Mary Magdalene, and she alone, was present at all the most important events of Jesus's ministry. It was to Mary Magdalene that Jesus first revealed his Resurrection, for example. Why was Mary Magdalene so important unless she was Jesus's wife, and how did her real status become so distorted by orthodox Christianity?

Anti-feminism in orthodox Christianity has been noted by very many theological experts and writers and it apparently stemmed from the belief that the "Second Coming" was expected to occur very soon after the Ascension. That being the case, there was no justification for bringing more children into the world because a certain percentage of them were destined to be damned. The reproductive capacity of women was, therefore, of very little value to the early Church. At best it was useless because the Second Coming was expected almost hourly, and at worst it tempted people to commit sin and to bring sinners into the world. This seems to be the foundation for anti-feminism in Christianity and it lingered even when the Second Coming failed to occur quickly. This, and nothing explicitly written or directed in the Scriptures, accounts for the celibacy of Roman Catholic priests; and this accounts for the low status of women throughout Catholic Europe during the time of absolute Church dominance. Given such a perspective, it becomes clear how even the wife of Jesus could become denigrated, and her existence finally denied altogether. It becomes clear how Mary Magdalene could come to be regarded as a prostitute in popular orthodoxy, even though the actual Scriptures nowhere describe her that way. But this anti-feminist perspective became so firmly entrenched within the celibate-and-priest-dominated Roman Church that in medieval Europe shelters for wayward women came to be called "Magdalenes."[23]

It is impossible to assess whether the tale of the Holy Grail is true, but there is the possibility that it preserves more truth than the religious dogma that millions cherish today.

When the dynasty of Godfroi de Bouillon lost Jerusalem to the Saracens in 1187 A.D., a unique opportunity for a more harmonious world very possibly perished along with the short-lived kingdom. For, if the tale of the Holy Grail is truth, then this bloodline incorporated within itself the legacy of Abraham, Solomon and David as well as Jesus Christ. A de Bouillon kingdom in the Middle East, and the way the Templars were already starting to change Europe could have reconciled Christian and Jew as well as speed up the tempo of the Western World's social development.

Perhaps such a Middle Eastern kingdom could have done more.

In addition to the genetic legacy of Christianity and Judaism the bloodline of de Bouillon boasted just as close kinship to the ancestry of Mohammed. Although it is almost unknown or unappreciated in Europe, it is a basic belief of the Islamic world that Mohammed, too, sprang from the line of Abraham. The line of David and Solomon issued from the union of Abraham and Sarah, while the lineage culminating in Mohammed issued from the union of Abraham and Hagar.[24]

Nowadays, and since the Babylonian "editing" of the Old Testament, Jews are fond of asserting rather smugly that while Sarah was Abraham's wife, Hagar was only Abraham's concubine. Abraham lived around 2000 B.C. and was part of a Middle Eastern culture of rather primitive nomadic herdsmen. They probably lived much the same way as the Bedouins of today, and were probably polygamous. Looking back four thousand years, it is impossible to know the actual relationship between Abraham and Sarah on the one hand, and Abraham and Hagar on the other. What was the difference between a "wife" and a "concubine" in a primitive nomadic culture? There very probably was no difference at all. And as for "marriage," what rites would have been performed? Certainly not Jewish ones

Ruins of Montségur castle in the French Pyrenees, last stronghold of Cathar heretics and reputed sanctuary of the Holy Grail. Troubadour Wolfram von Eschenbach, author of *Parzival*, referred to the citadel as the fortress of "Munsalvaesch" ("World-salvation") and states that the Holy Grail had been hidden in Montségur under the guardianship of Knights Templar. The castle was commanded by the lady-warrior, Esclarmonde de Foix, and fell to the forces of the Vatican on March 16, 1244.

because they had not yet been invented. Despite Jewish propaganda, which dates from the Babylonian Captivity and rabbinical "editing" of the Old Testament for the purpose of preserving a sense of cohesion among the displaced Jews of the time, there's no valid reason for supposing that Mohammed's line was any less legitimate than the one leading to David and Christ.

An opportunity to reconcile all three great religions of the West perished with the loss of Jerusalem in 1187, and Godfroi's lineage also lost its security. As I have related previously, the pope called for a crusade to exterminate the Cathars, and representatives of the de Bouillon bloodline who had returned to southern France, just 22 years later. This was the so-called Albigensian Crusade.

The Cathars, after an heroic 35-year defiance, were utterly crushed by forces of Rome and northern French barons. Thousands were killed in the warfare, or massacred after surrender. Cathar *perfecti* were tortured hideously and then burned at the stake. The last Cathar stronghold, the castle of Montségur, was taken on March 16, 1244. All of the surviving defenders were tortured and then burned alive, but it is said that they sang as they burned at their flaming stakes. It is said that the soul of Esclarmonde de Foix ascended to heaven in the form of a dove. It is said that the heretics were tortured so cruelly so that the Inquisitors could find out the truth of the Holy Grail and ascertain whether any of the Holy Blood had escaped from southern France and Montségur. Legend insists that the "Holy Grail" was taken to safety by four knights, whose names are known to history, just two days before the fall of Montségur. It may be then, that some of the descendants of the Holy Blood escaped again.

Not all of the Cathar heretics were exterminated, of course. Some individuals and entire families survived. They dispersed to find safety from the Inquisition. They professed orthodoxy, but they maintained, in secret, the beliefs outlined in the previous pages. In order to recognize each other as hunted refugees, Cathar families often changed their names to some other name reflecting Cathar symbolism. Many chose "Dragon" or "Mondragon" as a new name that would communicate their religious beliefs to other refugee heretics. Others chose the dove as a basis for a new family name. In the history of Europe's "Age of Discovery" we find an inordinate

number of people named after doves and dragons. Sir Frances Drake
(from the Latin *draco*—dragon) is one example. A mysterious figure
named "Mondragon" was Samuel de Champlain's sponsor in help-
ing Champlain to become an explorer, while Don Francisco Coloma
(Spanish for "Dove"), a Knight of Malta, also helped Champlain to
become experienced as an explorer.

And, finally—have you not already guessed it with these
clues?—Christopher Columbus seems to have been born of a heretical family too. Columbus is Latin for "Dove."

Chapter 5

Two Columbuses!
One Master Mariner

After the previous pages' glimpse into the historical, cultural and politico-religious conflicts that may well have provided secret motivations for Columbus's voyage of 1492, it should logically be the appropriate point to turn to Columbus's birth and boyhood in Genoa.

Unfortunately, we cannot do that. The reason is simple: there is no proof that Christopher Columbus was born in Genoa in 1451, the son of Dominico and Susanna. There may well have been *a* Christopher Columbus born to this couple, the father may well have been a humble wool-carder (not shoemaker), and this Christopher Columbus might also have even gone to sea in Genoese ships as many lads did. But there is no guarantee at all that this Christopher Columbus, if he ever existed, was the one who crossed the Atlantic in 1492.

In order to grasp the complications that Christopher Columbus of history presents, we must jump ahead to the year 1476. Our traditional Christopher Columbus would have been twenty-five years of age in this year and he was supposed to have been an accomplished mariner within the Mediterranean world. In 1476 he was part of a trading convoy of five vessels bound from Genoa to Flanders and England. This little merchant fleet had hardly cleared the Straits of Gibraltar when it was attacked by pirate vessels. History does not reliably record how many of the merchant vessels may have been sunk or damaged or captured, what the pirates' casualties may have been, or how many men on both sides may have been lost. We know only that Christopher Columbus of tradition found himself in the water, clung to a piece of wreckage, and began to swim for the coast of Portugal about six miles away.

He made it. The Christopher Columbus of history emerges with the man who dragged himself ashore on the Portuguese beach. From that seemingly low ebb in the fortunes of his life, he began his documented rise to fame in Portugal and Spain. From the time he reached the safety of the beach, he started to become the Christopher Columbus of our tradition and history. Rising toward fame, he later told of his Genoese birth, boyhood, youth and maritime experience. He told his sons Diego and Fernando. Fernando wrote that Columbus, his father, chose to tell the world about himself. Fernando's biography of his famous father, the *Life of Colón*, is the foundation of our traditional picture of Columbus.

Yet, in all that Columbus himself indisputably wrote, there is but one brief mention of Genoa and nothing suggesting that he was born there.[1] Further, in Genoa itself there is no record of Christopher Columbus the mariner.[2] History relies solely upon what Columbus told Ferdinand ("Fernando") as a child, and what the son wrote when much older. And what Columbus told Fernando may have been less than the truth because of the bald fact that Ferdinand was illegitimate. His mother was Beatriz Enriques de Harana, a *"converso,"* a Jew who had voluntarily and supposedly adopted the Roman Catholic faith. She was also a close relative of one of the two Harana financial moguls who sponsored Columbus's voyage. Both Ferdinand's own personal safety, and his claim to Columbus's legacy, depended upon his knowing much less than the truth about his famous father and his mother.

Who was the man who dragged himself ashore on the Portuguese beach in September of 1476? History does not know.

Understandable obscurity is deepened by the name of the pirate who attacked this merchant fleet. He was a fairly well known swashbuckler of the era and went by the name Coullon. Coullon is the French analog for Columbus, and both mean "Dove."[3]

In short, the Columbus of Genoa was pirated by a Columbus of France—and only one man swam ashore to make history. Was this man our traditional Columbus of Genoa, or was he the Columbus who was a French pirate and master navigator *on the Atlantic*, and a man of proven nerve and daring?

No one knows. Only one thing is certain. The French pirate disappeared completely from the stage of history in September 1476, and Christopher Columbus "of Genoa" makes his entrance at the same time. And it must be said, for it is simply a fact, that some of the daring nautical exploits attributed to "Columbus," not to mention some amorous ones, remind one of a swashbuckling pirate much more than a merchant skipper from Genoa whose youth was so unremarkable that there are no records of his existence in his native town.

For example, according to the *Life of Colón*, "Columbus" was hired by René d'Anjou, in the year 1472, to sail to Tunis and capture the Aragonese galleass, the *Ferrandina*.[4] That is, Columbus was hired to pirate this vessel in the struggle between the Angevins and the Aragonese for the control of Naples. Before 1472, our traditional Columbus of history had never claimed to have been master of a vessel. This piracy, then, was Columbus's first claimed voyage as a full captain. The situation bears careful consideration. Would an obscure merchant captain be commissioned to do a job of piracy on his very first voyage as sole master of a vessel? It is possible, of course. But, much more likely, a king like René d'Anjou who was a redoubtable and knowledgeable fighting man himself would have entrusted such a mission to someone experienced in the task at hand, piracy. Then, is it not more likely that French René d'Anjou would have favored an established French pirate than a Genoese?

This is one of the orphaned facts about the life of Columbus that has been glossed over by most biographers. Here's another one. The very next year, 1473, Columbus made a voyage to Chios, one of the Aegean Islands. The *Life of Colón* gives few details about this voyage. Now, it may be only coincidence, but it is nonetheless a fact, that Chios was a garrison of the Knights of St. John of Jerusalem, that "brother-Order" of knighthood created by the de Bouillon dynasty along with the Templars. It is also a fact that, according to the story of the Holy Grail, Anjou was a center where some of the Holy Blood settled immediately after evacuation from Arthur's Britain. Indeed, the secret of the Holy Grail was preserved in Anjou as in very few other places. The most famous troubadour of all, Wolfram von Eschenbach, wrote in *Parzival*:

> Kyot [i.e. Giot of Provence—Author's note], the well-known master, found in Toledo, discarded, set down in heathen writing, the first source of this adventure...
>
> A heathen, Flegetanis, had achieved high renown for his learning...was descended from Solomon and born of a family which had long been Israelite...wrote the adventure of the Grail...A host of angels left it on earth. Since then, baptised men have had the task of guarding it...
>
> Kyot, the wise master, set out to trace this tale in Latin books, to see whether there had ever been a people dedicated to purity and worthy of caring for the Grail. He read the chronicles of the lands, in Britain and elsewhere, in France and Ireland, and in Anjou he found the tale.[5]

Whether we like it or not, we find that our Columbus made a voyage in 1473 to an outpost of the Knights of St. John, and the previous year had pirated a ship on behalf of René d'Anjou. Again, it may be only coincidence, but it is also simply a fact, that both incidents are at least associated with the complexities of the Holy Grail story. Also, both incidents seem anomalous within the context of the traditional story of Christopher Columbus that scholars have chosen to accept. And, although these two incidents are related in Fernando's *Life of Colón* as experiences in Columbus's life, some biographers have chosen not to mention them at all.

The unspeakable possibility must be very clear to anyone familiar with mystery stories and detective novels: was the Christopher Columbus "of Genoa" a new alias created for a daring French pirate who was chosen to undertake a desperate and complicated mission? Is the Columbus "of Genoa" a total myth for all practical purposes? Even if such a person existed, perhaps some run-of-the-mill Genoese merchant skipper who actually died in some unrecorded marine disaster at age 25 had his life story borrowed in order to clothe a French pirate with a new identity. And, as unlikely as it may seem, was this French pirate somehow connected with the intrigues and conspiracies of the Holy Grail lineage?

We will recall that the Holy Grail was supposedly spirited out of doomed Montségur two days before the surrender by four chosen knights. This was in 1244. Did the Holy Blood survive the Albigensian Crusade? Were operatives working on behalf of the survivors 230-odd years later? Was Columbus such an operative?

A respected French historian, Abbé Casanova, discovered that a family named Columbus did settle in the French town of Calvi and left significantly more documentation of their existence than the Columbuses of Genoa. The pirate, Coullon, who eventually Frenchified his family name from the original Latin, sprang from this family. We are faced with the historical irony that there is more documentation about the French pirate Columbus than about our Genoese Columbus.

Where does this leave us? Our position can be accurately described in one word: helpless. History can have no certainty whatever about Columbus's origins or place of birth; no certainty about his childhood and youthful maritime experience. Only by taking selected facts from the *Life of Colón*, and by ignoring others just as well documented, have later biographers been able to offer us the traditional Christopher Columbus. But he does not exist. He may never have existed.

All that history can properly maintain is that the epic story of Columbus begins with the man who swam to Portugal in September 1476, whoever he may have been.

History can properly assert a corollary fact about this man: he was a master mariner and had had, at some point in his life, access to considerable education which he later, and continually, enhanced with private study. The Columbus who arrived destitute and half-drowned on a Portuguese beach could write Latin rather well; and he could speak and write in several contemporary languages of his time, including Arabic, apparently; and whoever he was, he was familiar with the maritime technology and navigational techniques of his age.

Rather than speculate upon who this man may really have been, it seems more profitable simply to accept him as "Columbus" and to describe the ships and navigation of his era, for it was this nautical foundation, after all, that he utilized to cross the Atlantic in 1492 and to navigate his way among the uncharted islands of the Bahamas and

Greater Antilles. The basic fact about Columbus remains: he was a master mariner in his time, and we should understand the nautical resources that were at his disposal in the second half of the 15th century.

It must be said at the outset that 15th-century European naval architecture was considerably inferior to that of other contemporary, so-called civilized regions and, sometimes, even inferior to the vessels of some so-called more primitive peoples.

We may recall our globe-trotting Arab friend, Ibn Batuta, who was so shocked at the behavior of Malian women. Before Ibn Batuta travelled to Mali, he had travelled to the Orient and had spent some years there. At last, when in Canton in China, he decided to return home to his native Morocco and therefore went down to the waterfront to book a westward passage on one of the huge Chinese junks of the mid-13th century. Ibn Batuta was tardy in booking his passage on the loading vessel. His travel memoirs describe his anger at the fact that he could not reserve a suite of staterooms with private baths and running water for himself and his harem. All of the choice accommodation had already been taken. Ibn Batuta and his women made a less-than-luxurious trip across the Indian Ocean to Oman, and he continually complains about his plight in numerous pages of his diary.

A century before Columbus's three tiny ships crossed the Atlantic, Chinese "ocean liners" were plying back and forth across the Indian Ocean on fixed schedules. Some of these vessels were about 300 feet long, and about as wide as the length of Columbus's *Santa Maria*, which was an estimated $77^1/2$ feet overall. These huge junks had up to five decks of passenger accommodation, plus cargo space, and some of the first-class cabins were equipped with bathrooms and running water. These huge vessels had five masts that were arranged asymmetrically along the length of the ship so that the sails would aerodynamically enhance the draft of the airflow for each other according to the venturi principle. Further, each mast supported a huge "battened lug" sail whose shape could be altered to the correct aerofoil curve by hauling on the parrels, ropes that curved the battens in the sail. All of this demonstrates that the Chinese had discovered the aerodynamic principles about how sails actually work as early as the 13th century, but probably long before.

Western yachtsmen discovered the same principles only in the 1930s because of a series of scientific experiments undertaken by the New York Yacht Club.

The most famous Chinese skipper on the Indian Ocean run in the 14th century was Cheng Hi who made no less than 13 recorded round-trips between Canton and Arabia and East Africa between 1325 and 1350 A.D. One of the Chinese products most coveted by the East African Zanj consumers was not silk, but porcelain tableware. So much Chinese porcelain was imported into East Africa that archeological sites in Somalia, Kenya, Tanzania and Mozambique are often conveniently dated by the style of Chinese porcelain found in them.[6]

These huge ocean-going junks had disappeared by Columbus's day. In that mysterious way in which cultures seem to evolve and change like living organisms, about 1375–1400 China turned inward and ceased its expansive phase. It became the isolated and self-satisfied "Middle Kingdom" (between earth and heaven) that Europeans rudely penetrated one hundred years later. But, before this inward-turning, Chinese junks had sailed widely. How widely? No one knows for sure, but perhaps across the Pacific to America.

The junk concept was evolved in North China and Manchuria and the original junks are more or less represented today by the vessels built in Antung up to the 1940s. These "Antung junks" incorporated all of the distinctive features that eventually made all junks so seaworthy: the battened lug sailing rig; watertight bulkheads; the deep-immersion rudder that acted also as a combined keel and dynamic stabilizing vane; the totally flat bottom which allowed cheap and strong construction and which, when the deep-immersion rudder was retracted, offered no resistance to storm waves passing beneath the vessel. Although Chinese naval architecture contradicts many of Europe's shipbuilding dogmas, the fact remains that junks demonstrated exceptional sailing efficiency combined with great seaworthiness and inexpensive construction. It is said that a well-found Antung junk, with its deep rudder retracted and its bluff bows kept head-on into the waves, could weather anything that nature had to offer. Perhaps it is enough to say that the junks evolved in the North China Sea and served mariners there for perhaps three thousand years without significant change; and to note that the North China Sea is the stormiest in the inhabited world with an average of 27 typhoons per year as compared with an average of eight hurricanes per year in the Caribbean.

Manchuria and North China coasts are swept by the clockwise-flowing Kuroshiwo Current, which eventually washes the West Coast of Canada, the United States and Mexico. Any disabled junk caught in this current would eventually end up in North America. Indeed, the occasional storm-damaged Chinese or Japanese fishing junk still ends up in North American waters, often with survivors aboard. In British Columbia, I know from personal experience that Japanese glass-globe, fishing-net floats can be collected off the west coast of Vancouver Island.

Did the Chinese and/or Japanese, too, discover America across the Pacific? It is said that the Chinese (Buddhist) monk, Fo-Hi, crossed the Pacific around 450 A.D. and this tale is supported by the fact that Chinese coins of about that date have been found in Acapulco. Then, a Japanese noble supposedly discovered land across the Pacific and returned to Japan to collect "10,000 youths and maidens" for a massive colonizing attempt. Ships carrying these colonists set off into the Kuroshiwo Current and were never heard from again. Did these colonists reach North America's Pacific coast? Perhaps. Ethnographic experts have observed much Japanese genetic and cultural influence on existing Northwest Coast Indians.[7]

There is no doubt that oriental naval architecture was superior to that of Europe during most of recorded history up until the medieval period when Columbus sailed. Then, for cultural reasons still curious and unknown, ship-building and ocean voyaging of Far Eastern peoples rapidly declined in the 14th century.

As was mentioned previously, Arab naval architecture was also superior to that of Europe in Columbus's day. All Arab sailing ships are popularly called "dhows," but in fact there were many types called by many names depending on the hull form, number of masts, and so on. All these vessels had one thing in common, though, they employed the triangular "lateen" sail which was also sometimes used by European ships in a somewhat inefficient way. Used correctly, however, with one lateen sail drafting another on multiple masts, the rig was very efficient indeed and could be used in a number of variations to suit wind conditions. One of the few

European sailing experts to have sailed "dhows" extensively was Britain's Capt. Allan Villiers, the man chosen to sail the *Mayflower* replica across the Atlantic. Just before World War II, Villiers shipped aboard a number of traditional Arab vessels and made passages across the Indian Ocean and along the East African coast. In his enjoyable and knowledgeable book, *Sons of Sinbad*, Villiers confirmed that a correctly handled lateen rig "pulled like a mule" and could sail up to 45 degrees into the direction from which the wind was blowing. This feat of windward sailing was not matched by European vessels until about 1650, and then these were pleasure vessels called *jachts*, copied from Arab and Indonesian boats and first introduced into Holland. Our modern word "yacht" derives from this Dutch type of pleasure boat. But the Arab lateen-rigged merchant vessels could sail efficiently to windward for centuries before Columbus.

In a modern experiment, a traditional Omani "boom" was replicated by Tim Severin and sailed from Oman to Canton.[8] A "boom" is a three-masted cargo ship that is "double-ended," or sharp at both bow and stern. It was constructed as a genuine replica in the traditional way, which is to say that its planks were sewn together in the manner described by Marco Polo. Coconut-fiber rope called *coir* was used for this sewing and the builders assured Severin that the stitched-together vessel would last for a century in salt water if properly laid *coir* rope was used and not hemp. Even the best quality hemp rope was no good for underwater stitches. Although Marco Polo made critical remarks about the sewn boats of the Arabs, Severin's replica vessel proved that this was not a weak method of construction at all, and could at least rival medieval European techniques of fastening planks with wooden pegs ("tree nails") and crude metal rivets. Construction of this replica vessel, and an account of its voyage to Canton, is documented in *The Sindbad Voyage*. From this experiment we know that *Sohar*, as the replica boom was named, was a much more efficient sailing craft than any of the several replicas of the *Santa Maria* that have crossed the Atlantic.

It may be of interest to some readers that the technique of sewing a boat together has been widely adopted by designers working for today's World Bank and United Nations development organizations. One of the priorities among developing nations is a revitalization of village fishing, or "artisanal fishing" as it is called in the aid and development business. A major difficulty in modern artisanal fishing reconstruction programs is the acquisition of suitable small craft for village fishermen. In many cases, the village fishermen must now go much further offshore than traditionally to catch any fish because of inshore depletion of fish stocks by trawling. Then, in many other cases, the traditional boat-building materials themselves have been depleted by modern forestry operations. The challenge is to design and construct small fishing boats that are even more seaworthy than traditional ones, but remain cheap and simple to make.

The Arab technique of sewing planks together has helped to meet this challenge, although the traditional construction has been refined with modern methods and materials. Perhaps Gifford Technology of Southampton, England, was the first group to perfect the "stitch-and-glue" method of boat-building for plywood catamarans intended to be built on the beach by village fishermen in Sri Lanka and India. The modern variation of the old Arab method is to stitch plywood panels together with galvanized wire and then to seal the joint with fiber-impregnated epoxy resin. After the shell, or hull, of the boat is completed in this way, then the internal frames and supports are dropped in and fastened to the hull in the same manner. It is a fast, inexpensive and exceedingly strong way of making a small fishing boat, and in general technique it follows the Chinese and Arabic practice of making the hull first and then adding the internal frames rather than the traditional European method of making the frame first and then fastening the hull planking to it. After Gifford Technology pioneered this modern refinement of the medieval Arab sewing method, Impex Southern, also of England, and my own Canadian-based CanTriad Export company adopted the technique.[9]

Personal experience has given me a healthy respect for the notion of sewing a boat together, however weak such a boat-building method may seem to the average Western reader and will certainly seem to any yachtsmen who may read this book. Nonetheless, modern "stitch-and-glue" results in very strong hulls, and compound curves can be incorporated very easily into any design. Stitch-and-glue makes strong hulls, and it can also result in very sweet-looking ones. It is a method that is very suited to the backyard designer-

Michael Bradley's recently constructed expedition barge, *Nepenthe*, which employed the "stitch and glue" method of construction.
Photo: Deanna Theilmann-Bean

builder of recreational boats as well as to professionals in the development/aid business. Although Gifford Technology invented the stitch-and-glue method using galvanized wire, my own experience is that actual "rope" in the form of braided nylon cord is just as strong. The practical advantage of stitch-and-glue is that an entire hull can be constructed in just two or three days by a couple of dedicated workers. We owe this efficiency in hull construction to the medieval Arab manner of sewing a ship together, a technique first described, with horror, by Marco Polo.

During the 15th century, even some supposedly primitive peoples boasted watercraft that were superior to the ships of Europe in at least some respects. In South America, mariners of the Inca-dominated Andean cultures navigated the Pacific on giant balsa rafts equipped with sails and rigging. These could be up to 70 feet in length and about 20 feet wide, and were capable of carrying up to 30 tons of cargo.[10] These rafts were used for fishing up to one hundred miles offshore in the Humboldt Current and for trading from Chile to Panama. Andean traditions state that fleets of such rafts crossed the western Pacific with colonists for the Polynesian islands, and discovered the isolated Galapagos group, and Easter Island, on the way. The exceptional sea-going characteristics of these giant Andean balsa rafts was proved by Thor Heyerdahl when he crossed the Pacific on *Kon-Tiki* in 1947. Like the Arab ships and the Chinese junks, Andean balsa rafts also boasted excellent performance in the art of sailing into the wind. Andean sailors used "guara boards" stuck down into the water between the logs of the raft in order to guide the raft on any desired course up to 45 degrees into the direction from which the wind was blowing. Early Spanish accounts marvelled at this feat, which the European ships could not duplicate, and the windward sailing ability of these rafts was finally demonstrated for modern naval architects and Pacific archeologists by a series of experiments performed by Heyerdahl in 1953. Previously, when numerous guara boards had been excavated from Andean-culture graves, they were thought to be shovels of some kind and were labelled "agricultural implements" by Western experts. Now, thanks to the practical experiments of Thor Heyerdahl, we know that the Andean peoples were a maritime culture of great sophistication for a purely "stone-age people," and that these Inca-ruled cultures first discovered and settled the Polynesian islands.

Andean colonization of Polynesia entailed open ocean raft voyages of four thousand miles before the first Pacific islands were reached. These unrecorded voyages represent the longest known passages out of sight of land. Before Europeans crossed the Pacific in 1519, Andeans had done it about a thousand years earlier.

Before turning to European shipping of the medieval era, it is only fair to mention that another contemporary culture was making longer voyages in ships of about the same length as European ones. This culture was the Polynesians themselves. Although Heyerdahl has demonstrated that the Polynesian islands were colonized first by mariners from South America, he has also shown that a second wave of immigrants reached the islands about 1100 A.D. from North America's Pacific coast.[11] These later colonists were apparently related to the Haida, Kwakiutl, Nootka and Salish Indians of British Columbia, Alaska, and Washington state. They used giant double-canoes to reach the islands, not balsa rafts. The double-canoes were hollowed out of huge Douglas Fir and Sitka Spruce trees that were, and are, native to the northwest coast of North America. Typically, double-canoes might be about 40–50 feet in length and 15–20 feet wide, but the largest ones were almost 70 feet in length and about 30 feet wide. This is nearly the length of the *Santa Maria*, and almost exactly the length of the *Niña*, although the carrying capacity of these double-canoes was very much less than that of European ships of the same length. In compensation, however, Polynesian double-canoes boasted much greater speed. Modern catamarans developed from Polynesian double-canoes because American servicemen stationed in the Pacific saw these vessels in use by islanders during World War II. Some of these servicemen, those who were boating enthusiasts, returned home determined to reproduce double-canoes with modern materials. This post-war experimentation resulted in the multi-hull revolution in modern yachting.

Naturally, traditional Polynesian double-canoes were not as fast as modern catamarans and trimarans, but they were a lot faster than any other known type of vessel in the 14th-century world. Speeds of perhaps 10–12 knots could be sustained for long periods under reasonably favorable conditions. Under exceptional conditions European caravels and Arab dhows could match this speed for a short time, but the average sustainable speed was only about 4 knots. During the 1200s and 1300s, Polynesians in their double-canoes undertook a series of remarkable and epic voyages: they sailed from Hawaii to Tahiti and back; they discovered New Zealand and settled it; they sailed westward to Fiji and eastward perhaps as far as the South American mainland. During these two centuries Polynesians developed regular navigational schools on the major islands and a guild of master navigators evolved. Epic poetry preserved not only the record of the voyages themselves, but also preserved precise sailing directions that had made the passages possible. Several modern experiments, in both yachts and replica double-canoes, have vindicated these traditional sailing directions, proving that the epic voyages did take place.[12] The Polynesians sometimes made purposeful voyages of exploration, but more often made long ocean passages simply to visit relatives or to obtain flowers they loved or medical herbs they needed.

Strangely enough, the great age of Polynesian voyages seemed to end about 1375–1400 A.D., just when the great era of Chinese voyaging ended, just when Arab maritime spirit seemed to decline, and even when the Andeans seemed to have ceased long passages on their balsa rafts. In some uncanny way, maritime people all over the world seem to have abandoned their expansive and adventurous spirits at almost the same historical instant, as if clearing the stage for Europeans.

For their part, the Europeans made their way cautiously and somewhat hesitantly into the floodlights of maritime history, almost reluctantly. This is understandable because their ships were woefully inadequate.

European ships can be somewhat arbitrarily and imperfectly divided into two main categories: long, slim, low-hulled ships of the Mediterranean that were equipped to sail but often relied upon oars—"galleys"; and round, tubby, high-hulled ships of the Atlantic that were powered by sails alone, albeit very inefficient ones— which we can call "knorrs" for convenience, after the Scandinavian type that developed from the Viking merchant ships. Broadly speaking, it can be said that the evolution of European ships into vessels capable of exploring the world came about through the gradual blending, or melding, of these two types. Aside from two very different types of hull shape, Mediterranean and Atlantic Coast ships differed also in how the planking was fixed to the frames. In general, ships of the Mediterranean had planking that butted along the length of the vessel, making a smooth hull, and this was called "carvel" planking. The planks on northern and Atlantic Coast vessels overlapped in what is called "lapstrake" planking. Yet another difference between the two types was the Mediterranean ships typically carried an Arab lateen rig while Atlantic vessels universally had a simple square rig.

It is tempting to suggest that the first reasonably effective blending of these two types took place in Spain and Portugal for the simple geographic reason that Iberia is at the junction of the Atlantic Ocean and the Mediterranean Sea. Today, sailing vessels are differentiated by the type of sailing rig they carry, but this was not so in Columbus's time. Vessel nomenclature referred to sailing rig, hull planking, hull shape and regional types in a confusing medley of names that offered no real classification system and made little sense at the time, let alone for modern scholars. Columbus's flagship, the *Santa Maria* was called a "ship" or, in Portuguese, a *nao* [which may be a Portuguese attempt to pronounce *knorr*—Author's note]. It was something of a blend of the Atlantic and Mediterranean types, but had more North European tradition in its lines than Mediterranean influence. Apparently, the *Santa Maria* was carvel-planked—the slim concession to Mediterranean developments—but otherwise it might have been depicted on some town seal of the Hanseatic League. She had a high sterncastle, a real North European forecastle, and it *looked* like a castle's battlements, and two masts rigged with simple square sails while the rear-most (mizzen) mast carried a lateen sail of inadequate proportions.

According to the best modern estimate, which is acknowledged to be the research of José María Martínez-Hidalgo of the Maritime Museum in Barcelona, the *Santa Maria* was 77.4 feet in overall length and obviously considerably shorter at her waterline, 26 feet in beam (width) with a draft of 6.9 feet, displacing a total of 202 tons. If you discount bow and stern overhangs so that you notice only her *waterline* length, and then consider that the *Santa Maria* was thought to be 26 feet side, it will strike you how tubby this vessel really was. She was only about two-and-a-half times as long as she was wide! It is difficult to see how she could have sailed at all except with a following wind, and then she would have lacked directional stability. Thankfully for Columbus, however, his route to the New World from the Canary Islands was entirely within the zone of brisk following trade winds, and the *Santa Maria* performed well enough on the actual ocean passage. It was among the high islands of the Greater Antilles where she came to grief, mountainous islands that caused fickle winds with which the *Santa Maria* simply couldn't cope. She was wrecked on Christmas Eve, 1492, when she ran aground on the north coast of what is now Haiti. One of her anchors may have been discovered, but the wreck itself has not yet been pinpointed. This is significant, for it may indicate that one or more anchors were set out in a vain attempt to control a ship by anchor-cables that could not be controlled by sails and rudder. Long before the wreck, Columbus admitted that the *Santa Maria* was not well suited to exploration, something of an under-statement.

The type of vessel which more perfectly blended the Mediterra-

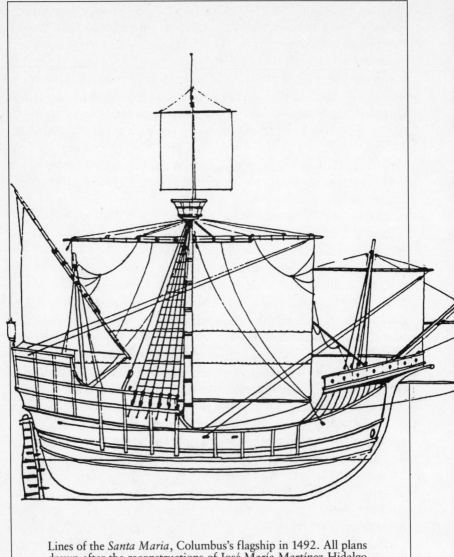

Lines of the *Santa Maria*, Columbus's flagship in 1492. All plans
drawn after the reconstructions of José María Martínez-Hidalgo
of the Maritime Museum in Barcelona. Although Martínez-Hidalgo is the world's acknowledged authority on the Columbus
ships, and although his reconstructions are based on detailed
research of medieval naval architecture, no one can be certain that
Columbus's ships looked exactly like these drawings.

Courtesy: The Maritime Museum of Barcelona and José María Martínez-Hidalgo

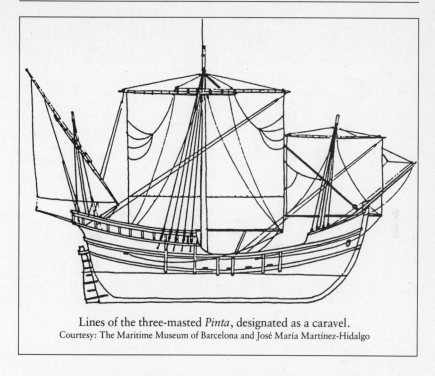

Lines of the three-masted *Pinta*, designated as a caravel.
Courtesy: The Maritime Museum of Barcelona and José María Martínez-Hidalgo

nean and Atlantic ships, and which eventually made the 15th-century European voyages of discovery possible, was the so-called "caravel." No one knows what this word means, exactly, but it probably derived from the carvel-style planking of the hull. Caravels presented very little standardization among themselves. Both the *Pinta* and the *Niña* of Columbus's little fleet were "caravels" according to the nomenclature of the time, yet they differed greatly. The larger *Pinta* had but three masts while the tiny *Niña* had four. Further, as the vessels were originally rigged when Columbus first saw them at Palos, the *Pinta* carried square sails on her two front masts and a small lateen on her mizzen, while the *Niña* carried lateens on all four of her masts.

In spite of these important differences, which would put the two ships in entirely different classifications by modern standards, there are similarities which serve to show how greatly the caravel had evolved from its purely Mediterranean and Atlantic ancestors. Much reduced are the stern and fore castles of North Europe, and so the

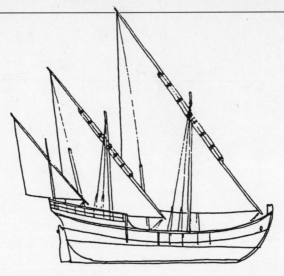

Lines of the *Niña*, also designated as a caravel. When this plan was drawn it was known that this ship had originally been rigged with lateen sails on all masts, but it was assumed that the *Niña* had only three masts like the *Pinta*. But very recent research by Eugene Lyon of the National Geographic Society revealed that this smallest of Columbus's three ships actually had four masts with lateen sails originally on each.

Courtesy: The Maritime Museum of Barcelona and José María Martínez-Hidalgo

difference between overall length and waterline length is much less. The hulls of both the *Pinta* and the *Niña* display a sensible compromise between the high hulls of the Atlantic and the extremely low hulls of Mediterranean galleys. At the same time, gone is any provision for being rowed in the Mediterranean tradition. *Pinta* and *Niña* are pure sailing ships, are moderate compromises incorporating lines that are pleasing to the eye, and simply look seaworthy. In the caravel, Europe had at last come up with a sensible, efficient and seaworthy ocean-going ship. Yet, the fledgling nature of European maritime effort is betrayed by the size of these caravels: they were tiny. Both the *Pinta* and the *Niña* displaced between 50 and 60 tons and were between 60 and 70 feet in length. They were much narrower, in proportion, than the *Santa Maria*. This made them handier as sailing vessels, but also made them very small ones. Cheng Hi's Indian Ocean junks were 10 times as large in terms of capacity,

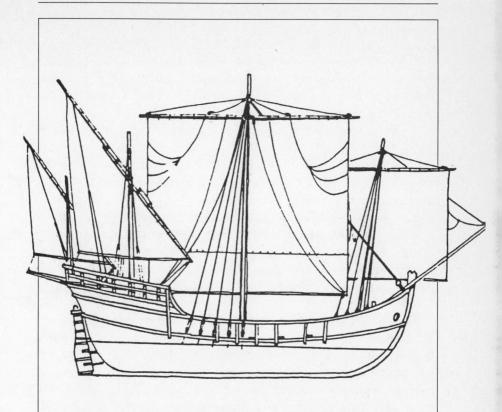

Niña, correctly drawn with four masts, but showing also the conversion to square rig on the two foremasts that Columbus ordered on Gomera (Canary Islands) for the Atlantic passage. It is unknown whether the *Niña* may have reverted to an all-lateen rig once Columbus arrived in the New World. Certainly, the captain would have kept these lateen sails and reversion to the original lateen rig would not have required more than a day—the conversion to square rig required only one day, according to Columbus's log. A lateen rig would have made *Niña* more efficient in variable winds of island-hopping and especially under the high coasts of Cuba, Haiti and the Dominican Republic. All we know from Columbus's comments is that *Niña* was his favourite vessel as a sea-boat, although the *Pinta* was somewhat faster. This little ship, only 67–70 feet long, made nine Atlantic crossings! Columbus chose her for his 1493 and 1498 voyages and Spanish records show that she carried cargo to Hispaniola at least two other times between 1494 and 1498. She was sold in Santo Domingo in 1499 and may have been lost on her return across the Atlantic to Spain (her 10th crossing).

Courtesy: The Maritime Museum of Barcelona and José María Martínez-Hidalgo while the average Arab dhow or baggala would have been three to four times as large. Yet, these tiny caravels were the best ships Europe had in 1492. Europeans worked wonders with them, not because the caravels themselves were barely adequate for the challenge that confronted them, but because the men in the caravels were incredibly determined to meet any challenge.

Oceanic exploration required navigational expertise as well as seaworthy ships. If it can be said that European naval architecture was just barely adequate to cross oceans in comparison with the ships of other maritime peoples, it must be acknowledged, at least, that in matters of navigation Europeans lagged behind no one in 1492. This was not because Europeans had made any special effort in navigation, but simply because everyone confronted a barrier to further progress. It was fairly easy to arrive at the barrier, and Europeans did so shortly after the Chinese and Arabs. Stalled at this barrier along with other seafaring peoples, Europeans were their equal.

The great barrier was that no one could determine longitude, the position east or west of a given point, with any accuracy. All adept mariners knew that the determination of longitude involved the accurate measurement of time and, in the 15th century, master navigators simply accepted the fact that their world had no way of measuring time with sufficient accuracy. The barrier of longitude determination wasn't broken until the mid-1700s and the invention of clocks accurate enough to keep time to the second.[13]

That being the case, navigation was confined to techniques that were finite in number and fairly easy to attain by all the navigators of the seafaring world.

A medieval navigator's reputation depended upon thorough mastery of two absolutely crucial pillars of existing knowledge: he had to grasp the "motions" of the North Star; he had to grasp the principle of the magnetic compass and understand its vagaries. After mastery of these two fundamentals, he could add many supporting struts to his professionalism.

First, the North Star. Polaris didn't possess primary importance for the medieval navigator simply because of the obvious fact that it is almost, not quite, due north when seen from any position in the northern hemisphere. Its primary importance was that a navigator could ascertain his latitude, his position north of the equator, by observation of Polaris. Even by 1492 geographers and geometers had divided the earth into degrees of longitude and latitude. From a pole to the equator is one-quarter of the earth's circumference, a quarter of a complete circle, or 90 degrees. For convenience, 0 degrees represented the equator and 90 degrees represented the poles. An observer on the equator would see the North Star barely kissing his northern horizon. An observer at the North Pole would see Polaris directly over his head. An observer anywhere between these two extreme points would see Polaris at some specific height above his northern horizon.

The trick for the medieval navigator was to measure this height in degrees. The answer or result was his latitude in degrees north of the equator. By the medieval period this measurement had been made for all the major seaports of the northern hemisphere, as well as for many other prominent places such as capes, bays, river mouths, peninsulas, conspicuous landmarks of all sorts and some navigational hazards such as particularly dangerous rocks and shoals. Because latitude could be determined by a measurement of Polaris above the horizon, but longitude could not be determined in any definitive way, the medieval navigator employed what is known as "latitude sailing".

This is simple to understand. The mariner immediately sailed north or south to attain the latitude of the place he sought, and then he sailed east or west as the case might be until he reached it. The key to this navigational method was the ability to measure height of the North Star above the observer's northern horizon. An instrument had been developed for doing this. It was called an astrolabe, and it was next to impossible to use at sea. Nonetheless, a competent navigator had to make measurements that were somewhat accurate because the entire technique of latitude sailing depended upon it.

An inevitable complication existed for the medieval mariner just as it still bedevils modern ones. Polaris is not *exactly* above the North Pole. It is one-quarter of a degree off center. Even if, by some miracle or accident of good fortune, a navigator made an accurate measurement of the height of Polaris above his horizon, he would still be one-quarter of a degree in error. Since one degree on the surface of

A rather complex 15th-century astrolabe such as a cosmographer
might own. It could make a number of celestial observations, not
just the North Star's altitude, and a tangent dial enabled algebraic
calculations to be made for greater accuracy. Such an astrolabe was
not intended to be used at sea, but designed to be suspended from a
stable support on land. With such an instrument, a cosmographer
of the time like Regiomontanus or Zacuto could predict the exact
time of eclipses and draw fairly accurate mathematical grids for
mapmaking.

Courtesy: Maritime Museum, Greenwich, England

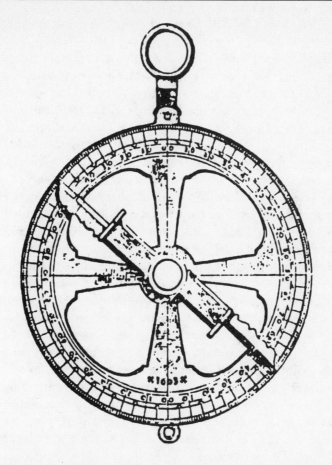

A much-simplified astrolabe for use by mariners was intended
primarily for measuring the height of Polaris above the horizon.
The method was to hang the astrolabe from a bracket on one of the
ship's masts because the instrument had to be in a perfectly
perpendicular position before its measurements would be accurate. Obviously, however, even the slightest wave motion would
transform the ideal of perpendicularity into its opposite . . . a
pendulum! On the open ocean calms are rare. A large swell with
wind-waves on top is more the usual situation. Trying to use an
astrolabe at sea offered much comedy and equal frustration.
Nonetheless, sometimes navigators achieved surprisingly accurate
measurements by no doubt making "mental allowances" for the
instrument's motion, or taking averages.

Courtesy: Maritime Museum, Greenwich, England

the earth is equal to 60 nautical miles, the inevitable error amounted to 15 miles. This could be a crucial error if hazards lurked in the vicinity.

A solution to this problem existed, although it called for more star lore. Polaris is the last star in the Little Dipper's "handle", and the other stars of the constellation seem to revolve around Polaris during the night, and Polaris itself also describes an apparent and very small circle in the sky. But the position of the entire constellation does not change with respect to Polaris and so the attitude of the Little Dipper as it appears in the sky can tell the navigator whether Polaris is one-quarter of a degree "above" north, one-quarter of a degree "below" north, "side by side" with north, or somewhere in between. A navigator had to memorize the various positions of the Little Dipper in the night sky so that he could make the appropriate correction of up to one-quarter of a degree to his astrolabe observation.

Polaris had lesser, but still important, relevance to the navigator because the *counter-clockwise* wheeling of the Little Dipper around it during the night gave an accurate measurement of elapsed time. As an aid to memory, Polaris was imagined to be centered on the body of a man with (sometimes) outstretched arms and legs. This divided the man's figure into eight points if one also imagined a line extending horizontally through the man's hips and another line descending from the head all through the body and extending down between the legs. Each section from point to point encompassed 45 degrees. Since the stars appear to revolve through 15 degrees in one hour of time, each 45-degree section of the man's body represented three hours. This was called "The Regiment of the North Star" and was used by all navigators to calculate elapsed time at night. The only other time-keeping device of the period was a sand glass that was (usually) designed to be turned every half-hour. Custom demanded that a bell be rung when the glass was turned, which is why to this day there are "eight bells" in the normal four-hour watch. The Regiment of the North Star offered more accurate keeping of time, when it could be used, because a ship's motion affected the rate at which sand trickled through the glass and, in any case, the man on watch might not notice exactly when the sand had run through and be tardy in turning it over. Columbus refers to all of these problems in keeping time by ampolleta (sand glass) when he

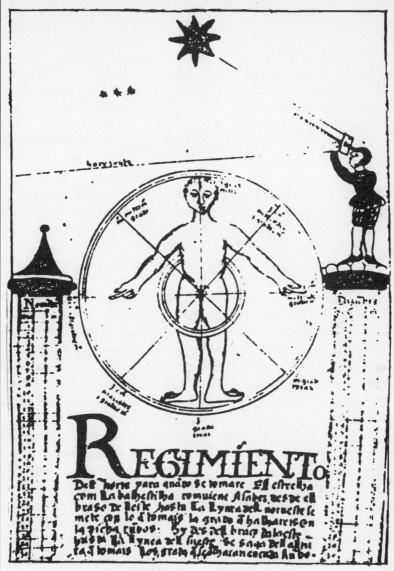

A "Regiment of the North Star," in Spanish, that arranges the man's figure somewhat differently than described in the text, but retaining the all-important 45-degree angles which each represent three hours of elapsed time.

Courtesy: Maritime Museum, Greenwich, England

wrote in his 1492 Log for December 13 that the daylight hours had been 20 glasses long "unless some error was made because the glass was not turned quickly enough or because some of the sand did not run through."[14]

Medieval European mariners had compasses and knew roughly how to use them, as did their colleagues in the Arabic and Far East regions. In fact, at one time it was thought that the concept of the magnetic compass had come into Europe via the Arabs and had originated in China. Nowadays, though, it is considered more likely that seafaring peoples discovered the secret of the compass independently. *Lodestone* is Norse for "leader-stone" and from this it is conjectured that in Europe the compass was first discovered in Scandinavia whereas if it had come into Europe due to Arabic transmission it would certainly have retained its Arabic name, just as so many other navigational terms derive from Arabic.

Some surviving medieval compasses have the needle suspended by a thread from a peg in the center of a directional dial, but others were apparently just wooden bowls with a directional dial around the rim. The bowl was filled with water and a sliver of magnetized iron was inserted into a straw or reed. The reed floated on the water and oriented itself in a north-south direction. Navigators could then determine not only north, but their vessel's course in relation to north. A circle was, and is, divided into 360 degrees, but the dial on a medieval compass's rim was not. It was divided into just 32 points.

This came about through both traditional and practical reasons and lingered in nautical custom until about a century ago. The tradition of 32 points derived from charts made before compasses came into general use. These points represented not directions, but "winds" that would blow a ship to a certain destination. When compasses were introduced, the 32 points were retained but changed into directions. Two of these points separate 11 1/4 degrees, and each point had a directional designation which navigators had to memorize. Reciting these designations clockwise around the compass was called "boxing the compass." Starting at North, the next point would be "North by East," "North Northeast," then "Northeast by North," then "Northeast" and so on around the compass to "Northwest by North."

In practice, courses like "Southwest by West" were sufficient

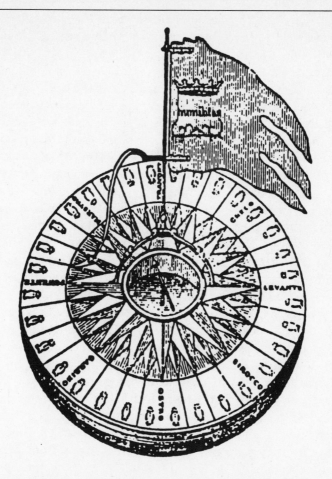

A 16th-century marine compass in which the magnetized needle is suspended by a thread from a central wooden peg. This compass is already divided into 32 "points," but the nomenclature indicates names of winds, not names of direction. This compass is transitional to more modern types: within a century the "points" will all be directional indicators.

Columbus's compass would have been more primitive than this one, possibly only a wooden bowl in which the magnetized needle was floated inside a straw or reed resting on water. The rim of the bowl would have been divided into equal divisions, but not necessarily 32 of them, and the divisions would have been named after winds.

Courtesy: Maritime Museum, Greenwich, England

because of the inaccuracies involved in reading an early compass at sea due to wave motion, and because of the impossibility of holding an early ship to any more accurate course. To set and hold a compass course within 11¼ degrees was considered good enough.

Aside from wave motion, compasses are affected by two other things which were not well understood by medieval mariners. First, there's *variation*. Compasses point to the magnetic "North Pole," not to the geographical North Pole. No one knows the geophysics that create earth's magnetic poles, but it is known that the magnetic poles seem to revolve around the geographic ones. Only if the compass, magnetic north and the geographic North Pole are all in a straight line, *and if the compass is south of the other two*, will the compass point due north. Obviously, this will be a rare configuration and there will usually be a variation between magnetic north and "True North" or geographic north. Further, this amount of variation changes annually by a small quantity as the magnetic pole revolves around the geographic one.

In Columbus's day, variation in the Mediterranean ranged from five to six degrees east of north, but this was unknown and ignored. In the process of crossing the Atlantic, variation changes from being easterly in Europe to being westerly toward America and, of course, Columbus had no way of knowing or suspecting this.

Everyone knows that a piece of iron or steel brought near a compass will cause the needle to swing away from its undisturbed magnetic bearing. This is called *deviation*, and early mariners were aware of it. They were careful to keep metal away from a compass when they were using it. What they did not suspect, however, was that the metal fittings of the ship, however large or small, from nails to cannons, conspired to create a local distortion of the earth's magnetic field. This distortion maintained a certain shape around the ship that was determined by the major metallic objects on board, like cannons, which were confined to one place on the vessel. One might say that this distortion invisibly "mirrored" the shape of the ship magnetically. Not only did this invisible distortion cause deviation from a normal orientation of the compass needle toward magnetic north, but, even more devilishly, the amount of deviation depended on the ship's own orientation within the earth's magnetic field. Which is to say that "deviation varies as per ship's course."

Deviation is not usually large, perhaps only from one to three degrees on average, but that can make a big difference in miles of error if a course is held for a long time. Medieval mariners did not suspect the phenomenon of a ship's having a distorting effect on the magnetic field and so they could not compensate for it as modern yachtsmen do.

In spite of all this, the compass represented a treasure for navigators because it could yield direction during both daylight and darkness. It came to be slavishly followed. On his 1492 voyage, Columbus encountered westward variation in mid-Atlantic for the first time in any known European's experience. He then took an observation of the North Star—but not to check the compass! He took the observation to prove that the star had moved, and not the compass needle. When his improved astrolabe called a "quadrant" tended to indicate that there was something new and strange going on with the ship's compass, Columbus decided that there was something wrong with the star and his quadrant instead. He stowed the quadrant for the remainder of the voyage. Indeed, there was something new and strange happening with Columbus's compass. It was reacting to westward variation. Columbus, thinking he was sailing due west, was actually sailing somewhat southwest. Over the length of the 1492 voyage, thirty-two hundred miles, this resulted in his ending up some 240 miles to the south of his assumed latitude. One would have thought that he could have corrected his error once he reached land and was able to hang his astrolabe from a tree. Free of wave motion, he could have obtained an accurate measurement of the North Star. He did, but some psychological block caused him to read the astrolabe incorrectly to support his dead-reckoning and his compass. All navigators for the next generation committed the same errors, or "psychological blocks," so that early maps of the New World almost always placed the Americas four to six degrees too far north in relation to Europe and Africa. As Robert H. Fuson comments in the Introduction to his new translation of *The Log of Christopher Columbus*:

> As a matter of fact, *all* the early 16th-century Mediterranean charts place Cuba *north* of the Tropic of Cancer. [Italics in the original—Author.][15]

Aside from the two indispensable techniques of star lore and compass lore, a medieval navigator had to be able to calculate his ship's speed through the water by dropping a wooden chip, or "log," overboard at the bow and counting the time required for the ship to sail past the chip. In Columbus's day, this timing was done by counting pulse beats or by reciting a chant. It gave a very approximate idea of the ship's speed, and this was used to estimate the distance made good over a given course. The medieval mariner had to be able to estimate the distance to land seen from the crow's nest of his ship. He could glean much information from the behavior of birds: birds that roosted on land, but which fed by day on the sea (such as pelicans, for example), always flew toward land at nightfall. An accomplished mariner could sometimes read wave-patterns and know that there was land in some specific direction.

Medieval navigation may seem vague and imprecise to modern readers consciously or unconsciously steeped in the scientific method, and it was. Many navigators lost their ships because of ignorance and error. There are wrecks aplenty. On the other hand, there was, and is, something almost supernatural about a true master mariner. He *knows* where his ship is, however unlikely that might seem to a modern landsman and sceptic. Allan Villiers, equipped with accurate charts and a good sextant was able to verify time and again that the very best *nakhodas* ("pilots" or "navigators") of Indian Ocean dhows were invariably within five miles of where they said they were. These master mariners possessed neither charts nor sextants, only their primitive compasses and a mind full of lore. When Villiers asked how they knew their position so closely they would reply: "I just know."

Professor E.G.R. Taylor, a student of ancient navigation, described this *knowingness*:

> For every master and pilot prided himself on knowing exactly how much way his ship was making. He knew the ship, he considered the wind, he watched the sails, he watched the water. In fact it was a matter that just could not be explained to the landsman. A good sailor knows his ship, and that is all.[16]

Whoever it was that swam ashore to become the Columbus of history, he was *that* kind of exceptional master mariner. He *knew*,

and he placed more faith in that than in all the primitive instruments
he had aboard. Again, Robert H. Fuson comments:

> Columbus always rates the highest accolades from scholars
> when it comes to his seamanship. He was, without question,
> the finest sailor of his time. Perhaps he was the greatest dead-
> reckoning sailor who ever lived. His navigation to the Azores,
> through one of the most terrible storms that residents of those
> islands could recall, is sufficient proof of his ability.[17]

Columbus's ability as a practical sailor, as a master in the
"haven-finding art" as navigation has been called, has never been in
question. But his motivations must be questioned. Why did he
undertake the 1492 voyage across the Atlantic? The argument of
this book, already hinted, is that he was commissioned to find a
refuge for Jews, Moors and Cathar heretics who were all associated
with what might be called the "Holy Grail Complex."

Yet, as a master mariner, Columbus above all men would not
have undertaken such a voyage, even for a noble cause, without
knowing that there was land within reach of European caravels of
the time.

Conventional history insists that Columbus sought to reach
China and the Spice Islands. And conventional history, backed up
by Columbus's own words, holds that to his dying day Columbus
really believed that he had reached Asia. In fact, it has been the
fashion to criticize Columbus for his ignorance, his failure to
appreciate that he had not reached Asia but had discovered a New
World. Historian Elizabeth Miller wrote: "When he left Palos he
was the foremost thinker of his day; when he landed on Watlings
Island he was a bewildered, ignorant man on the threshold of
immense facts."[18] Another historian, Frederick Pohl, quoting Miller,
adds that it was "a threshold he never passed."[19]

Is that view of Columbus correct?

I do not think it is, and on this opinion hinges the credibility of
this book. It was true, as we shall see, that Columbus argued,
apparently in error, for a world that was too small by some 6000
miles in his various presentations to gain Portuguese and Spanish
support. He consistently used the very few facts and opinions that
seemed to support his ideas, and just as consistently ignored the

many more facts that contradicted his concept, in order to argue that Asia was only about three thousand miles from Iberia and not the actual 9000 miles.

He had to do this, as ridiculous as he seemed to contemporary experts, for two very good reasons: everyone wanted to reach "Asia" and nowhere else; it was simply a fact that a European caravel could not deliver a crew alive to any landfall nine thousand miles away because the ship could not make sufficient speed or carry sufficient food and water.

Therefore, if his expedition was to gain support, Columbus had to hope that his determination, and Spanish desperation to duplicate Portuguese success, would weigh against all the very valid objections.

My point is that Columbus, master mariner, would not have set out if he knew the voyage to be a real impossibility, and he would know better than anyone. He must have known for certain that there was land to the west, that it was within the reach of the ships of his day, and he must have known as well as any other expert of his day *that this land could not be the Indies or "Asia."* But, this new western land which could not be "Asia" *could be a haven for religious refugees if only Columbus were successful in extracting certain concessions from Spain.*

Columbus partly countered objections to his truly impossible project by saying that he "might discover some very beneficial island or continent...about 750 leagues to the west"[20] where the ships could re-provision in order to continue the voyage to "Asia." Columbus discovered precisely this, and precisely that distance westward. Is that a happy coincidence, or did he know that some vast unknown land lay that distance away from Iberia? Legal documents suggest strongly that he knew about this unknown land. In the agreements signed on April 17th, 1492, ("The Capitulo") and on April 30th, 1492, ("The Titulo") the strange fact is that more attention is given to the rulership and jurisdiction of problematical lands that might be discovered en route than to a division of spoils from wealthy Asia. Is this not a strange emphasis considering that any new lands were, in the minds of experts other than Columbus, utterly hypothetical? And is this emphasis not strange considering that the entire thrust of the expedition was to reach the "Indies"? It must be considered a strange emphasis, and yet it was crucial for Columbus to extract a guarantee of his own rulership and jurisdiction over any new lands discovered before reaching "Asia" *if he knew it was there and needed to control it for an urgent reason.*

There is one major aspect of navigation that has not yet been dealt with, and that is the matter of charts. It seems beyond question that some charts available to Columbus showed the American continents. These were secret charts known only to very few persons, but there is no doubt that they existed because documents refer to them. Christopher Columbus had such a chart, and consulted it on September 25 during the 1492 crossing. The incident is mentioned in his Log. In fact, he ordered a change of course to conform to the chart. This was 17 days before the fleet sighted land.

In his various presentations to Portugal and Spain, Columbus dared not refer to these charts that showed a vast new land across the Atlantic *that was not Asia.* He dared not refer to them for two reasons.

First, of course, if the existence of this land could be shown plausibly on charts that had some credibility, Columbus himself would have become unnecessary to Spain. Some less troublesome adventurer could be sent on the voyage instead, and no concessions or rulership or jurisdiction or nobility would have to be made to him. The alternate adventurer could simply be paid for his services; paid generously, perhaps, which would still be less expensive than what Columbus demanded.

Second, if Columbus had revealed the existence of these charts, and thus his ownership of them, he would have branded himself as a heretic. The reason for his is that the priceless charts came from a thoroughly heretical source.

Apparently, from the evidence that exists, the charts could only have been provided by the Knights Templar.

Chapter 6

Lapsus Calami

Robert H. Fuson, member of the *National Geographic*'s 1986 project to research Columbus's life and discover the real location of his "San Salvador" island landfall, writes in his new translation of *The Log of Christopher Columbus*:

> This veil of mystery surrounding Columbus' personal background is not simply an accident of history; it is in large part Columbus' own doing. Fernando tells us in his *Historie* that his father elected to leave everything pertaining to his birth and family in obscurity. Even this, however, would appear to be an understatement. There is ample evidence that Columbus altered his identity . . . [1]

Even a few short years ago, such a statement would not, and could not, have been written by anyone remotely associated with the prestigious and ultra-conservative National Geographic Society. As late as November 1975, the lead article in the *National Geographic* still towed the traditional line of our schooldays Columbus "of Genoa" popularized by Samuel Eliot Morison and accepted Morison's opinion that Columbus landed on Watlings Island.

Now, though, because so many facts have been swept under the carpet of history that it has become unsightly with lumps, even a *National Geographic*-associated scholar like Fuson is compelled to admit that nothing is quite so straightforward as it seemed about Columbus. In *The Log of Christopher Columbus*, Fuson even concedes that Columbus very possibly came from a Jewish family, a possibility first raised by the research of Salvador de Madariaga (1967) in his *Christopher Columbus* and 13 years later re-hashed and sensationalized by Simon Wiesenthal in his *The Secret Mission of Christopher Columbus*.

Revelations of this sort, even partly endorsed by someone like Fuson and the National Geographic Society, may seem like more than enough shock for the average reader to absorb about someone so "familiar." Columbus may have been *Jewish*? At the same time, Jewish readers can accept that easily and with satisfaction, and may not be inclined to go any further: "Of course, it's only right that someone as famous as Columbus was Jewish! We knew it all along!"

Unfortunately for the non-Jewish and Jewish-partisan readers alike, there are yet more curious facts and mysterious associations swirling around the life of Columbus than scholars like Robert Fuson, Salvador de Madariaga and Simon Wiesenthal have revealed and which an organization like the National Geographic Society so cautiously concedes. While doing great service by recovering *some* of the facts from beneath the carpet, these "New Columbus" biographers have nonetheless chosen to leave some other facts under there still in order to keep their pet theories and speculations undisturbed by anomalous data. As these data are retrieved until the carpet is properly flat and lumpless, we may perceive a pattern that makes sense about what might be called the "*New*-New Columbus."

This pattern will suggest that Columbus was part of a noble conspiracy to discover a haven for religious refugees of the heretical "Holy Grail Complex" of belief. And, whereas it is true that *some* of these heretics came originally from a Jewish background, others and the majority of them seem to have come from Cathar "Christian" and Islamic backgrounds. This "Grail Religion" was a body of supposed fact and associated beliefs and loyalties which could *truly* convert someone from previous orthodoxy of one of the three great Western religions; it did not mirror the polite farce of "conversos" to Spanish-style Roman Catholicism that some Jews and Moslems professed openly while secretly practising another faith.

Since it is known that some of the "Grail Complex" heretics came originally from Jewish backgrounds, there would not be cause for surprise if Columbus happened to come from a Jewish background too. But that does not necessarily mean that he was a Jew any longer

in any meaningful, modern or orthodox sense, any more than he was
the good Roman Catholic he professed to be. He had come into
contact with a complex but very plausible body of fact and traditional
lore that compelled him to transcend his original Jewish, Christian
or Islamic parochialism in a more universal and cosmopolitan view
of human development and human destiny. If Columbus did originally come from a Jewish family, and there is good evidence that he
possibly, or probably, did, it does not seem as if he remained what
could be called "Jewish." In modern terms, he may well have
represented a neo-Catharism similar to the contemporary "Jews for
Jesus" movement which has caused so much consternation within
the modern North American Jewish community. From the orthodox
Jewish perspective, Columbus was most probably a "heretic," just as
he was probably a "heretic" from the orthodox Roman Catholic
point of view. At least, this is what some still sub-carpet data suggest.

From the beach where he came ashore after the pirate attack,
Columbus made his way to Lisbon. Columbus was destitute and,
luckily for him, his relative, Bartolomé, operated a bookstore and
map-making business in Lisbon. Columbus found employment
there, and also became exposed to the books and maps that supposedly formed his idea of sailing west to reach the east. But, as Robert
Fuson admits a bit plaintively, "even Bartolomé's life has been
obscured."[2] Samuel Eliot Morison, relying upon Fernando, repeats
the tradition that Bartolomé was Columbus's *younger* brother.
Other biographers make him an *older* brother, while Frederick Pohl
in *The New Columbus* argues that Bartolomé was Columbus's
uncle. The truth of the matter is simply that we do not know who this
Bartolomé was any more than we know who Columbus was.

All that we can safely assert is that Bartolomé did apparently run
a bookstore and map-making business in Lisbon, that Columbus
became associated with him immediately, and that both Bartolomé
and Columbus had mysterious commercial and social power that has
never been explained, as subsequent events make abundantly clear.

Within four or five months of his arrival in Lisbon, Columbus
shipped aboard a vessel bound for Flanders and England. In February 1477, according to Fernando, Columbus was in Iceland, or
"Thule" as Fernando called it. Many scholars today doubt that this
voyage to Iceland ever happened because, obviously, February

would not be the month to visit the place. Fernando says that the sea was not frozen in the vicinity of "Thule," and this does not accord with Iceland in February. Supposedly, too, according to Fernando, Columbus may have sailed "100 leagues" beyond "Thule." Scholars are willing to concede that Columbus may very possibly have visited Britain and, if so, he doubtless visited the port of Bristol. The simple truth of the matter, again, is that we don't know where Columbus went in 1477.

If Fernando's mention of "Thule" is a genuine clue that Columbus made a voyage into northern waters in 1477, Columbus's destination hinges on the meaning of "Thule." This was an ancient and anomalous word to use in the 16th century when Fernando was writing, or even in the late 15th century when Columbus related this tale to his son. For the Greeks of the 4th and 5th centuries B.C, "Thule" simply meant a vague someplace far to the north, about as far north as one could travel because of the ice and snow. In 325 B.C the geographer and explorer, Pytheas of the Greek colony of Marseilles, made a voyage to England and to "Thule." Unfortunately, all of the works of Pytheas have been lost, about a dozen books, including his *On The Ocean*, which describes this voyage. However, the works of Pytheas were very well known in the Ancient World and many writers quoted from them. There is little doubt that Pliny, writing in the 1st century A.D., was quoting Pytheas when he said:

> The outermost of all known lands is Thule. At the time of the solstice, when the sun passes through the eye of the crab, there are no nights there. In winter the day lasts only a short time, whereas the nights are very long. Many people even assert that this is the case for six months without interruption.[3]

Two hundred years later, the geographer Solinus, again probably quoting from Pytheas, says:

> From the Orcades [i.e. Orkney Islands—Author's note] to Thule is five days' and five nights' sail. Despite its northerly position, Thule is fertile and rich in late-ripening fruits. From the beginning of spring onward the inhabitants live with their cattle. They feed on milk and vegetables, but store up fruit for the winter.[4]

This "Thule" would seem to be Iceland from the sailing directions, but it is not. Iceland does not seem to have been inhabited at all in the time of either Pytheas or Solinus, and was not really known until Irish monks reached the island about the 7th century A.D. and even their visits were sporadic. One cannot say that Iceland was truly *inhabited* by people, such that their lifestyle could be generalized, until the Norse colonized it around the 9th century A.D. The only inhabited place in northern Europe that fits the description of Pytheas as quoted by Pliny, Solinus et al., is Norway at about 64-degrees north latitude in the region of Trondheim Fjord, and this identification of "Thule" is accepted by most scholars.

In the 15th century, Norway and Iceland and even Greenland were well known, at least to geographers and mariners, and they had names: Greenland was "Engroneland"; Iceland was "Islandia"; and Norway was "Norumbega." "Thule" was still sometimes used, but it had been pushed even further north by more specific knowledge. In the 15th century, "Thule" was a place in the *far north* of Greenland. It was still a vague and somewhat mythical place which simply designated "as far north as it is possible to go." But it was in Greenland, and it remains there. Today, Thule is a radar station.

If Columbus was not simply being coy with Fernando in using an obsolete and rather meaningless word like "Thule," but was truly giving the destination of his 1477 voyage, then Columbus must have been in Greenland—but hardly in *February* of 1477. It is worth noting that sometimes during the medieval period, but only rarely, northern Scotland and the Orkney Islands were sometimes called "Thule."

The use of the word "Thule" by Columbus and later quoted by Fernando, would seem to indicate that Columbus intended to communicate the knowledge that he had sailed "far north" of England without being too specific about it. This is about all that can be said. But even this much may prove to be suggestive, as we shall see.

By 1479 Columbus was back in Portugal working as a Lisbon bookseller and map-maker. In that same year he married Doña Felipa Perestrello e Moniz, and this must stand as yet another anomalous fact in Columbus's life. This girl was not a nobody in Portuguese society, but a member of what might be termed the middle-rank nobility. Her father, a decade in his grave in 1479, had been Perestrello, one of the "re-discoverers" of the Madeira Islands who had been made governor of Porto Santo.

Scarcely two years before, Columbus had come ashore supposedly destitute and, in any case, claiming no noble title. One cannot really expect that he and Bartolomé made so much money in the bookselling and map-making business, or that Columbus made so much money by shipping out on trading vessels, that their wealth could overcome their lack of social status. Portuguese of the 15th century were no less obsessed with lineage and nobility than other Europeans. How, then, could a presumably poor or, at best, "middle class" Genoese castaway manage to marry into the Perestrello aristocracy so quickly—or at all? Gianni Granzotto writes:

> . . . for Columbus the marriage represented a step upward in Portuguese society. It was hardly a common occurrence for a young immigrant just settled in Lisbon to marry the heiress to an aristocratic name.[5]

No, it was hardly a common occurrence, and Granzotto can suggest nothing better to explain it than the speculation that Doña Felipa must have been an ugly girl who could attract no better suitor. According to Granzotto, the widowed single-parent Doña Moniz must have married Felipa to the Genoese castaway in desperation! But there may be another explanation.

Robert Fuson gives the hint:

> Was Columbus really the son of poor woolweavers? How did he acquire his considerable education? How could a commoner, and a foreign one at that, marry into the Portuguese nobility? How was Columbus able to move among royalty as a peer? Was the Admiral of higher birth than many suppose? Frederick Pohl thinks so. Others, as well, hint at a blood link to the royal line.[6]

Columbus at least possessed a regal *appearance*. Fernando, Las Cases and Oviedo all agree that Columbus was of greater than average height, well built, with pale blue eyes and blond hair and an aquiline nose. By the time he was 30, his originally blond hair had turned completely white and by the time of the 1492 voyage, when most scholars make him 41 years old, his white hair had become speckled with grey. Appearance, of course, does not necessarily mean anything, yet this complexion is not what we normally expect of Mediterranean Jews, or Sephardic Jews, who came into Iberia from Palestine during the Diaspora. Some people said that Columbus's hair, blond in his youth, had a distinct reddish tinge.

If appearance means anything at all, the description of Columbus at least suggests a Celtic or Nordic genetic heritage, not a south European one. He could have come from the Celts of the Pyrenees Provençal culture; or from Brittany and Anjou where Viking raids of the 8th–11th centuries had left a Nordic genetic legacy; or he could have come from Sicily, which the Norse king Roger (1130–1154) had conquered with his many Nordic vassals and nobility, or from Mallorca, which also acquired a Nordic-looking aristocracy when Roger's ancestors decided to take that island. Indeed, in private correspondence with me, Michael Baigent, co-author of *The Holy Blood and The Holy Grail*, tends to think that Columbus may have been born on Mallorca where, just behind the Templar castle in the capital town of Palma, there was a district in which resided a number of cartographers recruited from all over the known world.[7]

It is at this point that several apparent digressions must be made in order to retrieve some seemingly Columbus-related data from beneath the carpet. But the digressions are only apparent ones, and their true relevance will suggest itself strongly in the following pages.

First, there is nothing mutually exclusive about the possibility that Columbus may have been both a "pirate" and also related in some fashion to "Grail Complex" nobility of which there were dozens of secret or semi-secret lineages. But to explain why piracy was apparently respectable within the "Grail Complex" scheme of things, we must return briefly to the Albigensian Crusade and the fall of Montségur.

It will be recalled that the Cathars were defeated, their *parfaits* tortured and burned alive, and yet there remains the claim that the Holy Grail itself was taken to safety by four knights just two days before the stronghold of Montségur surrendered. If we are indeed correct in regarding the Holy Grail as being a bloodline descended from Jesus, then this means, most probably, that one or more children representing the most direct descent from Jesus were evacuated from Montségur and taken to some place of relative safety.

The bloodline survived, according to tradition, and the Templars (and Knights of St. John of Jerusalem) were sworn to defend it above all else.

Although many Templars participated in the defence of Provence during the 35-year Albigensian Crusade, and although many died at Montségur, they still retained a European organization of great military strength and equal wealth. No combination of monarchs, and not even the Vatican, was anxious to try conclusions with them. Nonetheless, the Templars were marked for destruction.

The blow fell on October 13, 1307, when King Philippe IV ("le Bel") of France ordered simultaneous raids on all the Templar priories in his country. Hundreds of knights were captured, including the Grand Master of the Order, Jacques de Molay. They were all tortured, sometimes for months and years continually, in order to extract from them the secret of the Holy Grail and its whereabouts. The Grand Master, Jacques de Molay, was given special attention and suffered years of agony. But it is said that none of the Templars revealed the desired information.

In 1312, Philippe de Bel pressured Pope Clement V into disbanding the Order throughout Europe even though it was already effectively crushed in France itself. In 1314, Jacques de Molay who had suffered in Philippe's dungeons for seven years—he'd been blinded by red-hot irons thrust into his eyes, his genitals had been boiled in oil and then pulled off with cords, most of his bones had been broken or dislocated on the rack—faced his last torment: he was roasted alive over a slow fire by order of king and pope. This barbarous destruction of a human being was never to be forgotten.

Knights Templar, now officially disbanded, dispersed all over Europe as hunted men. But, for fighting men all over Europe, these refugee knights still commanded immense respect. They were welcomed in many places and given sanctuary as heroes. Some joined the Teutonic Knights and fought against Mongol and Tartar incursions in Eastern Europe; some went to Hungary and fought against Turkish expansion; some went to Scotland, and particularly to the family seat of the Saint-Clairs in Rosslyn; some went to Portugal.

Many experts think that the esoteric cults of Freemasonry, Rosicrucianism and the Illuminati of Bavaria are actually neo-

Templar organizations that were formed to preserve and popularize secret Templar knowledge.[8] Certainly, it cannot be mere coincidence that the Saint-Clairs of Rosslyn, long-time paladins of the dynasty of Godfroi de Bouillon, also became hereditary leaders of Scottish Freemasonry.[9]

In some places, however, the Templars were welcomed and did not have to cloak themselves with too much secrecy. Portugal was such a place. The Knights Templar retained something of a cohesive organization there and merely changed their name to "The Order of the Knights of Christ," and they found royal support to which the Church could only turn a blind eye. First, King Alfonso IV of Portugal became the Grand master of the "new" Knights of Christ. Later, Prince Henry The Navigator was also Grand Master of the Order.[10]

The destruction and dispersal of the Knights Templar had at least three direct and important repercussions in Europe, of which the most visible and least important was an upsurge in "piracy." When King Philippe ordered the dawn raids on October 13, 1307, the Templar fleet based at La Rochelle somehow got advance warning. The entire fleet set sail, escaped Philippe's net, and has never been heard from since. This fleet very possibly carried some of the Holy Blood to safety—or, at least, that's a geographically reasonable speculation since La Rochelle is a port on the extensive Garonne estuary, and the Garonne River wends its way deep into the Pyrenees. If descendants of Jesus were evacuated from Montségur in March of 1244 they probably hid in numerous secret Pyrenees caverns for months or even years, and some troubadour poetry refers to this. But true safety meant being taken out of France eventually, *and even out of Europe ultimately*. The Garonne River was the obvious route to reach the Templar fleet at La Rochelle, with a sanctuary at the town and fortress of Angoulême which may have been used as a haven for two or three generations. So long as the Templars remained a cohesive and independent Order, there was hope that the de Bouillon lineage could successfully hide secretly in Europe and begin the process of recouping its fortunes. But with the dawn raids of October 13, 1307, and the effective destruction of the Templar core, the only recourse was evacuation. So, the Templar fleet set sail a few hours before the raids, and it is not irresponsible to suggest that at least some of these Templar vessels carried "The Holy Grail" because guarding it was *the* task of the Templars.

Other vessels, however, seem to have been used as the Holy Blood's navy, to strike back at the hated Roman Church and the monarchs and countries loyal to it. An upsurge in European piracy begins from this time and the pattern of it suggests that many pirates were not mere freebooters who would attack anyone, but very curious "pirates" who confined their attentions to Vatican and loyal-Catholic shipping. Later, of course, Captain Drake ("dragon") would elevate "piracy" to big business, but he preyed only upon Spanish-Catholic ships once the Inquisition had been established in the New World.

Everyone knows that the proper pirate flag is the "Jolly Roger," a black flag with the "skull and crossbones" in white. What most people do not know, however, is that this same "skull and cross-bones" is carved on many Templar and Freemason gravestones. it is nothing more or less than the old Templar "cross pattée" rendered in human skeletal material with the knobs of the leg-bones being the "pattées" of the Templar cross. The message of the "skull and crossbones" is abundantly clear: a "neo-Templar" vow to oppose the Roman Church *to the death*, and thus the symbolism of human bones on both the flag and the Templar and Freemason gravestones. Experts might quibble with this interpretation were it not for the fact that the "Roger" who was so jolly appears to have been Roger of Sicily, a Templar, who conquered Sicily during the time of the Kingdom of Jerusalem. Roger naturally had a fleet, and the skull and crossbones first flew on his vessels. He also established a navigational school on Sicily, and one isolated from the Vatican by both sea and his fleet, which invited Jewish and Islamic geographers as consultants. The Arabic geographer, Ibn Idrisi, was attracted to Roger's court and produced a "celestial disc" and a "terrestrial disc," both in silver, which represented respectively all the astronomical and geographic knowledge of the day. Idrisi and Roger also produced the important navigational treatise called the *Al Rojari*. In passing, it should be explained that Roger was considered jolly because his court at Palermo was not only bright with geographical knowledge, but also lively with culture and music. Roger was fond

The skull and crossbones on a Masonic tombstone near Rosslyn, Scotland. Were some pirates flying the "Jolly Roger," the Holy Blood's navy?

Photo: Courtesy Michael Baigent

of Islamic and ancient Hebrew love-poetry, with a taste for beautiful women to match the allusions in it.

So much for pirates and the Jolly Roger. It is easy to see that a "pirate" working on behalf of the Holy Blood could very well come from some noble or royal family. In the Europe of Columbus's time, about three centuries after Roger of Palermo, René d'Anjou was much like a reincarnated Roger. Even in his own era, René d'Anjou was called "Good King René" because of his just and enlightened rule and his court, too, sparkled with knowledge and culture as few others in Europe. According to troubadour poetry, the first Frankish knight of the Holy Grail was Perceval of Anjou, and there can be little doubt that René d'Anjou was not only aware of the Holy Grail story but was a part of it himself. It will be recalled that René d'Anjou commissioned our "Columbus" to pirate the galleass *Ferrandina* belonging to Catholic Aragon in 1472. This seems to have been in the grand tradition of Roger of Sicily, "Coullon/Columbus" and Drake—the freelance navy of the Holy Blood striking back at the established might of Roman Catholic countries, particularly Spain. So, within the perspective of a secret and on-going conspiracy of the "Grail Complex" versus the Roman Church and its Inquisition, our Columbus could well have been a "pirate" and also of noble blood.

It was stated that Templar dispersion had three immediate repercussions in Europe of which an upsurge of "piracy" was only the first and least important in the 14th and 15th centuries.

A second repercussion, and a much more important one, was that wherever the Templars dispersed with some cohesion, *voyages of Atlantic exploration immediately followed*. In Portugal, it will be recalled, the Templars didn't go underground at all, but merely changed their name to the "Knights of Christ" and King Alfonso IV immediately became this "new" Order's Grand Master. Is it mere coincidence that King Alfonso IV also immediately began the Portuguese policy of sending ships out into the Atlantic? As the German historian Paul Herrmann wrote in his *Conquest By Man:*

> King Alfonso IV (1325–57) seems to have initiated long voyages to the west, probably the Canaries, as early as the first quarter of the 14th century. This tradition was taken up and continued by Prince Henry the Navigator (1394–1460) with the

aim of finding a seaway to India round the southern tip of Africa.[11]

Is it just coincidence that Prince Henry the Navigator was also a Grand Master of the Knights of Christ?

It was also noted that Templars fled to Scotland and were able to maintain some cohesion there under the protection of the famous Saint-Clairs. There is a Templar cemetery on the Saint-Clair domain at Rosslyn, which is a tourist attraction today. In Scotland, the Templars did not apparently try to organize themselves into a new Order of knighthood but elected instead to spread their secret doctrine more widely by creating Freemasonry, again under the leadership of the powerful Saint-Clairs.[12] Is it sheer coincidence that voyages to the west set out from Scotland within a generation after Templars had established themselves there?

A very obscure aspect of navigational history now confronts us. A voyage to the west from Scotland apparently reached the New World sometime between 1350 and 1370. Indeed, this voyage is important from one point of view. A survivor of it described the land across the Atlantic as Nuovo Mundo, a "New World," in literally those words, a realization that has been universally credited to Amerigo Vespucci 160 years later. We do not know anything for certain about this mid-14th-century voyage except that it took place and that the new lands seem to have been explored in some detail *over a period of some thirteen years!* At least one of the crew travelled from somewhere in New England or the Canadian maritime provinces all the way south to Mexico and back. His descriptions of the Indians and also of the Mexican civilization are accurate, and this cannot be the case unless he'd been there. This survivor recognized this land as a "New world" because he had seen it extensively and was intelligent enough to realize that the inhabitants and the cities didn't match Europe's idea of Cathay and the realm of the "Great Khan."

This voyage of 1350–1370 A.D. inspired a second voyage, which was made in 1398–1400 by Earl Henry Saint-Clair (or "Sinclair") with the stated purpose of establishing a colony there. Sinclair's expedition landed in a place called "Estotiland" which, because of its unique open pitch deposits, has been positively identified as Nova Scotia by Dr. William H. Hobbs, a geologist at the University of Michigan, in 1951. The whole idea of the Sinclair voyage seems to have been to found a colony or "city" in this new land, and the existing account of the voyage states that this was done.[13]

In 1974 the apparent remains of a 14th-century castle were discovered in mid-peninsular Nova Scotia and reported to the provincial government. In 1981, I was asked to look at the site by Nova Scotia's Ministry of Culture, an investigation that lasted until April 1983. The results of this research cannot be covered in detail in this book about Columbus, but the investigation is the subject of Holy Grail Across The Atlantic, which was published in Canada in September 1988. It can only be said here that the remains of a pre-Columbian European fortification apparently do exist on a hilltop location in Nova Scotia; the ruins appear to be rubblework construction appropriate to Sinclair's late 14th-century era, and typical of other Northern Scottish and Scandinavian fortifications of the period; and that several other sites were also discovered which seem to have been lookouts for the main fortress or settlement. The two-and-a-half-year investigation recommended excavation of the site by archeologists from the Nova Scotia Museum, but this has not yet been done. I hasten to point out that the other sites seemingly associated with the major mid-peninsular construction were not discovered by me and my associates, but by Frederick Pohl and a team from the University of Maine in 1959–1960. There is also evidence, again mostly uncovered if not actually discovered, by Frederick Pohl, which indicates that the Sinclair expedition at least casually explored as far south as Massachusetts.[14]

Can it be mere coincidence, then, that transatlantic expeditions sailed from Scotland, as well as from Portugal, just as soon as refugee Templars had established themselves in these two countries?

I think this is stretching "coincidence" a bit far. These transatlantic initiatives are, at least, correlated with Templar arrival in Scotland and Portugal. Although correlation is not necessarily causation, it seems reasonable to conclude that, somehow, Templars were at least influential in inspiring these voyages.

Several questions immediately spring to mind. Why were Templars seemingly associated with transatlantic voyages from 14th-

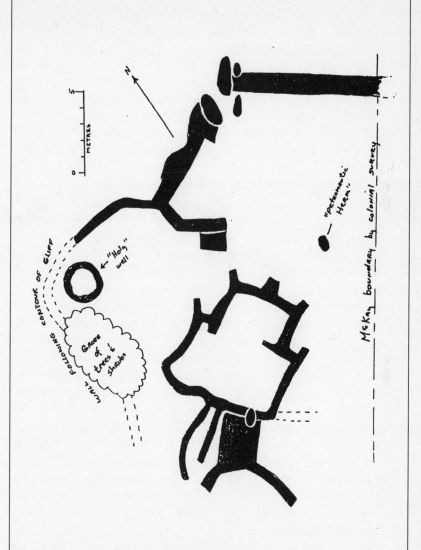

Northwest corner of apparent ruined castle in mid-peninsular Nova Scotia, which the author investigated for the Nova Scotia Ministry of culture during 1981–1983. This site plan was drawn by a Halifax civil engineer to the author's measurements of the ruins. Illustration from *Holy Grail Across The Atlantic*.

century Portugal and Scotland? What were the explorers seeking? Why did they obviously expect to find it across the Atlantic?

I think that some of these questions can be answered plausibly.

The answers, though, will impart a new and perhaps uncomfortable emphasis to Europe's so-called "Age of Discovery" and Columbus's role in it.

Templars had been created by the second King of Jerusalem, Baudoin, the younger brother of Godfroi de Bouillon. The whole mission of the Knights Templar was to protect the dynasty of de Bouillon. That was their entire reason for being. This dynasty had been all but destroyed during the Albigensian Crusade, and the position of any survivors became more precarious with the crushing, dispersal and disbanding of their Templar guardians. But the Templars were nothing if not utterly loyal and courageous. They had always been hand-picked for just those qualities.

If transatlantic expeditions set out from Portugal and Scotland shortly after refugee Templars arrived in both places, it is reasonable to speculate that Templars were attempting to find a haven for the survivors of the de Bouillon dynasty that these knights were sworn to protect. Survivors evacuated from Montségur, if there were any as legend maintains, desperately needed a secure refuge from the Inquisition. No place in Europe could really be considered safe in the long term. All of Europe was dominated by the Roman Church. Fringe areas, like Portugal and Scotland, might be "safe" in the short term but only as temporary springboard to some more secure haven. The south-eastern part of Europe and the Mediterranean was no haven because the Saracens controlled it. Central and northeastern Europe were out because these regions were fighting for their very existence against the Mongols, Tartars and Turks. There was only one direction left: west. Westward, across the Atlantic, there might be a land free of the Roman Church, where a truly secure haven could be established.

Did Templars have any reason to suspect, or to know, that there was such a land across the Atlantic?

Yes. There is strong evidence, short of absolute proof, that the Templars had knowledge of land across the Atlantic. This brings us to the third, and most important, repercussion of the Templar dispersion. Not only did Templars apparently influence transatlantic probes just as soon as they arrived in Portugal and Scotland, but all of Europe was suddenly flooded with sea-charts of inexplicable accuracy. These charts are really the most important result of the Templar dispersal because they accomplished two things: they greatly facilitated purely European trade and commerce by sea, and thus contributed to the further decline of feudalism; non-European portions of these same charts really made the European "Age of Discovery" possible because they showed the whole world, and also showed new land across the Atlantic.

Within a generation after Philippe le Bel pressured Clement V into disbanding the Templars, maps called "portolans" began to be distributed throughout Europe. One of the earliest portolans is called the Dulcert Portolan of 1339, which appeared just 27 years after the Knights Templar were disbanded. Scholars of navigation have consistently tried to ignore the portolans because of the problems they present. It is accepted that they did exist, but the problems they represent have been swept under the carpet. Only two experts have truly grappled with the mystery of the portolans, but academia as a whole has turned a blind eye toward their conclusions.

Stated simply, the mystery of the portolans is not so much that they appeared so suddenly in 14th-century Europe but that they are inexplicably accurate. It will be recalled that the barrier to medieval navigation was that longitude, the position east or west of any given point, could not be determined with any accuracy. The key to finding longitude by celestial observation was some method of keeping time with extreme accuracy. Clocks of such sophistication simply did not exist in the medieval world, and navigators had to wait until 18th-century technology supplied them.

The mystery of the portolans is that they *are* accurate in terms of longitude and, although they appeared suddenly to the medieval world, no one person, culture or civilization of the 14th century could have produced them.

The Scandinavian scholar, A.E. Nordenskiöld, studied all the portolans he could find in the 1890s. After analysing hundreds of these charts from scores of European museums, Nordenskiöld concluded that all of the portolans had been copied from just one original chart. This original chart was highly accurate in terms of both latitude and longitude. In fact, it was more accurate than some

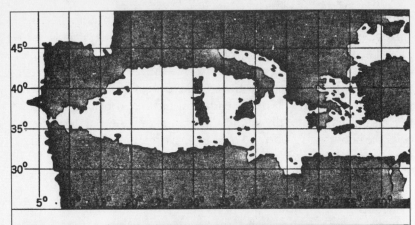

Ptolemy's 2nd century A.D. Map of the Mediterranean (top) compared with the Dulcert Portolano of 1339 A.D. The Ptolemaic map shows great distortion and yet it was considered the best rendition of the Mediterranean available *by European geographers*. The portolan is almost modern in its accuracy, but portolans suddenly turned up in the hands of common mariners, not academics.

Just as the Templars assisted merchants on land in the 13th-century by constructing warehouses, guarding merchant pack-trains and issuing letters of credit, it is possible that Templars assisted mariners in the 14th century by releasing the European portions of secret world maps of inexplicable accuracy.

Courtesy: Charles Hapgood and the Chilton Book Company

maps made in Nordenskiöld's own day. Other portolans replicated this accuracy to a greater or lesser extent depending on the care taken in the copying—but one and all were much more accurate than maps made by Ptolemy, and far more accurate than products known to have derived from the medieval period.[15]

A modern expert, Prof. Charles Hapgood of Keene State Teacher's College in New Hampshire, took up, in the 1950s and 1960s, where Nordenskiöld left off in the 1890s. Hapgood arranged to have his analyses checked by the Cartographic Section of the U.S. Air Force's Strategic Air Command (8th Reconnaissance Technical Squadron). Like Nordenskiöld before him, Hapgood could only conclude that all the portolans seem to have been copied from one original because they all displayed the same peculiarities. Hapgood also concluded that a portolan known as the Ibn Ben Zara Chart, dated to 1487, was the best one and had been most carefully copied from the original. It was probably not *the* original, but it best replicated the original. Hapgood says of it:

> I had been attracted to a study of this portolan because it seemed definitely superior to all other portolan charts I had seen in the fineness of the delineation of the details of the coasts. As I examined the details in comparison with modern maps, I was amazed to see that no islet, however small, seemed too small to be noted...The grid worked out for the map revealed, indeed, a most amazing accuracy so far as the relative latitudes and longitudes were concerned. Total longitude between the Sea of Azov and Gibraltar was accurate to half a degree.[16]

This is an error of only 30 miles over an east-west distance of over 3000 miles, and is better accuracy than can be claimed by road maps of the 1950s and 1960s.

All of the surviving portolans are centered on the Mediterranean world. They show only "Europe" from the Atlantic Coast, through the entire Mediterranean, and usually also include all of the Black Sea. Occasionally, as with the Ibn Ben Zara chart, they extend further north to the Sea of Azov. One or two of the portolans even extend eastward to include the Caspian Sea. Always, the longitude is inexplicably accurate.

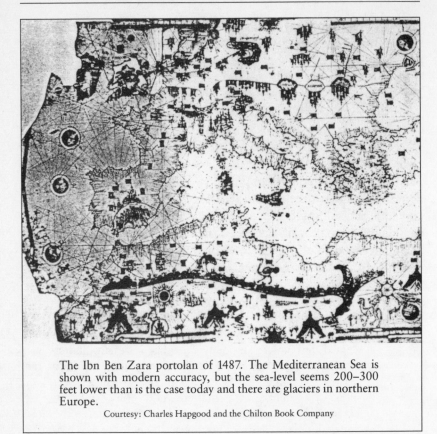

The Ibn Ben Zara portolan of 1487. The Mediterranean Sea is shown with modern accuracy, but the sea-level seems 200–300 feet lower than is the case today and there are glaciers in northern Europe.

Courtesy: Charles Hapgood and the Chilton Book Company

A crucial question begs to be asked. Although the surviving portolans depict only "Europe," did the source map from which they all derive depict a much larger area? In fact, could the portolans have been copied from just the "European" part of a larger map that showed the entire world?

This question is crucial indeed. If the portolans represent just the small "European" portion of some larger world map, or "mappamundi" as academics would say, then the corrolary must be that the rest of the world would be depicted as accurately as the small European part. In short, if there was a mappamundi source it would have accurately shown Europe, Asia, Africa and the Americas because there's no good reason to assume that the remainder of the world would have been drawn any more or less accurately than the European portions which survive. There's a subtlety to this situation which should be emphasized. If a source mappamundi existed that showed Europe, Asia, Africa and the Americas *then the owners of this priceless map-of-the-world* could see clearly that there was land across the Atlantic, but that it was not Asia.

Was there ever such a world map? Did Templars get possession of it? Did they bring copies to Portugal and to Scotland which served as guides for Atlantic voyages in search of a religious haven *in the New world, and not in Asia*?

I believe it is justified to assume that it is probable, with this probability verging on certainty, that Templars did possess such a map of the world. The reason for stating this so strongly is simply that modern scholars have found precisely this kind of mappamundi in Middle Eastern archives. Specifically, two very intriguing maps of the world have been found: the Hadji Ahmed Map was discovered in 1860 in what is now Lebanon; then, in 1929 the Piri Re'is Map was discovered in the old Imperial Palace in Constantinople. Before looking at these maps and their unnerving implications, something should be said about the methodology of medieval and early Renaissance cartographers.

Supposing that a map-maker of the 15th or 16th century possessed a very accurate map that he could copy, he would still be inclined to "improve" on it based on the best contemporary knowledge available to him. Look at the situation from the cartographer's point of view: he may have a map showing the whole world and places that had not yet been discovered, but he had no idea how accurate this map might be. He knew well enough how accurate his own charts were. Not very accurate at all. Why should he assume that his priceless mappamundi was any more reliable than the best maps of his own age? He had no good reason to make any such assumption, and therefore he had every right, and even an obligation, to correct matters to the best of his ability.

For places that were unknown by reason of inaccessibility, such as northern Greenland, for example, or for places depicted on the mappamundi that had not yet been discovered, the map-maker had no choice but to rely on his source map. But when it came to places that the cartographer thought he knew, like the Atlantic Coast of

Europe and the Mediterranean area, he felt an obligation to improve things from the best knowledge available to him. Unfortunately for the medieval or early Renaissance cartographer, and unfortunately for modern scholars, 15th and 16th century knowledge and map-making techniques were no match for the accuracy of certain maps that were in the hands of some map-makers of the 1400s and 1500s. The mysterious source maps were always accurate, while the map-maker's own attempts to improve on them with current knowledge always resulted in distortions that stick out like the sore thumb of ignorance. When we look at the Hadji Ahmed Map, and at the Piri Re'is Map, we have to bear this in mind.

First, the Hadji Ahmed Map. This was drawn by a mediocre Arab geographer, only obscurely known to history, who operated out of Damascus. It is dated 1559 and it shows the entire world in a somewhat fanciful type of projection that is more art than science and which was typical of Arab chartwork of the mid-16th century. A *careful* look at this map will show that Hadji Ahmed "improved" the Mediterranean according to Ptolemy, and thus distorted it, and also drew Africa according to the best Portuguese information that he could get, and distorted Africa too in a manner completely typical of the mid-16th century.

But now look at North America and South America. They have an almost modern shape, and should be compared with Mercator's Map of South America drawn 10 years *later* from contemporary explorers' information. Thankfully, Hadji Ahmed apparently had no access to contemporary maps and charts of the Americas and so he was stuck with simply copying some mysterious mappamundi in his possession. This map was more accurate than the best information available in 1559 and so Hadji Ahmed's Map looks very modern. It shows Baja California, which had not been mapped then. It shows the Northwest Coast of North America, including Alaska, which had not been discovered then. It shows the Hawaiian Islands in the Pacific, which were not discovered until two hundred years later. It shows a sprinkling of islands in the Pacific, a sort of vague and suggestive rendition of the Polynesian Islands, but they had not been discovered yet. It shows Antarctica clearly, and even a suggestion of the Palmer Peninsula, and that had not been discovered then either. I've used "discovered" in this paragraph to mean,

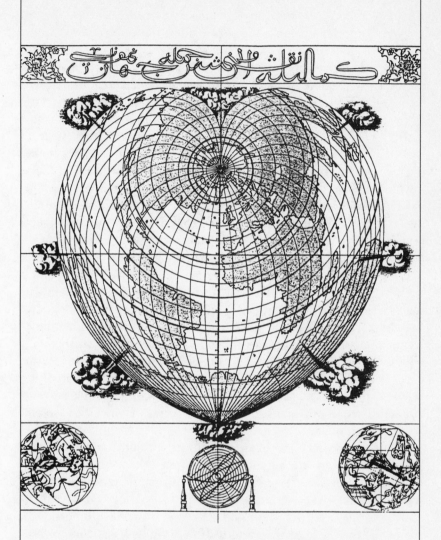

The Hadji Ahmed world map of 1559. The general continental shapes were not bettered for another century, but the sea-level seems too low on this map, as is the case also on all portolans, and some portions of now-flooded continental shelf are shown as land. There is no Bering Strait between Alaska and Asia, but a correct depiction of the Bering Land Bridge and other now-sunken continental fringes.

obviously, *discovered by Europeans or Arabs* from which Hadji Ahmed could have gleaned information.

The Far East, insofar as it can be made out in this curious "split-apple" projection, is distorted but reasonably accurate. But the strange and unnerving thing about this map is the region of Alaska and Asia. The curve of the Aleutian Islands is depicted accurately, but there is no Bering Strait and the whole area is land. This part of the map depicts how the world of that region actually was—but 10,000 years ago! This map shows the "Bering Land Bridge" between Asia and North America, *and shows it correctly.* Up until the 1958 Geophysical Year, scientists always thought that the "Bering Land Bridge" had been exactly that, a "bridge", which is to say a rather narrow connecting link between Asia and Alaska. But soundings taken in 1958 proved conclusively that this land connection had not been a narrow "bridge" at all, but an expanse of land of subcontinental proportions that included all the area north of the curving Aleutian chain and the Alaska panhandle. In short, it had been exactly as shown on Hadji Ahmed's Map. This fact almost defies speculation. Or, is it just a coincidence? Perhaps a mediocre map-maker, not knowing how Asia and North America actually terminated, decided to make things easy and simply joined then. This is a valid possibility, but its probability diminishes as we look at other details. This map, like all the portolans, and particularly like the best of them, the Ibn Ben Zara Chart, shares a peculiarity that characterizes all portolans: the general accuracy is there *but the sea level seems too low.*

On the Ibn Ben Zara Chart, most of the islands of the Aegean which exist today are all shown a bit larger than they are today, while there are some "extra" islands that do not presently exist, but which would exist if the sea level dropped by about 200–300 feet, and which *did* exist ten thousand years ago near the end of the Ice Age when the sea level was exactly 200–300 feet lower than today. Also, on the Ibn Ben Zara Chart, we see that some river deltas, like those of the Nile and the Rhône, are shown significantly smaller than they are today as if the rivers were younger and had just commenced flowing after the ice retreated.

On the Hadji Ahmed Map, we see the same phenomenon replicated in other places besides the Aleutian area. There's a large bump on southern California extending out into the Pacific, and this is the actual location of a bit of continental shelf that was above the sea ten thousand years ago. Looking at Northeast North America, we can see an inlet that represents either the Bay of Fundy or the St. Lawrence estuary, but Nova Scotia and Newfoundland are joined together. This would have been the case ten thousand years ago because the Grand Banks of Newfoundland and the George's Bank off Nova Scotia would have been above sea level. Professor Steve Davis, of St. Mary's University in Halifax, Nova Scotia, has just caused a stir among Canadian archeologists with his announcement that human artifacts have been dredged up from the George's Bank by a scallop boat. Davis dates the find to about ten thousand years ago. People inhabited this now-drowned land. Although the Canadian newspapers naturally headlined the discovery with sensational allusions to Atlantis, the artifacts discovered are primitive fish-processing utensils very similar to those used by today's Eskimo people and by the vanished Beothuk Indians of Newfoundland.[17]

Since these sea-level problems are common to all the portolans and to the existing mappamundi from which the portolans seem to have been excerpted, are we to believe that the earth was accurately mapped ten thousand years ago and that a few copies survived into the medieval period?

The Piri Re'is Map found in 1929 presents an even greater puzzle. It was drawn in 1519, the year that Magellan's expedition set out to circumnavigate the world. But this expedition did not return to Europe until 1521 and so the Piri Re'is Map could not have relied on information derived from this voyage. According to marginal notes presumably made by Piri Re'is himself, his map was based on "the map of Columbus" and on other maps "dating from the time of Alexander the Great." Note that Piri Re'is does not say a map *by* Columbus, but a map *of* Columbus. Piri Re'is was first an Islamic pirate and then a Turkish admiral, and he might have been in a position to know, or guess, what sort of map Columbus had and from which mappamundi it had been copied.

In any event, this map caused a stir in both diplomatic and geographic circles because it showed American continents with incredible accuracy. The problem with this was that the American *continents* had not yet been discovered, or even coasted to any great

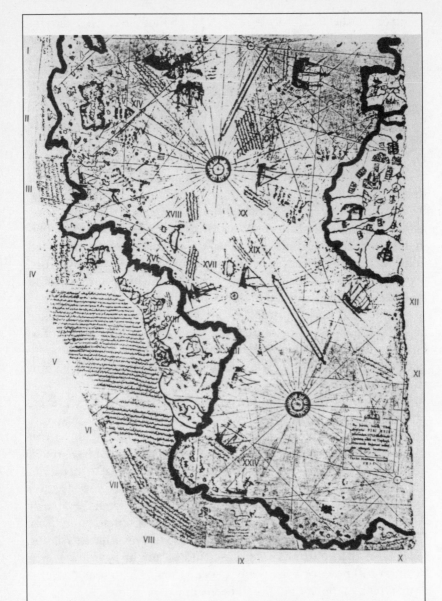

Surviving portion of the Piri Re'is Map of 1519, now a treasured possession of the Library of Congress. I have darkened the coastal outlines to show the continental profiles more clearly than in the faded original.

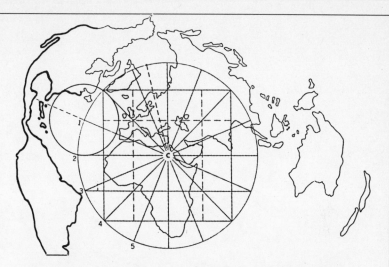

The Piri Re'is shape of North America and South America im-
posed on an "Azimuthal Equidistant Projection" of the world.
This is not really as difficult as it sounds! *Azimuth* is an Arabic
astronomical and navigational term meaning the angular distance
between the horizon and the observer's zenith. *Zenith* is another
Arabic astronomical and navigational term meaning a point directly over the observer's head. Therefore, in "Azimuthal Equidistant Projection" simply pretend that you're suspended high above
some convenient point on earth and that the horizon is equally
distant from you all around. Then, pretend that, somehow, the
surface of the *whole earth* has been miraculously split open and
spread flat so that you can see even land masses that were on the
other side of the earth. The most convenient point for doing this
happens to be directly above the Great Pyramid near Cairo in
Egypt. The reason for this is that the Great Pyramid happens to be
located at the centre of the earth's land masses and the earth's
surface can be "split and flattened" with the least distortion if
viewed from this point. If you are successful in imagining this
projection, you will immediately see that the coastline of North
and South America of the Piri Re'is map, which I have emphasized
to make it clearer, is remarkably similar to the same coastline
shown in a modern Strategic Air Command "Azimuthan Equidistant Projection" of the world. It is this similarity of the Piri Re'is
map and modern ones that raise the question of how the Piri Re'is
projection appears on a map drawn in 1519, but based on even
earlier ones. At some time in the past was the earth surveyed from
space? Whatever the answer, experts have concluded that the Piri
Re'is map must have been based on aerial photography of some
sort to present so accurate a representation of the American coast
as seen from a great distance.

Illustration from *Holy Grail Across The Atlantic* by the author, but based on the
research of Charles Hapgood.

Modern U.S. Air Force Equidistant Projection map of the world centered "near Cairo" (i.e. centered on the Great Pyramid). Note that the shape of the American continent is almost identical with the geography of the Piri Re'is Map.

Illustration taken from *Holy Grail Across The Atlantic* by the author, but based on U.S.A.F. standard-issue map.

extent, in 1519. Europeans were just then feeling their way out of the Caribbean. Cortez landed in Mexico the same year this map was drawn, 1519. Pizarro had not yet met the Incas of South America. What, then, could be the sources for this map? American Secretary of State of the time, Henry Stimson, began a flurry of correspondence with Turkish authorities that lasted during much of the 1930s.[18] Stimson urgently requested the Turks to conduct a careful search of all their old archives to see whether any similar maps might come to light. The Turks complied, or said they did, but nothing else like the maps of Hadji Ahmed or Piri Re'is turned up.

The Piri Re'is Map does show the New World coastline with incredible accuracy, but it may not seem that way to the average reader! It was self-evident to cartographic experts of the 1930s, however, because they were able to recognize immediately that the Piri Re'is Map had been drawn according to a very special sort of projection: azimuthal equidistant projection. I have tried to explain this, and to demonstrate it visually, in the accompanying illustrations. A careful look at these illustrations, and a serious reading of the descriptions, will clearly convey the staggering implications of this map. Cartographic experts were, and are, both amazed and puzzled by it.

Professor Charles Hapgood spent a great deal of time analysing the Piri Re'is Map, and the Strategic Air Command endorsed both his methods and his startling conclusions: the Piri Re'is Map could only have been drawn using data from aerial photography! The reader is referred to Hapgood's *Maps of the Ancient Sea-Kings* for a much more detailed discussion of this map.

Henry Sinclair had a map, too, when he set sail for Nova Scotia in 1398 and, very possibly, the previous 1350–1370 expedition had the same map or another copy. This map comes down to us as "The Zeno Map of the North," and was drawn by a Venetian navigator in Sinclair's service, Antonio Zeno, sometime around the year 1400 A.D. But it is obvious from a detailed study of this map, which Hapgood recounts in detail, that Antonio Zeno's map was actually copied from some other highly accurate chart that was drawn on a conic projection. Antonio did not understand this projection, which is understandable since it was not supposedly "invented" until three centuries after his death, and he also "improved" things from his

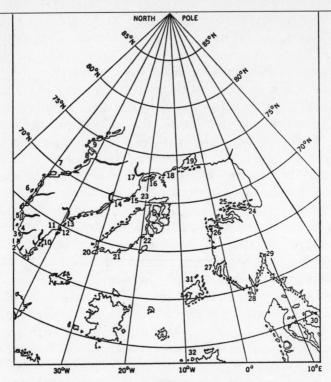

The "Zeno Map of the North" included in the account of Henry Sinclair's transatlantic voyage of 1398 A.D. In this illustration, the map has been transferred to a modern conic projection by Prof. Charles Hapgood with the assistance of the Strategic Air Command. The result is that 32 mapped places are accurate in both latitude and longitude, including eight points in northern Greenland where no known European had ventured in the late 14th century.

The "Zeno Map of the North" is attributed to the Venetian cartographer and mariner, Antonio Zeno, and dates from between 1400 and 1404 A.D. But to have accurately mapped places that had not yet been discovered, Zeno must have had a highly accurate source map from which to copy, a map similar to those of Hadji Ahmed and Piri Re'is. How did such a map end up at Rosslyn in Scotland with the Saint-Clairs? The most reasonable conjecture is that the source map must have been brought to Rosslyn by refugee Templars who are known to have arrived there between 1307 and 1330.

The imaginary Atlantic islands and crude coast of Denmark are Antonio Zeno's own contributions to this map.

Courtesy: Charles Hapgood and the Chilton Book Company.

own knowledge when he could. On this inexplicable map, northern Greenland, where no known European had ever been, is depicted with great accuracy while the various Atlantic islands and bits of North America are not so accurate because Antonio "improved" the geography from his own knowledge and map-making skill. How did a highly accurate map of the North Atlantic get to Rosslyn of the Sinclairs in the 14th century? Is it probable that it arrived with refugee Templars.

The reason for assuming this is simple and, I think, justified. Two mappamundi turned up in Middle Eastern archives relatively recently: the Hadji Ahmed Map in 1860 and the Piri Re'is Map in 1929. There must have been many more such maps in those same Middle Eastern archives about 900 years ago when the Templars captured and sacked many Saracen towns and cities. It is a virtual certainty that at least some similar maps were discovered by the de Bouillon dynasty. Their value would have been appreciated at once. Had the Kingdom of Jerusalem survived, its wealth and future prosperity would have obviously depended upon trade and commerce, not upon agriculture. Palestine was as arid in the 12th century as it is today. Anything that could give the de Bouillons an edge in trade would have been a treasure, and the Templars would have been given the task of guarding it.

But then the de Bouillons lost Jerusalem. They fell back on Provence to be massacred during the Albigensian Crusade. Some few representatives of this supposed Holy Bloodline allegedly survived, but then the Templars themselves were crushed and dispersed. The maps would then have an even greater worth than they had back in Palestine. The fundamental survival of the "Holy Grail" depended upon them. If there was land across the Atlantic, as both the Hadji Ahmed and Piri Re'is Map show, then a truly secure haven from the Inquisition potentially existed. It was the Templars' job to find that haven if at all possible, and so they fled to Scotland and Portugal with their precious maps. Probes were immediately launched out into the Atlantic.

We know that Henri Saint-Clair had such a map because it was included in the documented account of his voyage known as *The Zeno Narrative*.

It is absolutely certain, too, that the royalty of Portugal had maps that showed discoveries "in advance." Some navigators made a *lapsus calami*, a "slip of the pen," from time to time which gave the secret away. Here's a slip made by Pigafetta, a navigator attached to the 1519 Magellan expedition:

> The sentiments of every person in the fleet were that it [i.e. "The Strait of Magellan"—Author's note] had no issue in the west; and nothing but the confidence they had in the superior knowledge of the commander could have induced them to prosecute the research. But this great man, as skilful as he was courteous, knew that he was to seek for a passage through an obscure strait: this strait he had seen laid down on a chart of Martin de Boheme, a most excellent cosmographer, which was in the possession of the King of Portugal.[19]

Where had this chart come from? No one knows for certain. There is no proof, but it seems at least probable that this chart came into Portugal with refugee Templars—just as it seems equally probable that Henry Sinclair's map of the north came to the Rosslyn refuge with dispersed Templars. The coincidences are at least highly suggestive even if they do not constitute absolute proof.

Columbus had a map of some sort. If our conjecture is at all valid, it may have been very similar to the maps of Hadji Ahmed and Piri Re'is. Both of these show the New World, and neither confuses the Americas with Asia. Hapgood observes that Columbus would not have understood the projection employed on a map like the Piri Re'is óne, but that mattered little. The relative distances are accurate in azimuthal equidistant projection. Columbus would have recognized Europe and the Mediterranean world easily enough and could have worked out a rough scale for the entire map based on the European distances he knew. He would know the direction to sail in order to reach the New World and he would know approximately, say within 10 percent, the distance to his destination.

We have skirted the uncomfortable topic of how, where and when these inexplicable mappamundi *originated*, and have concerned ourselves only with copies made in medieval times and with the use to which these maps were put. It seems highly probable that the Templars found such maps in the Middle East, but how did they get *there*. I think there can be several possible explanations of varying appeal, but that none will prove to be particularly palatable to conventional historians.

Since these maps were found in the Middle East, the simplest explanation is that some unknown and unsung Arab geographer of genius compiled the original mappamundi from which the portolans were exerpted and which Piri Re'is and Hadji Ahmed copied. It is true that an Arab cartographer named Abulfeda, somewhat obscurely known to history, asserted that voyages around the world had been made as early ad 1300 A.D., and it is worth nothing that Abulfeda knew that the earth was a sphere. Arabs sailed out of Canton, China, as early as 800 A.D., and it is possible that some exploratory probes were made out into the Pacific where contact might have been made with the Andeans who'd reached the Polynesian Islands by raft three hundred years earlier. As Heyerdahl has shown, Andean linguistic elements in modern Polynesian languages still exist and include many South American words. The name of the sweet potato, *kumara*, for example is the same in Fiji as it is among the Quechua-speaking Andean Indians today. But further, some Polynesian songs, legends and sagas seem also to date from the Andean colonization and have not been wholly submerged by the later immigrants from North America's Pacific Coast. These legends preserve some idea of South American geography and even many place-names that can be found in South America today only slightly changed. If Arabs reached out into the Pacific they may have been able to chart the Pacific Coast of North America themselves by using the Kuroshiwo Current, and have drawn South America based on Polynesian descriptions of it.

On the other side of the earth, Arabs penetrated into West Africa and learned of Malian voyages across the Atlantic. It might have been possible to have drawn a roughly accurate profile of the New World's Atlantic coast because of African information that has since been lost. Only meagre scraps of African maritime lore have survived for historians today, but perhaps much more was available to Arabs in the 9th and 10th centuries. Perhaps, then, it would have been barely possible for some Arab cartographer to have drawn a roughly accurate world map as early as 800 A.D. or so. This still doesn't explain how the longitudes of the portolans are so accurate, why the sea-level seems to be lower, and the apparent fact that some maps seem to reflect aerial photography in their projections. A "straw grasping" answer to this is that the Andean peoples are known to have constructed giant hot-air balloons for the purpose of allowing dead Incas to rejoin their "father," the sun. A replica balloon was built and flown by the Explorer's Club and their only difficulty was obtaining modern fabric that was woven as finely as fabric recovered from Andean graves. Apparently, this ultra-finely woven Andean cotton was used specifically for making the hot-air balloons. The Explorer's Club balloon was able to carry a crew to an altitude of several thousand feet. Maybe, and it is admittedly grasping at straws, Andeans or Arabs used such balloons to draw segments of coastline accurately and these correctly rendered coastlines ended up on Arab charts.

Another explanation, and one pioneered and preferred by Charles Hapgood himself, is that there was a relatively advanced civilization somewhere on earth during the last Ice Age, and that these mysterious maps derive from that lost culture. In support of this notion, it must be admitted that there are anomalous artifacts reposing in the world's museums that hint at some technologically advanced civilization which existed before the present cultural cycle began about 4000 B.C. in Sumeria and Egypt. One artifact is an aluminum-link belt found in a Chinese grave dating to about 250 A.D., and aluminum requires great amounts of electricity to separate the metal from bauxite ore. There is no doubt at all that the Indian epic, *The Mahabarata*, describes flying machines called *vimanas*, weapons that were not developed again until the 20th century and other anomalous technology. All of these things perished in a "world war" that took place ages ago, according to the poem. *The Mahabarata* itself dates from perhaps 500 A.D. in written form, but its oral sources are believed to reach back to 1000–1500 B.C. or even earlier.

There are other possible explanations which may come to the minds of some readers, but which do not bear discussion here. But, whatever the ultimate answer, it cannot be denied that these maps exist and they should not exist if conventional history is a correct and complete view of human development. Columbus had a map of some kind. He refers to it. If it was like the Piri Re'is and Hadji Ahmed Maps it would have shown both Asia and the New World as completely separate geographic entities.

The significance is twofold: first, it indicates that Columbus knew where he was going, and it was not to Asia; second, it indicates that Columbus seemed to have had very high connections indeed among a Templar-associated "underground" that included nobility and even royalty stretching back to *the* most illustrious European royalty, the Kings of Jerusalem. Columbus may not have been of noble or royal birth himself, but the "noble conspiracy" of which he seems to have been a part was formed solely for the preservation of the most royal, most revered bloodline in the Western World. As a chosen operative of this conspiracy, Columbus enjoyed what today might be called "major clout" among ordinary nobility and run-of-the-mill monarchs.

This may explain his marriage to Felipa de Perestrello e Moniz in 1479. As a dowry, although it was never described as such, the bride brought with her all of her father's journals and sea-charts. These may have proved more priceless than gold to Columbus and his secret supporters.

In late 1479 or early 1480, Columbus and his wife moved to the Madeira Islands. And it was there, in 1480, that Columbus's first son, and only legitimate one, was born, Diego.

In later life Columbus claimed to have sailed from the Madeira Islands as far to the south along the African coast as the Portuguese had ventured. This means, if it is true, that Columbus sailed to the outpost of La Mina, now Elmina, Ghana. He certainly was familiar with African yams, African manatees, the major rivers and many languages of "Guinea." Columbus must have shipped aboard these voyages from the Madeira Islands. And, according to Fernando, it was in the Madeiras that the great revelation happened:

> . . . He inquired into the voyages the Portuguese then made to Sào Jorge de Mina [i.e. "La Mina"—Author's note], and along the coast of Guinea . . . He began to reflect that, as the Portuguese travel so far to the southward, it were no less proper to sail away westward, and land might in reason be found that way. That he might be more certain and confident in this particular he began to look over all the cosmographers again whom he had read before, and to observe what astronomical reasons would corroborate this project; and therefore he took notice of what any persons whatsoever spoke to that purpose,

and of sailors particularly, which might in any way be of help to him. Of all these things he made such good use that he concluded for certain that there were many lands west of the Canary Islands and Cape Verde, and it was possible to sail and discover them.[20]

This is a familiar quotation from Fernando's *Life of Colón* and, indeed, I can't think of one popular biography of Columbus that hasn't used it. Yet, this passage conceals within itself at least two suggestive clues which have eluded the notice of most commentators. The first clue is that these lands were west of the "Canary Islands and Cape Verde." Why west of these places in particular? Columbus then resided on the Madeira Islands and the New World was west of them as well. Why was he so confident that land lay west of the Canary Islands and Cape Verde unless he had somehow come to learn of the 12th-century Malian voyages *from Cape Verde* which discovered, at least, the North Equatorial Current and the heart of the Northeast Trade Winds?

We may recall that the Emperor of Mali, when relating his youthful experiences on the Atlantic, described the wind-driven current as a kind of river flowing in the sea. In later years, Columbus used exactly the same metaphor. Columbus described his sailing within the North Equatorial Current "as like navigating between the banks of a river."[21]

Perestrello, Columbus's deceased father-in-law, had sailed as far south as Cape Verde. Since all Portuguese voyages southward were also minor slaving expeditions, Perestrello might well have learned of the Malian voyages from black Africans captured in the region of Cape Verde. All of Perestrello's journals and sea-charts came to Columbus. Did Columbus know of the westward-flowing North Equatorial Current and the Northeast Trade Winds from accounts of captured Africans preserved in Perestrello's journals? In *The Black Discovery of America*, I argued that this African information might well have reached Columbus via Perestrello's journals. Perestrello also probably drew a chart showing just how far off the African coast, according to Malian traditions, one could expect to enter the current-and-trade-wind westward conveyor belt.

Aside from some Templar-provided map showing the strange New World across the Atlantic, it is very possible that Columbus had another, partial, chart of the Atlantic that indicated where the westward-flowing winds and currents would be encountered.

The second clue concealed within this passage from Fernando's *Life of Colón* could be considered another "slip of the pen." According to Fernando, Columbus "concluded for certain that there were *many lands* [Author's italics] west of the Canary Islands and Cape Verde, and it was possible to sail and discover them." Columbus used the term "many lands," and not the all-important word *Asia*.

If Columbus, by this time, had access to some Templar-provided map like the Hadji Ahmed one or the Piri Re'is one, he would have indeed known that there were "many lands" to the west: an entire new continent and many offshore islands. And he would have known, too, that these many lands were not Asia because Asia was also clearly shown on the same Templar-provided maps and shown to be different from the new lands across the Atlantic.

In hindsight, which is dangerous, Columbus's entire career since he arrived in Portugal in 1476 seems somewhat in the nature of a scientific experiment. First, he sails north to "Thule" where he could not have failed to have noticed the prevailing westerly winds blowing towards Europe and the warm westerly currents bathing Britain and Iceland: the Gulf Stream. Then, Columbus goes south, to the Madeiras, where he received many indications of eastward-flowing currents and winds. It is almost as if some organization with maps and knowledge of land to the west, an organization which might have even already established a settlement in northern latitudes, needed to solve a problem and, in order to do so, called in a master mariner to observe conditions personally and make an assessment.

Even assuming that a haven had been established in Nova Scotia for the most direct descendants of the Holy Bloodline, the pressing problem had not yet been solved. Henry Sinclair crossed the Atlantic to Nova Scotia in the teeth of the prevailing winds and, if he established the "castle" or city, he did so at a northern latitude which presented formidable, or at least less-than-ideal, climatic conditions for the Holy Grail refugees. This was better than nothing, and far better than the Inquisition offered, but it was not a final solution to the problem. Two further things were really needed before it could be said that the secret of the Holy Grail would be safe and potent, once again, in world affairs.

First, and above all, a safe and reliable method of dealing with the Atlantic had to be developed. Could the Atlantic be crossed both ways with relative ease, security and frequency? Could someone find the key to the Ocean Sea?

Second, of course, could some more hospitable land in the New World be found—a region that could be easily, securely and frequently reached from Europe; and just as easily, securely and frequently communicate with Europe? It almost seems as if that was the task that Columbus was commissioned to solve. He seems to have been supplied with Templar-provided charts showing some New World about 3000 miles across the Atlantic from Europe; then he went north to observe the prevailing westerlies; and then south to Madeira to learn about all the indications that the trade-winds-and-currents heading toward America seemed to begin about five hundred miles to the west of the Madeiras.

Columbus seems to have intuited the answer, the key to the barrier of the Ocean Sea. Land shown on Templar maps formed a diversion for the westward-flowing equatorial currents and winds so that these were deflected, in a circular and clockwise direction in order to return to Europe in higher latitudes. Then, if the Templar maps were correct, and the existence of the winds and currents both north and south seemed to verify their general correctness, then there *must* be land with more moderate climate than Nova Scotia roughly west of Cape Verde. If this land was, in reality, anything as extensive as the Templar maps indicated, then it would not be merely a religious refuge for a few direct descendants of the Holy Blood. It held room enough to be a New World in which "heretics" of all sorts could find freedom to practice their varying religious beliefs. The genuine Grail Complex might form the core of New World government and developmental guidance, but there would be room for other refugees from the Inquisition: orthodox Jews, orthodox Moslems and those Cathar-inspired (but not-quite-Cathar) Christians who were starting to call themselves "Protestants" against papal authority. All could be accommodated if the New World was actually as large as the lands shown on Templar maps and if the key could be found to the barrier of the Ocean Sea.

Before leaving this chapter, it should be emphasized that a careful scrutiny of the Piri Re'is Map and the Hadji Ahmed Map would have presented a dazzling possibility to Columbus and his hypothetical Grail Complex conspirator-colleagues. Both maps are, of course, drawn to a very large scale where one inch represents many hundreds of miles. They cannot offer local geography in exact detail. Yet both maps do indicate plainly enough that the new western lands become very narrow in modern Central America and, of course, this is actually the case. A map like the Piri Re'is one, drawn on azimuthal equidistant projection actually emphasizes this narrowness. Could there be a strait at this narrowest part of the new western lands? It might be too small to be shown on the large scale of the maps, but a break in the barrier coast might nonetheless be there. The land certainly thinned down to *almost* nothing before South America's considerable expanse continued southward. If there was a strait, then the conspiracy had not only a vast haven, but it also had an open-ocean passage to the true "Indies." Even with the caravels of the time, it might be possible actually to reach Asia if they were re-provisioned in the new lands. Refugees would then have not only the commodities of the new lands, but also access to Asian spice and riches. The possibility of a strait in Central America, I think, may have much to do with Columbus's rather desperate 1502 voyage which will be discussed later. He went straight for the Central American coast seeking a break in the land. He urgently needed a passage for legal reasons that will unfold.

But in 1484, Columbus seemed certain that he'd found the key to the barrier of the Atlantic, at least, and he went to Portugal to present his proposal to the king.

Chapter 7

The Portuguese Connection

If we allow ourselves to assume, for the moment, that Columbus was part of a great conspiracy to create not just a mere refuge across the Atlantic but an entire "New World" free of religious intolerance, a "New Jerusalem," then we can begin to appreciate the complexity of the conspiracy's problems. Let us further assume that by 1484 the first predicament had been ironed out to Columbus's own satisfaction and that he'd convinced his colleagues in the conspiracy that the key to the Ocean Sea had been found: the strange lands shown on Templar maps deflected the Atlantic winds and currents into a huge, circular clockwise-flowing system; it was possible to reach these new lands by sailing west in low latitudes near the equator and to return to Europe in higher latitudes nearer the pole, about the latitude of Britain. The existence of a clockwise-flowing oceanic system would seem to ensure relatively safe and frequent sailings between both sides of the Atlantic. Indeed, as Columbus must have known, the westward passage to the new lands would prove easier than the return voyage to Europe. In the southerly latitudes of trade winds and the North Equatorial Current, the climate was warmer and more pleasant and serious storms were rare during the proper sailing season. Columbus would have known this from his stay in the Madeiras. One could not say the same for the Atlantic in more northerly latitudes. Yes, the *prevailing* winds were westerly and would push a ship back to Europe, but they were neither so constant nor so strong as the trades. Then, the Atlantic in northerly latitudes could be stormy at any time of the year, and Columbus would have known this from his 1477 voyage but in any case this was the grim common knowledge of all Atlantic sailors.

The reality of transatlantic navigation, both north and south, was borne out in Columbus's 1492 voyage. Passage to America was both swift and pleasant, but the return trip to Europe was a nightmare.

Nonetheless, the key to the Ocean Sea had been discovered to the satisfaction of Columbus and his colleagues, or so we will assume.

Now, we can begin to appreciate the truly daunting dilemma that confronted the conspiracy. Even though the Grail Underground possessed some ships and "pirate" captains to sail them, their resources were insufficient to colonize the new lands independently. Further, if they did so the secret would inevitably leak out because of increased transatlantic traffic. Their colonies would become prey for any and all European powers which wished to conquer them. The Grail Complex was beyond the pale of European society, an underground organization that was represented by no nation and protected by no law.

If the new lands were to be colonized, the discovery of them and claim to them must be the acknowledged work of some established European nation-state strong enough to support and defend its claim to the new territories. The catch was that all suitable European nation-states were officially Roman Catholic in terms of religion; and therefore officially enemies of the Grail Complex.

This difficulty could be gotten around, perhaps, if Columbus could extract a legal agreement from the target nation-state that nicely balanced greed and independence: the nation sponsoring the voyage would get the lion's share of the wealth that could be extracted from the new lands, while Columbus would demand hereditary powers of vice-royalty and absolute governorship in the discovered territories. European monarchs would get the majority of the gold, but the conspiracy would secure a vast new world for heretics and dissidents to colonize. Played adeptly, the Church itself might even approve of this game because many heretics could emigrate and this would leave Europe itself free of them. Roman Catholic orthodoxy, at least in Europe itself, would be enhanced and strengthened.

In short, ahead of Columbus and his hypothetical conspiratorial colleagues stretched a tightrope. Only a superb balancing act of negotiation could bring success, and any mistake spelled disaster. Yet, the risk had to be taken sometime in the late 15th century. Sooner or later, the new lands across the Atlantic would be discovered *anyway* by expeditions of European nation-states. They would be claimed as a matter of course and fall under the inevitable domination of the Roman Church automatically. Columbus, if he could only extract legal guarantees of governorship and practical political control of the new lands, *might* prevent this. If there was, in fact, an underground Grail Conspiracy entirely devoted to founding a New Jerusalem of tolerance for all faiths, then the late 15th century was the time to gamble on Columbus's project.

The major difficulty with this project was simply that these new lands were not Asia. Aside from the fact that this was a secret that could not be allowed to come out, European nation-states were interested only in Asia. Since the fall of Constantinople in 1453, Europe had been starved for commodities that meant wealth, luxury and even health. The taste of spice was avidly sought, but some spices were also used to preserve meat for long periods of time. Spice could also cover the taste of tainted meat, on which most of Europe dined when meat was available at all. Spice was both a luxury and almost a necessity. In addition to spice, Asia produced silk, ivory, precious gems and many other commodities required for the display of wealth and power. But, since 1453, the Arabs absolutely controlled access to Asia, and Europe got what it needed, and wanted, at exorbitant prices or not at all. Getting to Asia by outflanking Arab control of the Middle East was the obsession of Europe. Getting to Asia by sea, since there was no possible land route open to Europeans, was the only maritime project worth considering.

In order to get support from any European nation-state, therefore, Columbus had to present his goal as being Asia and nothing else. And the problem here was that the new lands, which he knew he could reach, were not Asia. They were much too close to Europe to be Asia, and somehow, Columbus had to argue this awkward fact away.

In 1485, no educated person thought that the world was flat and certainly no reputable geographer thought so. Not only that, but the actual size of the world was known with fair accuracy. Frederick Pohl states the case, but from a conventional view of Columbus:

> Columbus estimated the earth's circumference as about three-quarters of its actual size, only 20,400 Roman miles, or 18,777 English miles, instead of the actual 24,902 English miles. From the Arabian cosmographer Alfragano he took the length of a degree to be only 56²/₃ miles, thinking these to be Roman miles instead of the much longer Arabic miles. He preferred the authority of Marinus of Tyre to that of Ptolemy, because Marinus said that Asia extended eastward half as many degrees again as Ptolemy said, and to this exaggeration of the land mass of Asia, he added Marco Polo's further exaggeration of the distance from China to Japan (i.e. 1500 miles—Author's note).
>
> The argument thus built up as to the short distance to India, with its error of over six thousand English miles, was the critical one in his attempt to persuade the king of Portugal to sanction and finance his proposed expedition, for there were many who thought they knew, and really did know, near enough to the actual circumference of the earth to declare his project impossible. Columbus said he expected to find land about "750 leagues" or 3000 miles to the west, for that was the distance he believed it was from Portugal to Japan, or even to the Kingdom of Cathay; but the members of the examining commission insisted that it was nearer to 8000 miles or more, and therefore an impossible distance.[1]

The reason it was an impossible distance has been covered previously: a caravel of the time could not sail quickly enough, or carry enough food and water, to cover more than about 4000 miles non-stop with a living crew. Since the Portuguese examining commission was correct in believing the distance to "India" to be twice as far, Columbus's proposal was rejected in 1485.

Columbus's formidable problem was plausibly to shrink the size of the earth in his presentations so that the new lands he knew existed could conform to Asia or the "Indies" in the minds of monarchs and their geographic experts. Conventional history tells us that Columbus was not successful in Portugal because of his failure to accomplish this geographic legerdemain, and so Portugal lost its chance to discover the New World.

Conventional history offers, in this case, mingled fact and fable. We have read the testimony of Pigafetta that the king of Portugal already possessed a map showing South America correctly enough to include the Straits of Magellan before Magellan's voyage sailed in 1519. The royalty of Portugal also had a map showing the termination of Africa before Diaz "discovered" the Cape of Good Hope in 1488. If, as I have suggested, Templars brought maps showing the entire world, and if the royalty of Portugal became Grand Masters of the reconstituted Templars known as Knights of Christ, then the king of Portugal knew very well that there was land across the Atlantic about "750 leagues" to the west as Columbus claimed. Indeed, much more tangible than maps, Portugal had actually reached these lands in the 1470s. There is suggestive evidence that Joao Corte-Real, father of the more famous Gaspar and Miguel, reached Newfoundland in 1473 as part of a joint Portuguese-Danish expedition. Portuguese and Danish co-operation is explained by the fact that the king of Denmark, Eric, was the uncle of Prince Henry the Navigator of Portugal and both men were interested in sponsoring voyages. Now, it cannot be denied that Joao Corte Real was rewarded by the king of Portugal with the Governorship of the Island of Terceira in the Azores for having discovered "Stockfish Land," or Bacalao. This was Newfoundland, named after the codfish ("stockfish") to be caught off the Grand Banks.[2]

At least some people in Portugal already knew about land to the west in northern latitudes for the very good reason that it had been discovered by one of their own captains, probably in co-operation with the German captains Pining and Pothorst, who sailed in the service of Denmark. Further, the Portuguese knew precisely what this land offered: fog, cold and codfish. As for Newfoundland codfish, the Portuguese had been catching them for a decade when Columbus made his presentation.

The point is that Columbus did not fail to convince the Portuguese examining commission that there was land to the west. They already knew it. Its only commodity was codfish, and so it naturally held less attraction than Asia. Portugal had limited resources and these were already totally committed to the long and costly effort to reach the "Indies" by way of Africa. In 1485, success was in sight and Portugal didn't need Columbus.

It might seem justified to criticize the Portuguese for being short-sighted. Perhaps the known western land held more of value than codfish? The only way to find out would be to explore it, and Columbus offered that opportunity. Perhaps, in more southerly latitudes than where the codfish thrived, the new lands might offer pleasant places for colonists and unknown wealth? That was a real possibility that must have occurred to both the king and to his examining commission. Yet, in a way, Portugal already had her hands full with her own "New World." Africa. Portuguese mariners not only tried to sail around it, they planted colonies on the way. Portugal was building an empire in a huge, unexplored continent and the country simply could not cope with the challenge of another empire across the Atlantic.

The true thinking of the Portuguese examining commission must have been that Columbus might well discover new and promising land across the Atlantic, but that Portugal was in no position to exploit it at the moment and, in any case, the examining commission *knew* that Columbus could not offer a *shorter* route to the "Indies."

Personally, because of certain anomalous events of the 1492 voyage, I'm inclined to think that there may have been yet another reason why the king of Portugal rejected Columbus's proposal in 1485. If this conspiracy construct has any validity at all, then Portugal must be considered to have been at least "sympathetic" to the Templars and to the underground Grail Complex, and also perhaps grateful. The Templars were welcomed and endorsed by royal approval in Portugal; voyages westward were immediately begun under Alfonso IV, possibly at the behest of Templars, and for all we know the Holy Blood may have found a very temporary refuge on the Azores before Sinclair found his Nova Scotia haven. In return, Templars may have given Portugal the key to spice wealth and an African empire by supplying the map that showed the Cape of Good Hope. The tale of the Zanj captain doubling the Cape in 1420 may well have been a cover story to explain this map.

Sympathy for the Templars and for any underground Grail Complex *could* be dangerous. Any obvious and provable association with Templar secrets and the Grail Complex *would* be danger-ous. Portugal could get away with African explorations and the

Templar map that inspired them could be passed off as data derived from a Zanj captain. But duplicating this success with Columbus and the New World might seem too much of a good thing. It might well kindle the suspicions of the Inquisition. It would certainly excite the greed and envy of other European states. There would be nothing to prevent the pope calling for a new crusade, like the Albigensian one, and envious and much more powerful kingdoms than Portugal would be only too eager to participate. Portugal could be devastated and partitioned, its independence lost and its colonies in Africa stolen. Riches of the African spice route, almost within Portuguese hands, would be snatched from Portugal's grasp for the benefit of crusading nation-states representing orthodoxy and greed. In short, what had happened to hapless Provence could also happen to Portugal. It was definitely best not to appear too success- ful, and not to betray any too-obvious sympathy for, or association with, Templars and the underground Grail Complex.

I cannot help but suspect that this sort of consideration, too, influenced the Portuguese decision to reject Columbus's proposal. The high-level Portuguese attitude toward Columbus seems to have been that his proposal offered an excellent chance of discovering a possibly valuable New World in southern latitudes across the Atlan- tic; that he was wished every personal good fortune in doing so; that Portugal could play no part in the project for many good and urgent reasons. . .but Portugal would like to know what happened if Columbus was able to mount an expedition. Portugal might be able to repay the Templars and their Grail Underground, someday, in return for information about what was across the Atlantic. This is, admittedly, speculation.

But it is fact that Columbus, returning from America in 1493, stopped first in Lisbon before sailing on to Spain! How could this be? Lisbon would be the last place that Columbus would anchor since, because of his own discoveries, Spain was now a serious rival to Portugal. His stated reasons for entering Lisbon were that he had no choice because of severely bad weather. He had experienced terrible storms and, in fact, entered the "river of Lisbon" in a gale. Columbus stresses the extremely bad weather in his Log, but the truth is that we cannot know how bad these storms really were, and neither could Ferdinand and Isabella of Spain. All we know is that

Columbus returned from the New World to Lisbon, of all places.

According to Columbus's own Log he wrote to the king of Portugal on Monday, March 4, 1493. The next day he had a visit from Bartolomeu Diaz, the famous discoverer of the Cape of Good Hope. On Friday, March 8, Columbus received a letter from the king in answer to the one he had written on Monday. Columbus was invited to visit the king and queen of Portugal and spent Saturday, Sunday, and Monday with them, March 9–12. From the Log of Columbus we read:

> Monday, 11 March 1493
>
> Today I took leave of the King, who gave me some messages for the Sovereigns on his part and showed me great kindness all the time. I left after eating and the King sent Don Martin de Norona with me. All his cavaliers came to accompany me, and they paid me honors for quite a period of time. I then went to the Monastery of San Antonio, which is a place near Villafranca, where the Queen was staying. I went to pay homage to her and to kiss her hands, for she had sent me a message saying that I was not to leave until she saw me. With her was the Duke and the Marquis, and there I received great honor. I took leave of her at night and went to Alhandra to sleep.

> Tuesday, 12 March 1493
>
> Today, as I was about to start from Alhandra to the ship, a squire from the King arrived and offered me, on the part of the King land transportation to Castile, if I desired to take that route . . .[3]

All of this sounds very civilized, if not downright friendly, and it makes no sense within the context of conventional history or even human nature . . . unless the king of Portugal knew very well what Columbus's voyage was really all about. What did the king and Columbus talk about for two days? The weather? The king already knew all about Columbus's project because he and his examiners had rejected it. The only topic of discussion likely was what Columbus had discovered. We are faced with the irony that Portugal, rival of Spain, must have been informed of Columbus's discoveries before Ferdinand and Isabella were. Columbus himself wrote in his Log: "His Highness should know that I did not come from Guinea but from the Indies,"[4] which is why Columbus wrote to the king of Portugal on Monday, March 4.

What was going on here? We do not know, and cannot know. All we can conclude is that Columbus's relationship with the royalty of Portugal seems "obscurum per obscurius," obscure enough and more.

Did Portugal repay our hypothetical Templar-guarded Grail Dynasty for the information that Columbus reported to the king of Portugal in March 1493? Perhaps. Just a year later, 1494, Spain and Portugal negotiated and signed the Treaty of Tordesillas with the endorsement of Pope Alexander VI. This is the famous agreement that "split the world in half" between Spain and Portugal. The Line of Demarcation in the Atlantic was far enough to the west so that all of Nova Scotia and Newfoundland fell to the east of it, in Portuguese territory. I suggested in *Holy Grail Across The Atlantic* that this division safely placed Henry Sinclair's castle settlement within Portuguese territory according to the geographical knowledge of the era and thus legally protected hypothetical Holy Blood refugees from attack by Spain and the Inquisition. Although these northern lands legally belonged to Portugal, the Portuguese made no serious attempt to colonize it or settle it. They fished off the Grand Banks, and on the George's Bank, but they made no attempt to claim the land in any practical way. If there were truly Holy Refugees in the mid-peninsular castle in Nova Scotia, they were ignored and left alone by Portugal and were safe from the incursions of the Spanish Inquisition.

Portugal's apparent apathy about its territories in Northeastern North America had another, and long-term, effect. Other European states felt more or less free to explore the area and eventually to plant colonies there: the English, the Dutch, the French and the Scots. As history knows well, many of these earliest colonists were heretics and dissidents fleeing from Roman Catholic persecution. The "Pilgrims" of Massachusetts are just one example, but one of national importance to the United States. "New Holland" became a haven for Dutch Protestants. New France became a haven for Huguenots. Is all this a coincidence? In the 16th century, Portugal became a powerful nation rivalled in European affairs only by Spain. Portugal *could have* colonized and defended her North

American possessions legally confirmed by the Treaty of Tordesillas and could have excluded the Dutch, English and French, just as Spain proved capable of excluding other European powers in Central and South America on her side of the Line of Demarcation.

But Portugal never asserted her claim to Northeastern North America. Is this a mere accident of history, evidence of Portuguese obsession with Africa and the Far East? Perhaps that is the answer.

But it is also possible that Portugal agreed not to assert any claims to this region because of a 14th-century agreement with the dispersed Templars and the Grail Complex they guarded. Perhaps Portugal turned a blind eye toward this heretic's haven in return for the maps and geographic knowledge that catapulted Portugal into an age of wealth and empire. It is at least possible that the religious and political freedoms that North Americans value so highly today were made possible by a pact between King Alfonso IV of Portugal and Templars, and that these freedoms derive essentially from the Holy Grail.

Chapter 8

Capitulations

Portugal had little to offer Columbus after his proposal was rejected in 1484. Perhaps, also, he needed a change of scene because of the death of Felipa. History is not absolutely certain, but she seems to have died in 1484 or 1485.[1] Columbus left Portugal in the spring of 1485 and settled just inside the Spanish border in the Franciscan monastery of La Rábida.

Our traditional story of Columbus describes him as a penniless man, standing at the door of this monastery with his motherless son Diego, as a supplicant seeking food and shelter from kindly monks. This can hardly be accurate since Columbus almost immediately began to demonstrate that mysterious capacity he had for making liaisons in high places. He may have lived with the monks of La Rábida, but he did not live like one. Within a couple of years he'd acquired a mistress, Beatriz Enríquez de Harana, and she bore him a second son, Fernando (or Ferdinand) in 1488.[2] She was not Columbus's only amorous conquest while he was in Spain, for sometime around 1490 he courted Beatriz de Bobadilla, Governess of Gomera in the Canary Islands and a lady-in-waiting to Isabella. On the 1492 voyage, Columbus tried to spend a month in the company of Beatriz de Bobadilla before setting sail from the Canaries, but was frustrated by contrary winds.

Then, sometime between 1485 and 1492 Columbus found the time to have an affair with the Marquise de Moya, reputedly the most beautiful woman in Spain who was, indisputably, married to the richest man in Spain. There are the inevitable rumours that

Isabella herself succumbed to Columbus's charm. No historical proof of such intimacy has survived but her support for his expedition, and her offer to pawn her jewels to finance it, are certainly suggestive. What woman would sell her jewels except to help a lover?

As things turned out, Columbus didn't need Isabella's jewels because he'd already obtained the backing of four Spanish financial moguls: Luis de Santangel, Alonso de Harana, Alonso de Carvajal and Diego de Harana. All of these men were "conversos," former Jews who had supposedly and voluntarily accepted the Roman Catholic faith. The exact identity of Columbus's mistress, Beatriz de Harana, seems to be something of a minor mystery, with some sources making her the daughter of Alonso de Harana, and others the sister of Diego de Harana.

Columbus also became friends with Don Luis de la Cerda, Duke of Medina Celi, who owned a fleet of trading ships. Columbus convinced him of the practicability of his project as early as 1486. Columbus now had the ships, and he had financial backing, and there would seem to have been no barrier to quietly undertaking the voyage as a private venture, and, it seems, the financial people were eager to do so.

Columbus, however, submitted his proposal to Isabella who saw him very promptly in 1486. But the voyage then became a matter of state, the project was again submitted to an examining commission, and Columbus was to wait six years for a favorable response. Tradition has him spending this time in poverty and frustration, but we have seen that this was unlikely. In actual fact, Columbus was placed on the royal payroll and did not suffer financially.

We should stop and take stock of all this. Columbus's marriage into Portuguese aristocracy may have been a fluke, but his similar amorous successes in Spain argue against this. Our Columbus cannot have been a quiet and rather dull Genoese captain whose first 25 years were so obscure and eventless that Genoa itself retains no record of him, or else we must suppose that the trauma of the pirate attack and the swim to the Portuguese beach changed the lad's personality significantly. The man who entered Portugal may have been a navigational genius with immense determination, but he was also a rake and an adventurer in the best senses of those words. Doña

Felipa seems to have satisfied him while she lived, for there is no strong evidence of any extra-marital adventures on Columbus's part between his marriage in 1479 and her death in 1484 or 1485. From Columbus's subsequent behavior, this argues against Gianni Granzotto's speculation that Felipa must have been ugly and unattractive. Not long after her demise, however, our Columbus moves to Spain and becomes an attractive rake and fascinating adventurer again, just as in Portugal; at least three notable women were eager to succumb to his charms, and perhaps a fourth in the person of Queen Isabella herself if the inevitable rumors and her own jewel-pawning behavior have any relevance.

We cannot be observing an obscure Genoese merchant captain here, the son of humble wool-carders. What we see, on the contrary, is someone absolutely unique within class-conscious and rather rigid European society of the 15th century. Our Columbus can move at will on the waterfront and in noble bedrooms with equal ease, and equal respect and success in both venues. More important, perhaps, he can also move from these disparate venues into the rarified socio-economic strata of Spain's top money-men. He can hobnob with dukes who own shipping fleets. He can, perhaps, attain the queen's own bedchamber through a liaison with a Governess of the Canary Islands who happens also to be a royal lady-in-waiting. How could a wool-carder's son achieve such sophistication? And how—as both Robert Fuson and Gianni Granzotto ask—could a wool-carder's son achieve Columbus's education?

Granted that Columbus possessed an imposing physique, though not an extraordinary one, we can only attribute his success to his own daring and nerve—but not only that. There has never been anything particularly strange about noble and royal ladies taking well-built swains as lovers, but this was done with discretion. Columbus's affairs were not those of a courtier gigolo; they seem to have been acceptable and, if they were recorded in Fernando's *Historie* and *Life of Colón*, which they were, no particular attempt was made to hide them. One might say that Columbus even *flaunted* them, for otherwise they would not have survived for historians at all. Considering that his actual mistress, Beatriz de Harana, was a "converso," this was flaunting in spades. The Inquisition knew well enough that "conversos" were something of a polite farce in Spanish society of the time. They were tolerated, with suspicion, only because they possessed the financial acumen that Spanish royalty needed and lacked. Columbus, aside from his imposing physique and rakish personality, must have possessed, as an "open secret," some claim to, or high-level association with, royalty of a caliber that the Spanish nobility and royalty of the era could not match. Otherwise, so many noble and/or wealthy women would have not dared to share a bed with him such that their relationships were known well enough to have come down to historians. There was only *one* lineage of royalty that could fit this pattern: the royalty of the Kingdom of Jerusalem. *The* royalty of the Western World.

Let's return to the incident of 1472 when Columbus was commissioned to pirate the Aragonese galleass, the *Ferrandina*. How *dare* Fernando write that in his *Life of Colón*? Ferdinand happened to be King of Aragon and this incident made Columbus a one-time enemy of Aragon. One would think that any such adventure would have been concealed, forever, by Fernando. Robert Fuson reflects the same psychology when he writes:

> Columbus may have at one time served a country at war with Spain, or a kingdom that would later be swallowed up by Spain. Even if he were originally of Spanish birth, the fact would avail him little if he had been on the wrong side of a political controversy.[3]

This statement reveals little appreciation for reverse psychology. If we are truly dealing with an underground representing *the* most illustrious royalty of Europe, and *the* most critical threat to the Vatican, then "the best defence is a good offense"—let it be known that the Grail Dynasty yet survives and that Christopher Columbus not only serves it, but has powerful allies in high places all over Europe. This, and perhaps only this, can explain Columbus's appeal to ladies in high places, to financial moguls and to Spanish shipowners. This might also explain King Ferdinand's general dislike of Columbus and his general opposition to supporting him, but also his reluctance to thwart Columbus in any significant way. Ferdinand seems to have washed his hands of the whole matter and let it be decided by his queen. Compared to Columbus's lineage, or to the one he may have served, Ferdinand must be considered "small potatoes" by comparison with the epic struggle, royalty and lineage of the Holy Blood. It is also possible that the Roman Church, and even the fanatics of its Inquisition, may have "backed off" in the face of Columbus's confidence with his choice of financial backers and mistresses. In a way, if our construct is correct, Columbus in Spain was serving notice that the Holy Grail Complex was alive and well. It could not command the power to confront the Roman Catholic Church in open conflict, but it was potent enough to scare the Vatican. In Columbus's time, offshoots of Catharism, more or less garbled, were again surfacing in the world. This would become known as "Protestantism" and emerge in northern France, Holland and Germany. Columbus may have been serving notice in Spain that he represented a formidable religious and political complex that the Church had thought it had confidently destroyed during the Albigensian Crusade.

Then, if conventional history is correct, and if Columbus actually thought that he was heading for Asia and its wealth, we may wonder why he and his financial and ship-owning backers didn't just sail away and acquire this wealth of Asia. The ship owner himself, Don Luis de la Cerda, Duke of Medina Celi, was anxious to launch the expedition immediately and had the ships to make it possible. If conventional history is correct, then Columbus should have jumped at this chance since (1.) he was bound for Asia, and (2.) he had private financial backing, plus the ships, to mount a lucrative voyage there. With the undoubted profits, if he was bound for those "Spice Islands," Columbus could have *bought* himself into the parochial Spanish nobility.

Yet, Columbus did not do this. Instead he walked the tightrope for six years. It was not personal wealth that motivated him. He had to achieve two things: official claim to the new lands by a powerful maritime European power; and legal guarantees of his family's actual *vice-regal* governorship of the new lands. Until he had accomplished that, the potential "New Jerusalem" could not exist. So, although Columbus could have made a personal fortune as early as 1486, *if he was truly targeted on the "Indies" as he claimed*, he waited for six more years to obtain the guarantees that he *thought* would protect the New World against incursions of the Inquisition.

King Ferdinand was the only strong card that the Roman

Church seems to have held in this entire subtle game. His personal opposition stalled matters until 1492, or six years after Columbus entered Spain. Ferdinand's apparent opposition was an important factor, but it must also be said that Spain's examining commissions reported precisely as the Portuguese ones had done. Nothing else could have been expected because the Spanish experts had access to the same geographical information as the Portuguese. Columbus's project was impossible to anyone who correctly knew the size of the world and knew roughly the distance from Iberia to Cathay.

Nonetheless, Columbus's project represented the only chance for Spain to duplicate Portuguese success, and an important event had occurred just two years after Columbus had arrived in Spain. In 1488 Bartolomeu Diaz had discovered the Cape of Good Hope at last. Diaz had actually sailed on the Indian Ocean—sailed for only a short distance, it is true, but there was no doubt in anyone's mind that this ocean washed the Spice Lands and led to Cathay. It only had to be navigated, but it was no longer unknown territory because Europeans knew that Arabs had navigated it for centuries. If Arabs could do it, then Europeans could do it. Diaz's success ensured Portugal's eventual success. Spain could not help but be acutely aware of this. And, perhaps, the Spice Lands were not the major factor after all. En route to them, Portugal had planted the seeds of empire in Africa and that continent held considerable wealth, and also a strategic commodity of the era as far as Iberia was concerned. Africa's huge tropical forests existed as an incipient fleet of gigantic proportions in the Iberian mind's eye. Whereas Iberia itself was severely arid and treeless in many places, Africa represented a Portuguese fleet that could come to rule the world. Spain, with increasing nervousness, shared a peninsula of Europe with the nation that promised to become the premier state of the Western World. Would Spain eventually be swallowed by Portugal? Or, put another way, and more ominously: how long could Spain avoid domination by Portugal unless Spain itself gained an empire?

Then, Spain had a thorn-in-the-side that Portugal did not suffer. Some of Spain was still controlled by Islamic Moors centered on the great fortress-city of Granada. Although it was the last Moorish stronghold in Iberia, it was in no mood to surrender. The mighty Alhambra still contained many confident warriors. Ferdinand and

Isabella did not have enough Christian knights and soldiers to take Granada by force, and would not for a generation, and the Moors knew it.

Spain was not whole in one other respect. Many Jews had come into Spain with the Moors. Their culture and their financial clout, both of which were appreciated by the still-undefeated Moors, represented not only a highly imperfect reality of religious orthodoxy that Rome tried vainly to ignore, but also subtly prevented Spain's financial resources from being concentrated in totally Christian and European directions.

Ferdinand, with the Church's guiding hand on his shoulder, may have demanded something of indisputable tangible benefit to Spain in return for his endorsement of the voyage and before he would give in to Columbus's rather unacceptable terms. *Ferdinand and the Church may have demanded that the surrender of Granada be a part of the deal.*

Is it only coincidence that Columbus met Ferdinand and Isabella for the last and ultimately successful round of negotiations, in Santa Fé? This was a dusty army town, or encampment, from which the forces of Aragon and Castile were somewhat ruefully besieging Granada. There, as we know, Columbus's project was (again) initially rejected and his demands were laughed off. What were his demands?

First, and probably least important, he was to be officially made a noble of Spain empowered to call himself Don Cristobal Colón, and his heirs and successors forever were to have that title. Second, he was to be Admiral over all "islands and mainlands" he might discover before reaching Asia, the same title to be held by his heirs and successors forever, which meant that he and his nominees would absolutely control all shipping to and from these hypothetical new lands. Third, he was to be Viceroy and Governor-General over all such lands, again powers to be hereditary or nominated by Columbus's heirs and successors forever, and all officials of these new lands were to be appointed by the monarchs of Spain from a short list of three candidates submitted by Columbus and his heirs and successors; in short, Columbus and his heirs and nominees would absolutely control the government of any new lands forever. Fourth, he was to have the option of paying one-eighth the costs of sending forth any ships to "his domain," and receiving one-eighth of the profits. Fifth, he was to retain, tax free, one-tenth of all the precious metals, jewels, spices and other valuable products which any new lands might produce.[4]

About Asia? Columbus asked Their Majesties for several copies of a "Letter of Credence" confirming him as an official explorer representative of Spain. These letters were to have blank spaces so that Columbus could conveniently fill in the names of any Asiatic potentates he might encounter. He asked also for a Latin passport entitling him to cross the ocean to the region of India ("ad parties Indie") and at the same time empowering him to take possession of, and govern, any "islands and mainlands" he might discover on the way as per the five demands outlined above.[5]

It is quite evident from all this that Columbus was much more concerned about the "islands and mainlands" he might reach en route to Asia than about what he would get out of wealthy Asia itself. And it is equally evident that his demands were, truly, unacceptable for any king. Columbus was asking nothing less than to be king of any new lands he might discover. Whereas these new lands might turn out to be of inconsequential size, or even non-existent, they could well turn out to be many times larger than Spain itself. Columbus's demands could make him and his dynasty more powerful than Aragon and Castile, more powerful than Ferdinand and Isabella. Quite naturally, Ferdinand had to refuse such preposterous demands, and was perfectly correct in doing so. Under the walls of Granada, then, Columbus was rejected for the last time. He saddled his mule and departed, making it clear that he was going to approach the kings of Portugal (again), France and England. He did not get that far. As we all know, Their Majesties reversed their decision after consultation with Juan de Coloma ("Dove" in Spanish), an influential courtier, and Luis de Santangel, Chancellor of the Royal Household and Controller General of Finance for King Ferdinand. As Fernando tells it:

> Upon this resolution, the queen immediately sent an officer post, to bring Columbus back, who found him on the bridge of Pinos, two leagues from Granada...Their Catholic Majesties...granted him all the articles and clauses he had demanded.[6]

What had happened? History may never know. But it is possible that Ferdinand and the Church made a demand of their own: that Columbus somehow arrange for the surrender of Granada.

Columbus was first rejected and then recalled in January 1492. The articles and clauses he demanded were not granted *immediately* by Their Catholic Majesties. Three months more were to elapse before the documents were actually signed. What urgent negotiations went on during this time? History does not know.

All that history knows is that Granada agreed to surrender peacefully on April 6, 1492, and, on that same day, Ferdinand and Isabella walked (cautiously) through the streets of the Moorish fortress in bloodless triumph under the eyes of many warriors garrisoned in the Alhambra. The next day, April 17, 1492, Their Catholic Majesties signed the so-called *Capitulations* with Christopher Columbus, the all important document granting his demands. Is this not a strange title for an agreement between monarchs and a humble Genoese skipper? Is it only coincidence that Granada agreed to surrender the day before?

On April 30, 1492, Ferdinand and Isabella signed another document, the *Titulo*, which actually empowered Columbus with all the titles and rights he had demanded in return for what "he had discovered." In the view of conventional history, the past perfect tense was used so that Ferdinand and Isabella could repudiate the deal if Columbus failed.[7] But the past tense may have been important to Columbus. It was the only way that the concessions would be legally iron-clad when he found the new lands that, we have strongly suggested, he *knew* existed and *knew* that he could reach. The only other way of writing such a contract would have been for the monarchs to have "promised" to grant Columbus's demands upon his successful return. Royal promises have often proved notoriously worthless. With the past tense wording of the *Capitulations* and the *Titulo*, however, Columbus had his demands legally wrapped up the instant he discovered any new lands.

With the agreement of Granada to surrender peacefully, Spain attained the potential for becoming cohesive politically, culturally and religiously instead of being fragmented. The king and queen, along with the Church, consequently achieved the confidence to promulgate an edict expelling all unconverted Jews from Spain.

These were mostly Jews who had lived among the Moors because the Moors themselves did not demand conversion. A deadline was set for these Jews to depart or else, August 3, 1492—the same day that Columbus weighed anchor to begin his epic voyage, an expedition that carried no Roman priest.

It may be merely coincidence, but we cannot escape the fact that royal endorsement of Columbus's project, and granting what he demanded, are closely associated in time and place with the submission of Granada and the expulsion of Jews. It all got thrashed out within three months in Santa Fé.

Spain had cleared its geographical and religious decks, so to speak, so that Portugal could be challenged and, at one stroke with Columbus's expedition, had simultaneously actually begun the challenge. Everything was combined into one package, more or less, and perhaps we are justified in asking a question: after six years of delay, and during the three or four months of rapid negotiations and great changes, did Columbus and his hypothetical conspiratorial colleagues lay at least some of their cards on the table? Did they reveal their evidence of a New World across the Atlantic, land that seemed extensive but which could not be Asia? Might they have shown their maps depicting this land?

I think this is a definite possibility that bears serious consideration. As monarchs, the prime concern of Ferdinand and Isabella must have been to preserve Spanish security. Their obsession with expelling Moors, accomplishing the surrender of Granada, and then expelling Jews demonstrates that their primary goal was obtaining, at last, some cultural, political and religious cohesion for Spain. Which is to say that their motivations were properly *geopolitical* rather than merely manifestations of greed and fanaticism— although these elements were present in significant quantity. But, it may have occurred to the monarchs as well as to their advisors that empire might proven more important than spice. Indeed, it may have occurred to them that in the longer term, commerce of a more general nature, not just the magic word "spice," actually depended on empire.

With an empire like Portugal's in Africa, Spain too could build thousands of ships and could enslave or recruit conquered peoples for many commercial and agricultural purposes. With an empire,

Spain could preserve its independence from Portugal. This was much more important than making contact with Cathay and obtaining a few shiploads of spice. According to European notions of the time, the Great Khan (or "Cam") was the most powerful sovereign in the world with all of eastern Asia as his sphere of influence. Even if Spain reached Asia because of Columbus's voyage, Spain could not reasonably expect to obtain an empire there. The Great Cam was too powerful, more powerful by far than Spain. By European views of the time, there was no room for a Spanish empire in Asia.

But new lands on Templar maps showed the potential of empire. From the prevailing European perspective of human creation and dispersal, which was the Bible, these new lands might not be inhabited at all because there was no apparent way for descendants of Noah to have reached them. On the other hand, if they were inhabited, and some Portuguese or Scottish information may have indicated this, then the people could not be sufficiently advanced to rival Spain. Aside from some hard data that might have reached the ears of Spanish experts from Portugal's 1470 probe to Newfoundland and Scotland's voyages to Estotiland, this fact seemed self-evident because these New World people had never crossed the Atlantic to visit Europe. In short, if there were people there, they could be conquered. Spain could have an empire to rival Portugal's; Spain could maintain its security against Portugal.

I think that we must grant the possibility, at least, of this kind of thinking between January and April 1492. A lot had changed since Columbus entered Spain in 1486. Bartolomeu Diaz had changed it in 1488. Perhaps some people were beginning to appreciate that the ramifications of rounding the Cape of Good Hope and of all those Portuguese outposts in Africa suddenly went far beyond "spice."

Columbus could have shown the maps and the new lands with some impunity. The lands were there on the maps, but they had long ago been mentioned by Classical writers with whom Spanish experts were familiar—Aristotle himself and Diodorus, the writers quoted in the first chapter. Yet, even if the lands were there, they had been reached only infrequently and sporadically. Columbus held his trump card, his real discovery: the key to the barrier of the Ocean Sea. One could build an empire with it by frequent navigation to the new lands. It is possible that Columbus showed the maps, but one card he could not have laid on the table was his secret of the Atlantic.

It is an awkward fact, and it can't be argued away, that the *Capitulo* and the *Titulo* deal at much greater length with new "islands and mainlands" that might be discovered en route than with the division of Asian trade profits. Columbus's demands, his emphasis on non-Asian territories, cannot have escaped the notice of Spanish legal experts. His emphasis did not hint, it blatantly proclaimed his own real expectations, motivations and goal.

Their Majesties and the Church may have thought this larger deal worth Columbus's demands. Columbus would have vice-regal powers in the new lands, yes, but he would remain Spanish and, in fact, become a noble of Spain. Even if the lands became a haven for heretics *religiously*, it might remain allied to Spain *politically* and, in fact, *belong* to Spain in spite of the governorship demands conceded to Columbus's dynasty. Spain would have an empire. Columbus would have his New Jerusalem, heretics could have a refuge, the Church could have Spain. It would have been a delicate accommodation, but a plausible one. Something has to explain the emphasis on "new islands and mainlands" in the *Capitulo* and the *Titulo*, and conventional history does not.

I do not argue that this larger accommodation was conceptualized; I suggest only that it might have been done and that it explains a few facts.

The bottom line, however, was that Columbus possessed the key to the barrier of the Ocean Sea and the conspiracy of which he may have been part possessed some power; but neither he nor the Grail Complex had the power to enforce agreements with Spain and the Church. It was a gamble that seemed necessary at the time, a risk worth taking. In the region that Columbus actually "discovered," which is to say Latin America, the gamble was ultimately lost. But in a larger sense his key to the barrier of the Ocean Sea ultimately won. Spanish-discovered lands did not become a New Jerusalem, but other places did.

As of April 30, 1492, whatever the nature of the deal that was actually understood between Columbus and Spain, he was free to mount his expedition. That same day, the Crown provided his ships.

The three ships of the Columbus fleet were obtained in the tiny seaport town of Palos de la Frontera. Apparently the town had committed some acts that were detrimental to the Crown. As punishment, the town had to provide two caravels whenever commanded to do so, for a period of up to 12 months. Furthermore, the town was ordered to pay all costs of equipping the vessels. On April 30, 1492, the Crown called in its marker and ordered the two caravels placed under the command of Columbus. The Council also authorized the payment of four months' wages to those who signed aboard and a decree granting amnesty to any criminal who volunteered to ship out on the voyage.[8]

Columbus obtained the *Pinta* and *Niña* in this way. As for the *Santa Maria*, she was named *La Gallega* and belonged to Juan de la Cosa. Columbus chartered this vessel, changed her name to the *Santa Maria*, and chose her as his flagship. As one preparation for the voyage ahead, Columbus had huge Templar crosses painted on the *Santa Maria's* sails.[9]

Modern financial experts have estimated that the entire cost of the expedition was 1,340,342 *maravedies* or about $63,000 in 1492 currency, which would have approximately the buying power of $700,000 in 1987 currency. Spain extracted from the New World 1,733,000 *maravedies* for *each maravedi* invested in the 1492 voyage, or about $22 billion in 1987 currency. Not a bad investment.[10]

Not all of it reached Spain, however. Once the Inquisition was established in the New World, a number of French and British pirates suddenly appeared to prey on Spanish treasure convoys. It has been estimated that at least $1.65 billion was pirated, of which about half ended up in England, or $800 million. Another $4.4 billion (estimated) was lost en route due to storms and other maritime disasters, of which most is thought to remain in the Caribbean and along the Florida coast; perhaps 10 percent of this has so far been recovered by treasure hunters, or $400 million.[11]

Roughly $16 billion may have actually reached Spain. It has also been estimated that Portugal netted about $10.2 billion from African gold, African slaves, African agriculture and forestry products plus profits from the spice trade. Something between $25–30 billion flowed into Spain and Portugal during the three centuries between 1500 and 1800. Britain, France and Holland extracted a few billion during this time from their colonies, but nothing like the Iberian haul.

This money went straight into the hands of kings, queens, princes, nobles and churchmen; but they, in turn, commissioned various categories of craftsmen to create things that would reflect their wealth, power and nobility: jewellers, weavers, armourers, painters. A bit later, this money went for entertainment as well: musicians, writers and books, painters, dancing-masters, sculptors and finally even to scientists and philosophers who could offer learning. Iberian wealth trickling through Europe gradually began to finance the Renaissance. Enough lingered, enhanced by British, French, Dutch and Italian colonization, to seed the Industrial Revolution and our modern world.

Columbus's key to the barrier of the Ocean Sea unlocked other barriers as well of which the Western World is still largely the beneficiary. For the majority of the world, though, Columbus's key proved to be a key that locked shackles of slavery and colonialism firmly onto millions of non-Europeans.

Chapter 9

The Best Laid Plans...

Columbus arrived at Gomera in the Canaries on August 12, 1492, nine days after his fleet had weighed anchor in Palos and had departed from Spain. The Canaries were plagued by fickle winds that year and these caused Columbus some anxiety for two weeks. First of all, the *Pinta*'s rudder had been damaged in the crossing from Spain, damage that Columbus thought to be purposeful sabotage, and the caravel ended upon on Grand Canary instead of Gomera with the *Santa Maria* and *Niña*. Three days later a brig left Gomera for Grand Canary and, as Columbus says in his Log entry for August 15:

> ...I seized the opportunity to send a man to assist Martín Alonso with the repair of the *Pinta*'s rudder. I wrote Martín a note saying that I would have gone myself if the *Santa Maria* were not such a bad sailer...[1]

Doña Beatriz de Peraza y Bobadilla, a young widow of Hernando Peraza who had been governor of Gomera until his recent death at the hands of rebellious natives, was now the governess of the island. When Columbus had arrived at Gomera, however, she was not in residence because she had taken a trip to Grand Canary. The fickle winds and calms delayed her return. On August 16th, Columbus's brief Log entry reads: "I passed yet another day at anchor, still with no sign of Doña Beatriz."[2] The next day, he confesses: "...I am beginning to fear for the safety of Doña Beatriz."[3]

He began preparations for the Atlantic crossing, and had some difficulties obtaining adequate provisions. He noted (September 4) that: "The Portuguese have wonderful facilities for provisioning ships, but they have had many years' experience. Everything considered, I have no complaints about the assistance I have received from the people of Gomera."[4] Doña Beatriz arrived back in Gomera on September 2 after almost three weeks' delay because of calms. She and Columbus were able to spend only two or three days together instead of the two or three weeks that Columbus had apparently anticipated.

During this time of preparation in the Canaries, Columbus had the pure lateen rig of the *Niña* changed to a square rig. Although the Arab lateen rig was much superior for windward sailing and for dealing with fickle winds, and although the *Niña* was the handiest of Columbus's three ships and his favorite by far, he apparently knew that he would have constant following winds all during his Atlantic crossing and that a square rig under these conditions would be better. The new rigging of the *Niña* was completed in just two days, on August 28 and 29, and I think this indicates strongly that some of the rigging must have been planned by Columbus before leaving Spain and that the sails, at least, had been prefabricated. This re-rigging of the *Niña* does not necessarily mean that her original lateen sails were abandoned on the Canaries and, indeed, it is hard to imagine her captain's leaving his expensive gear behind. Although Columbus's Log never explicitly says so, it is possible that the *Niña*'s lateen rig was used again once the Atlantic had been crossed because it would have been more efficient for inter-island sailing. The *Niña* certainly proved to be the best ship for island-hopping that Columbus had, and this may well have been due to a reversion to her original Arab rig. However, in the Log entry where Columbus informs us of his decision to square-rig the *Niña* for the westward crossing, he reveals that he knew the key to the Ocean Sea. He wrote on Saturday, August 25, 1492:

> I have determined that the most efficient action is to make a new rudder for the *Pinta*. Also, I have determined that the *Niña* should be square-rigged as the other ships . . . this will enable the *Niña* to follow the other ships more closely and safely in this belt of easterlies. These winds blow steadily from the east or NE every day of the year, and a square-rigged ship has every

advantage in these latitudes. We will return from the Indies with westerly winds...When I sailed to England with the Portuguese some years ago, I learned that westerlies blow year-round in the higher latitudes and are as dependable as the easterlies, but in the opposite direction.[5]

There is Columbus's key said succinctly in his own words. He was to discover that he was not quite accurate. The Northeast Trades that will blow a ship westward are almost utterly dependable and, moreover, blow with a comfortably constant force. In higher latitudes, westerlies prevail and will blow a ship back to Europe, but they are not so consistent or so constant in force as the trades. Then, howling gales can visit the North Atlantic blowing from any direction.

Nonetheless, this somewhat optimistic statement in Columbus's Log betrays astounding knowledge. How did he know that the belts of opposite-blowing winds extended across the entire Atlantic? Why had no other European navigator, and there were plenty of good ones, come to this conclusion before? Why was Columbus so certain that land lay three thousand miles to the west, when truly knowledgeable experts knew that the "Indies" were really almost six thousand miles further west, that he would risk his life and crew? Again, I suggest that answers to these questions are inter-related. Columbus seems to have had privileged access to some *map* that showed *extensive* land about three thousand miles westward, land that effectively formed a long north-south barrier on the western side of the ocean. Only an extensive north-south barrier would deflect North Atlantic ocean currents and winds into a clockwise circular system. A few islands would not do the trick. I have italicized the word *map* in the previous sentence because only a map could have suggested the existence of such a lengthy north-south land barrier in 1492. The Atlantic had been crossed a few times before Columbus, and he probably knew about some more recent crossings like that of Corte Real in the 1470s, but no previous exploration of the western lands had been comprehensive enough to provide a description of a continental north-south barrier to currents and winds. Quite obviously, if there had been any such comprehensive exploration, which would have required many voyages to piece the truth together, there would have been nothing left for Columbus to discover! So, his knowledge had to have come from a map.

Very obviously, too, Columbus had absolute confidence in this map. Why? The only possible answer would seem to be that this map also showed Europe, with which Columbus was familiar, very accurately. Perhaps Columbus would even have suspected, or known, that Europe as depicted on the map was more accurate than charts made in his own day. If so, then he would have had no reason not to trust what the map showed across the Atlantic. Still, he would have made all the verification that was available to him. He would have observed the winds both north and south. He did, and their pattern seemed to confirm the existence of some lengthy north-south barrier across the ocean which deflected the winds and currents into a clockwise system. In fact, the reality of some land barrier to the west was really the only possible answer to the opposite-blowing winds that he observed.

Critics may judge that this is circular thinking, and not only with respect to ocean currents and winds. But perhaps it is integrated thinking in which all the factors inter-relate to give mutual support to an entire concept. Columbus's conclusions seem to indicate that the map he had seen must have been related to the portolans because the accuracy of Europe was crucial for Columbus to accept the map at all. And, if it was related to the portolans, then the map came from the same mysterious class as the Piri Re'is and Hadji Ahmed Maps.

During these preparatory days in the Canary Islands, Columbus makes a couple of other references to western lands. In his Log entry for Sunday, September 2, 1492, Columbus wrote:

> ...I remember that when I was in Portugal, in 1484, a man came from the island of Madeira to ask the King for a caravel to go to the land that he had seen in the west. Also, people in the Azores say that they see land to the west every year. All these peoples see this land to the west under the same conditions and report it to be about the same size.[6]

What can this mean? First, I think that Columbus is being deliberately coy. He himself was the man who came from Madeira to ask the King for a caravel! This was in 1484 and his request was denied in 1485; he moved to Spain in the spring of 1486.

What about the western land seen from the Azores? It is not seen today for the very good reason that the Azores are 1650 airline miles from the nearest point in North America which is Cape Race, in Newfoundland. Columbus was being a bit coy again, for he can only mean that some people from the Azores made annual voyages to some specific landfall in the west and knew the local geography very well. Perhaps these Portuguese-governed people in the Azores sailed to Newfoundland's Grand Banks for codfish every year. This is a virtual certainty because of that 1473 Portuguese-Danish probe to Newfoundland for which captain Joao Corte Real was rewarded with the governorship of one Azores island. But could Columbus be hinting that some of these Azores mariners may have sailed to a destination somewhat south of Newfoundland—to Nova Scotia in order to maintain contact with Sinclair's fortress-settlement? These words of Columbus are intriguing, but can history ever know precisely what he was trying to say, or hint?

Thursday, September 6, 1492, was the day that the actual Atlantic crossing began. Columbus's Log:

> Shortly before noon I sailed from the harbor at Gomera and set my course to the west. I am somewhat disturbed by word I received this morning from the captain of a caravel that came to Gomera from the island of Hierro. He reported that a Portuguese squadron of three caravels is in the vicinity of Hierro, apparently with orders to prevent me from departing the Canaries. There could be some truth in this, for King John must be angry that I went over to Castile...[7]

This is more obscurity, or perhaps something penned for the benefit of Ferdinand and Isabella, since we have seen that Columbus returned to a cordial welcome *in Lisbon* after he returned from the Indies and that King John II of Portugal was very friendly to Columbus. Now, if Columbus was aware of a Portuguese squadron with orders to prevent him from leaving the Canaries, and if he really thought that King John was angry with him for going over to Spain, would Columbus have dared return first to Lisbon under any circumstances? However bad the weather might have been when he regained the European coast, surely Columbus should have risked shipwreck rather than enter Lisbon if the sentiments written in his Log are at all valid. Columbus and his crew could easily have "disappeared" in Lisbon, his ship could have been scuttled, and his discoveries could have been quickly appropriated by King John.

We will probably never learn the truth about Columbus's relationship with Portuguese royalty, but can only repeat that this association seems obscure enough and more so.

What is known is that 33 days after leaving Gomera, the *Niña*, the *Pinta* and the *Santa Maria* dropped anchor in the lee of "San Salvador" and Columbus took possession of it. In 1882 Gustavus Fox suggested that Columbus's "San Salvador" was Samana Cay in the Bahamas, but the authority of Admiral J.B. Murdock, J.B. Thatcher and Admiral Samuel Eliot Morison (also a Ph.D. in history) argued that the 1492 landfall was made on Watlings Island about one hundred nautical miles north of Samana Cay. To confuse matters, Watlings Island now has officially been named San Salvador. It appears, however, that Gustavus Fox was right. In 1986, the National Geographic Society used computers to analyse Columbus's route across the Atlantic and, much more important, his subsequent island-hopping from "San Salvador." Only Samana Cay satisfied all the requirements of Columbus's various courses when the computers took account of wind, currents and compass variation, and only if Samana Cay is accepted does Columbus's description of islands he visited afterwards make sense.[8]

On this first, 1492 voyage, then, Columbus discovered Samana Cay and then Fortune Island and Long Island, all in the Bahamas; then he crossed the channel to the northeast coast of Cuba, passing the Ragged Island Range en route (which Columbus called the "Sand Islands"), and then crossed the Windward Passage to the northwest coast of modern Haiti on December 6. On Christmas Day the *Santa Maria* was wrecked off the north coast of Haiti and, although Columbus salvaged all he could from the ship, he could not save the vessel itself. It is worth noting that the local Taino Indians, led by their chief, Guacanagari, did everything possible to assist Columbus. On Wednesday, December 26, Columbus wrote in his log:

> Today at sunrise the King of this country came to the *Niña*, where I was, and almost in tears told me not to be dismayed because he would give me whatever he had. He had already given two very large houses to my men, and he would give us more if we needed them. And yesterday he gave us as many canoes as we needed and the labor to unload the ship, and not

even a breadcrumb was taken. They are so loyal and so respectful of the property of others, and this King is even more honest
than the others.[9]

Losing the *Santa Maria* meant that Columbus was forced to
leave some of his men in the New World until another expedition
could rescue them. He therefore founded the settlement of Navidad
(Nativity) on Christmas Day when the ship was wrecked. This
settlement must have been near the Taino Indian village and also
quite close to the wrecked *Santa Maria*, and yet the site of it has
never been found. Columbus left between 39 and 42 Spaniards at
Navidad with strict orders as to how to behave toward the Indians.
Unfortunately, the Europeans did not prove to be so "loyal and so
respectful of the property of others" as the so-called savages of Haiti.
Unfortunately, gold had already been acquired from these Indians in
trade for hawk's bells. Men left at Navidad wanted more and, when
Columbus departed in the *Niña* to return to Europe, they began to
abuse the natives in order to get it. Finally, even these good-natured
and honest people could take no more. They massacred the Spaniards, razing Navidad—or so conventional history says.

Columbus certainly had his problems during Christmas 1492.
Martín Alonso Pinzón had deserted the fleet in the *Pinta* on November 22 and was not on hand to help salvage the *Santa Maria* or help
establish Navidad. Columbus could not be sure that the *Pinta* would
return at all, nor could he be certain that the *Pinta* would ever reach
Europe with news of the discovery. Aside from that, he couldn't be
sure of Pinzón's account of things if he did reach Europe safely. With
but one ship remaining, his favorite little *Niña*, Columbus had no
choice but to curtail his exploration of the coast and accelerate his
plans for returning to Spain. However, the *Pinta* met up with
Columbus somewhere along the north coast of the modern Dominican Republic. Pinzón claimed that he'd become separated acciden-
tally and had not deserted. According to Pinzón, he'd first sailed
north intending to return to Spain if he could and discovered a large
island on the way (Great Inagua), but then decided to return south in
order to search for Columbus, whom he sighted on January 6, 1493.

Columbus considered Pinzón's explanation to be a pack of lies,
and said so in his Log entry for Sunday, January 6:

Martín Alonson Pinzón came aboard the *Nina* to apologize, saying that he had become separated against his will. He gave many reasons for his departure, but they are all false. Pinzón acted with greed and arrogance that night when he sailed off and left me, and I do not know why he has been so disloyal and untrustworthy toward me on this voyage. Even so, I am going to ignore these actions in order to prevent Satan from hindering this voyage, as he has done up until now.

An Indian, among those I had commanded to Pinzón, told Pinzón that on the island of Babeque, there was a great quantity of gold; since the *Pinta* was light and swift, he wished to withdraw and go by himself, leaving me. I wished, on the other hand, to take my time and explore the coast of Juana (Cuba) and the Isla Española (Haiti and the Dominican Republic). After Pinzón went to Babeque, the Indian told me he found no gold. He then came to the coast of Isla Española because other Indians told him that there was on this island a great amount of gold and many mines. Because of these circumstances he came within 45 miles of the Villa de la Navidad more than 20 days ago. . . The *Pinta's* crew traded for a great deal of gold; for a piece of leather strap they were given good pieces of gold the size of two fingers, and at times as large as the hand. . . So, Lords and Princes, I know that Our Lord miraculously ordered that the *Santa Maria* should remain here because it is the best place on all the islands to make a settlement, and it is near the gold mines.[10]

There is an element of bafflegab in this Log entry. The monarchs of Aragon and Castile were interested in gold above all else and, whereas Columbus continually refers to it and promises that he can get barrels of it if only his co-captains would obey him, the fact is that Columbus poked along the coasts of Cuba, Haiti and the Dominican Republic. His Log entries are replete with descriptions of the people, valuable plants (almost invariably inaccurate), *and good places for settlement*. Although paying lip-service to his interest in finding gold, Columbus himself was obviously more interested in forging long-term and more or less equitable relations with the Indians. His behavior is absolutely consistent with his being an operative for colonists that regarded these new lands as a potential home for relatively few refugees who must, above all, maintain good diplomacy with the native inhabitants. Columbus was good at this.

But, of course, all of the people on this expedition may not have been part of the conspiracy and sympathetic to its longer-term goals. The two Pinzón caravels had been supplied by the Crown and, perhaps, *their* captains were given the strong royal hint to bring back as much gold as possible and to report on the exploitability of the people, never mind what Columbus might want to do.

The gist of Columbus's long Log entry of January 6, 1492, is that Martín Alonso Pinzón speeded ahead of Columbus's slow progress along the coast and succeeded in discovering the best Haitian source of gold (and mines) *before Columbus did*. Martín Alonso Pinzón also passed the site of Navidad *before Columbus did so* and passed by the place where the *Santa Maria* was wrecked *before it was wrecked*.

This is clear because Columbus wrote that Pinzón "came within 45 miles of the Villa de la Navidad more than 20 days ago." Columbus may have hoped that Their Majesties would skip over this passage and not realize the implications of it. Columbus was writing on January 6, and Navidad was founded the same day that the *Santa Maria* was wrecked, December 25. The Villa de la Navidad was but 13 days old when Columbus wrote on January 6, yet he admits that Pinzón was there "more than 20 days ago" *when the town was not yet in existence* and when the *Santa Maria* had not yet been wrecked.

In short, Martín Alonso Pinzón jumped ahead of Columbus's snail's pace and located the obsession of Spain, gold, before Columbus did, and also secured the lion's share of it before Columbus could. Perhaps Martín Alonso Pinzón did this on tacit orders from Their Majesties. It is also possible that Vicente Yañez Pinzón, captain of the other Crown-supplied caravel, was only apparently more loyal and obedient to Columbus: perhaps this Pinzón had been tacitly ordered to shadow Columbus, thereby appearing loyal, in order to report on what Columbus did. It is possible, in fact, that Columbus's only real allies were aboard the *Santa Maria*, a ship he had chartered himself with Santangel's money.

If that is a possibility, then perhaps history is justified in looking a bit more closely into the wreck of the *Santa Maria* and the founding, and supposed subsequent massacre, of Navidad.

The relevant passages are too long to quote directly from the

Log, but Columbus says that the *Santa Maria* "went upon the bank so quietly that it was hardly noticeable" and, "although there was little or no sea I could not save her."[11] Columbus immediately requested aid from the Taino chief with whom he had obviously established excellent relations:

> He sent all his people from the village to help unload the ship...The King displayed great haste and diligence, and everything was unloaded in a very brief space of time. He... guarded what was taken ashore in order that everything might be completely secure...I certify to Your Highness that in no part of Castile could things be so secure; not even a shoe string was lost.[12]

With so much efficient help and security, it is probable that the ship was stripped of everything of conceivable value. It is known that the ship's weaponry was taken ashore; and it is possible that the most crucial items of its rigging were saved along with other supplies and tools. Now, it is said by conventional history that roughly 40 men were left at Navidad, including Juan de Coloma ("Dove") who had intervened on Columbus's behalf during the 11th-hour negotiations at Santa Fé. And, according to conventional history, the place was razed and the men massacred, because they abused the Indians in greed for gold. In fact, the place was destroyed so thoroughly that modern archeologists have not been able to locate it even though one of the *Santa Maria's* anchors has been found and even though the location of the town was very well known. One must ask if Navidad ever existed for very long. Perhaps it was not intended to be a permanent settlement, but simply a place where another ship could be made using the *Santa Maria's* salvaged gear, but a vessel much handier than Juan de la Cosa's old tub. Perhaps selected people were left at Navidad among friendly Indians and with all the *Santa Maria's* salvaged weapons, provisions and equipment. They were stranded on a coast boasting some of the best ship-building timber in the world.

A Spanish-born Canadian researcher, Alexander Roncari, delved into stories and traditions that have survived among ancestors of Columbus's 1492 crew. His theory is that a vessel was built at Navidad, called the *Santa Cruz*, and that this vessel has been remembered for five hundred years in tales, stories and letters deriving from crew descendants.[13] Whether this is true or not, the fact remains that the well-equipped castaways at Navidad had an undisturbed year in which to build such a vessel and to sail into obscurity. If these people were hand-picked associates in the conspiracy, or even members of the Holy Grail lineage, they could have escaped to establish a refuge anywhere in the Caribbean.

The inhabitants of Navidad may not have been massacred at all, and the town may not have been razed by outraged Indians. The settlement may simply not have existed very long and the chosen castaways constructed their ship while sheltered in Taino houses donated by the chief. Perhaps there is no site for archeologists to find. Conventional history has it that Navidad Spaniards abused the Indians in their greed for gold and yet, as we have seen, Columbus was careful to take the greediest contingent, Martín Alonso Pinzón and his crew, away from the area en route back to Europe.

Columbus in the *Niña* and Martín Alonso Pinzón in the *Pinta* departed for their return to Europe from the *"Golfo de la Flechas,"* as Columbus called it ("The Gulf of Arrows"—now Puerto Rincón, at the northeastern extremity of the Dominican Republic). What was the precise destination of the two ships? Presumably Columbus intended to head north to pick up the westerlies in higher latitudes and this would have taken him to the vicinity of the Azores. The two caravels departed on their long journey on January 16, 1493. On Thursday, February 14, the two caravels became separated in a "frightful" North Atlantic storm which, as Columbus conceded, forced both vessels to run as best they might before the wind "for there was no other remedy." Columbus sought the haven of the Portuguese-governed island of Santa Maria in the Azores. He arrived in Santa Maria on February 18 and departed on the 23rd. The Log for these days recounts that Columbus was threatened by Portuguese authorities, but was not captured or detained as surely should have happened. He was allowed to depart in peace, and again one can only say that the situation is puzzling and everyone's motivations seem obscure.

It should be mentioned here that if Columbus displayed superb seamanship sailing in the uncharted West Indies, he did even better during the storms around the Azores. He had only a compass and was not sure of its variation or deviation; he could not use his astrolabe in the huge waves even if he trusted it, which he did not. He could estimate his position only by his knowledge of his ship: how fast was she travelling? how much leeway was she making? what were the currents? And he had to keep track of this estimation through numerous changes of course without any accurate way of telling how much time had elapsed on any one course. Two pilots from the Niña, Pedro Alonso Niño and Bartolomé Roldán, plus Columbus's own pilot from the *Santa Maria*, Sancho Ruiz de Gama, all agreed that the ship was 450 miles closer to Spain than Columbus thought. All the pilots were certain that the storm-tossed Niña was already well past the Azores when a haven was needed so urgently. Yet, Columbus's own dead-reckoning, put them near the island of Santa Maria, the easternmost of the Azores group, and he steered them right into it. This was an incredible performance considering he had had no "fix" on the Niña position, even by the rueful standards of the 15th century, for many days. He just *knew* where his ship was.

Yet, the fact remains, Columbus entered the Portuguese-con-trolled Azores Islands, the last place excepting only Lisbon itself, where he should have shown his flag. Did he really have no choice? Martín Alonso Pinzón's *Pinta* was tossed by precisely the same storm, and became separated from Columbus. Now, whereas the *Pinta* was very slightly larger than the *Niña*, and was acknowledged to be a faster sailing vessel, it seems also to have been acknowledged that the Niña was a better sea-boat for bad conditions. Yet, Martín Alonso Pinzón did not seek the shelter of the Azores. He carried on across the Atlantic to the port of Bayona in northwest Spain. Later, he must have run into the same storms as Columbus off the coast of Portugal but, unlike Columbus, he did not think of entering Lisbon. Pinzón pushed on for Seville. In fact, the *Niña* and the *Pinta* actually entered the port on the same day. It seems to me that Martín Alonso Pinzón must be given high marks for his seamanship as well. On two occasions he carried on to a friendly port when Columbus sought shelter in hostile ones—or, rather, ports that should have been hostile but proved not to be so *to Columbus*. Pinzón battled the same storms, but reached Spanish havens instead of grasping for Portu-guese ones. Columbus may well have been the "best dead-reckoning sailor who ever lived," but perhaps this is exaggeration. There were plenty of good navigators around who did very well with the primitive methods and technology at their disposal. Martín Alonso Pinzón was no slouch. He may have been, also, a more loyal servant of Spain than Columbus. At least, he seemed determined that no information about the "Indies" should fall into Portuguese hands.

It is admittedly speculation, but it remains worthy of consideration that Columbus may have decided upon a brief sojourn in Lisbon in order to protect himself upon his return to Spain. He did not know if Martín Alonso Pinzón and his *Pinta* had survived the storm off the Azores or not. Columbus put into Santa Maria for a few days. Therefore, if the Pinta had weathered the gale, she could have reached Spain before Columbus for all he knew. Earlier in his Log, when he was still off the north coast of Haiti and the Dominican Republic, he expressed concern about what the Pinzóns might say about him to Their Majesties in Castile. Then, there was the all-important fact that Martín Alonso Pinzón was bringing that mesmerizing commodity, *gold*, back to Castile, and Columbus had none to show himself. Indeed, all that Columbus could write plaintively in his Log was that a barrel of mixed sand and gold awaited Their Majesties in *their* city of Navidad some thirty-five hundred miles west of Seville. Pinzón had the hard goods: chunks of gold as big as two fingers, and some as large as a hand. Columbus himself admits this.

Also, from the Spanish perspective, which seems to have been one of the purest manifestations of sheer greed that history has ever witnessed, Pinzón had immediately grasped the relevant reality and was anxious to return to Spain while making every effort to avoid the rival Portuguese: there was gold in the new land, lots of it, and there were mines from which it must have come although the exact location of these mines was a bit hazy; then, there were people in the new lands who were no match for Spanish military technology, and that being the case they could be tortured to reveal the location of the mines and then enslaved to work them. That was the "bottom line" of empire, and Martín Alonso Pinzón could bring it back to Spain, with the precious metal itself. Columbus could not. Pinzón could also report truthfully that the expedition had seen no persuasive evidence whatsoever of the "Great Cam's" navy, army or administrative sovereignty. Either the "Great Cam's" dominion was a great deal more primitive than Spain had been led to believe (through the only half-believed observations of Marco Polo) and Spain might be able to conquer Asia—or, this was some other part of the world not subject to the "Great Cam" at all and therefore free for the taking. Either way, Pinzón could give a succinct "situation estimate" in which Spain was apparently in a "no-lose scenario."

Columbus, the leader of the whole thing, could return with only his Log, some Indians, no gold, and his opinion that he'd reached the "Indies." As for his Log, it was mostly filled with fairly insightful ethnographic information about the various native tribes he'd encountered, which would not have interested Ferdinand and Isabella at all; some highly inaccurate ideas about the botany of the region and his eulogies about the honesty and gentleness of the inhabitants—plus many lines of vituperation against the Pinzóns, but against Martín Alonso in particular. Given the possibility that the *Pinta* just might have weathered the mid-Atlantic storms and that Martín Alonso Pinzón might have reached Spain before him, Columbus must have been acutely aware of the weakness of his position.

His situation provided a subtle dilemma: there was a glaring loophole in his legal agreements with the Spanish Crown. This loophole was inevitable detritus from his secret knowledge, whether some of it may have been tabled in the hectic January–April 1492 negotiations in Santa Fé or not. A caravel could be sailed through this loophole, and Columbus was anxious to close it, at least temporarily and in his lifetime. All of his vice-regal concessions regarding control over any *new* "islands or mainlands" he encountered before reaching the "Indies" *were legally and absolutely dependent upon his reaching the "Indies" at some point.* If he could not prove, or establish a plausible claim, that he had reached an "outpost" of the "Great Cam"—or, at least that he could reach such domains in his lifetime—then both his personal dynastic wealth and concessions, plus his larger and perhaps conspiratorial geopolitical value, would become null and void. Columbus was on a tightrope, and in a "Catch 22," and here we have to give full marks for card-playing to Ferdinand and the Church. Even if, as has been suggested in previous pages, maps showing new lands that were not Asia but held the prospect of a Spanish empire comparable to Portugal's were shown to Spanish experts in a last-ditch attempt to get the expedition endorsed, a crucial fact remained: the new lands on the maps seemed to be a complete barrier to reaching the real "Indies" for neither the Piri Re'is Map nor the Hadji Ahmed one show any break at all in the continent lying athwart the Atlantic three thousand miles westward. Even though this new continent seemed narrow, according to a projection like azimuthal equidistant projection, this was all to the good for the Spanish Crown making concessions to Columbus. For, according to the best contemporary calculations as to the size of the earth, even if voyages could be launched from the west coast of this narrow (in azimuthal equidistant projection) new western continent, a 15th-century caraval could still not cross the other and unknown western Ocean (the Pacific) with a living crew. The distance was too far: about fifty-five hundred miles because of the distortion of azimuthal equidistant projection.

Ferdinand and the Church therefore felt safe in granting the demanded concessions to Columbus because he might find a new world and an empire for Spain, but would not have dominion over them until he'd reached the true "Indies," which were still too far distant to be reached by ships of the time. This was superb poker.

Now, Martín Alonso Pinzón could, and did, bring back evidence that these western lands held wealth, alright, but betrayed no indication of being the realm of the "Great Cam," the true "Indies." Columbus had to counter this, both with imaginative geo-historical allusions and with sheer military threat. He did both. First, he wrote that the island of "Cuba," as the local Indians called it, was probably a regional way of honoring "Kubla" Khan. . . a "Great Cam" who actually ruled at one time, and who had been in power when Marco Polo had visited China. Kubla (or Kublai) Khan had come to the throne in 1276 A.D, just before Marco Polo had met him. If he were a mortal man, Kubla would have been long in his grave by 1492. Yet, Marco Polo's story was about all that 15th-century Europe had. Polo had described Kublai's dominions in such extravagant terms that Marco was called "Master Million" when he returned to Venice—"master of a million lies." Yet, no one in Europe was sure. Maybe Kubla Khan had been such an exceptional monarch that his name had been adopted as an hereditary title? Perhaps all Khans ("Cams") were called "Kubla" by 1492? No one could say. Perhaps "Cuba" was a reference to Kubla. Who could say otherwise?

Then, there was the distressing thought that this "Kubla Khan" might be a Christian, a convert to Christianity known (vaguely) throughout Europe as the Prester John.[14] This aspect of medieval European belief need not concern us except to support the idea that, whatever the Spanish geographical experts thought, and whatever Their Majesties would prefer to believe from Martín Alonso Pinzón's account, there remained nagging doubts of a geographical/political/religious nature that argued caution. "Prester John" was not a monarch to be trifled with.

Columbus may well have fuelled these doubts with a naked power play which Spain could not ignore. By sailing into the Azores and Lisbon under a credible plea of foul weather, he protected his reputation as being a loyal servant-explorer of Their Most Catholic Majesties of Aragon and Castile. At the same time, however, by his name-dropping of being met by the king and queen of Portugal, he served notice on Ferdinand and Isabella that he had very good friends in the highest places of Portugal—as his own log, quoted in the previous chapter, documents clearly enough. Spain was in no position to contest the new lands with Portugal: Portugal had more ships; Portugal had spring-boards in the Azores and Madeiras; Portugal was friendly with Columbus. While Columbus might well have been eliminated on his return to Spain, and especially on the testimony of Martín Alonso Pinzón, since Columbus was now unnecessary to Spain's navigation to the new lands, it was the better part of valor to simply await developments. Columbus might well have actually discovered the "Great Cam's" outposts in far western Asia, so far as anyone knew *for certain* in Iberia, and this Khan might not only dispose of infinitely more military power than Spain could boast, but might also turn out to be the revered "Prester John" whom the pope himself was trying to locate. More pressingly important, Columbus demonstrated by a remarkable display of nerve and applied "reverse psychology" that right next door, in Portugal, he had friends who could snuff Spain's colonial pretensions in an instant. Whatever Martín Alonso Pinzón had to say, which many clear "Renaissance" heads might have endorsed, was put on ice for a few years because of both medieval geopolitical ignorance and *Realpolitik*.

Columbus was lionized upon his return to Spain by King Ferdinand, grandees and courtiers who must have secretly despised and doubted him, but his adept play of the cards at his disposal bought him almost a decade of security. But security is not co-operation, nor is it trust. We must suppose from subsequent facts that while Spain dared not make any overt moves against Columbus for more than six years after his triumphant return, Crown spies kept him under surveillance at home and on his subsequent voyages and did all they could to sabotage his ultimate goal of finding some strait in Central America that would lead to the true "Indies" and thus confirm his vice-regal powers.

If we look at the discovery voyage of 1492 from this perspective, we can reasonably conjecture that Columbus might well have continued to coast Cuba, Haiti and the Dominican Republic in his methodical way, gathering information for colonization. He might have established settlement anyway, even if the *Santa Maria* had not been wrecked. And, if our admittedly complex construct has any validity, he might also have made some sort of probe toward the narrowest part of Central America in hope of finding that strait leading to the ocean that lapped on the far-away shores of true Asia. If that was his intention, it was the machinations of Martín Alonso Pinzón that effectively scuttled these plans. Pinzón had deserted the fleet on November 22, sighting Columbus perhaps by chance, on January 6. Pinzón could desert again at any time and carry news of the discovery back to Spain as well as a negative report about Columbus's explorations. Therefore, after the *Pinta* rejoined Columbus on January 6, 1492, however that rendezvous actually came about, Columbus could not afford to let Pinzón out of his sight. And, knowing that Pinzón could, and would, desert again if any extensive New World exploration was attempted, Columbus had no choice but to curtail whatever more-ambitious plans he might have had and return to Europe as quickly as possible while taking what steps he could to consolidate his position with Spain. He might have hoped that succeeding voyages would present him with a fair chance of undertaking methodical explorations and also with some chance to find that potentially invaluable strait.

If this was, indeed, the bright hope of Columbus, it was gradually darkened over the course of three more voyages until it flickered out altogether in 1502: intrigues against him by the Crown; insubordination and disobedience by subordinates assigned to his expeditions; possibly his own lack of competence as a governor; the weather and primitive ships; and, finally, his own failing health—all seemingly combined against him.

On his second voyage, in 1493, Columbus discovered the islands of Dominica, Guadeloupe, Maria Galante, Santa Cruz and Puerto Rico. He also founded the first enduring European settlement in the New World, initially named "Isabella," on the north coast of Haiti not far from the wreck of the *Santa Maria*. This first Spanish outpost in the Americas (except for the abortive settlement of Navidad) immediately manifested all those ills characteristic of Spanish colonialism. Its European inhabitants displayed greed, corruption, lack of integrity and cruelty that later conquistadors apparently tried to emulate. Columbus has been blamed for this, by conventional history, because of his lack of competence as a governor and administrator. Conventional history says that Columbus placed his two brothers (!?), and others, in charge of Isabella, men of overweening ambition who fomented discord among themselves because of greed. The origin of these two "brothers" is, of course, even more obscure than Columbus's own history. We have no idea who they were. They may well have been Crown appointees attached to Columbus's expeditions with orders to extract as much gold as possible by enslaving the Indians, and with orders to create as much chaos as possible. Columbus may have been stuck with these men, while at the same time attempting to establish some genuine refugee colonists who came not to conquer, but to live. The genuine colonists may actually have been in the majority, and these people will be discussed later, but the few bad apples from the first, set Latin American history on an inhumane course. Conventional history cannot document whether greed and ambition were truly a part of Columbus's own legacy, or whether they derived mostly from Crown-appointed *agents provocateurs*.

On his third voyage, in 1498, Columbus discovered the islands of Trinidad and Margarita, and a bit more than two hundred miles of the coast of south America flanking the Gulf of Paria. This third voyage is interesting because Columbus seems to have been headed straight for the narrowest part of Central America where it joins the continent of South America. He did this taking a departure from the Cape Verde Islands, not from the Canary Islands as before. From this more southerly point of departure, *if he had a map like the Piri Re'is or Hadji Ahmed charts*, he could reasonably expect to avoid the now-familiar islands of Cuba, Hispaniola and the Bahamas and strike directly for the Central American isthmus. Unfortunately for Columbus, in that particular year the Northeast Trades did not apparently extend so far to the south as usual. This happens sometimes, as in 1951, when Atlantic yacht crossings were unusually long, due to lack of wind.

Columbus succeeded in completing the passage, and even made landfall on the South American coast which, if followed, would have led him to the modern Panama. Misfortune dogged this voyage. Because of the slow sailing, food and water were in short supply by the time Columbus reached South America. Then, he encountered the rough weather that the Gulf of Paria can dish out so frequently. His progress slowed and his provisions low, he had no choice but to turn north and head for the settlements on Hispaniola, now five years old. There, he could reprovision his ships.

Isabella had been founded by Columbus himself in 1493, but in the meantime yet another city had been established which offered a better harbor on the southeast coast of the island, Santo Domingo, present capital of the Dominican Republic. He arrived there on August 11, 1498, and walked into a precarious situation.

It must be recalled that Queen Isabella had ordered monthly voyages across the Atlantic in 1494. These vessels carried a mixture of adventurers and colonists and, by the time that Columbus reached Santo Domingo in August 1498 there were several hundred Spaniards residing there. One of them was named Francisco Roldán, one of the most obscure and intriguing figures in American history. He had been a kind of "assistant" to Queen Isabella, an *alcade*, before going to the New World. Once he reached Santo Domingo, he manifested curious and non-Spanish behavior. He rebelled against the official authority of the "Columbus brothers" and, with about a hundred men in his camp, he left the city to establish another settlement inland in the Xaragua region:

But there was also something different, even unusual, about Roldán's revolt. Roldán had what we might today call a romantic disposition; he was very attracted to the beauty of the land and to the gentleness of the Indians' customs. His sentimentalism had a social side to it. He preferred the savages and their way of life to the rules and obligations of the city.[15]

Specifically, Roldán was opposed to any form of slavery, and he was set on establishing a sort of independent commonwealth composed of Indians and Spaniards. We cannot ever hope to know what was really going on here. Supposedly, conventional history tells us that Roldán rebelled against the tyranny enforced by Christopher Columbus and his "brothers," the elusive Bartolomé of the Lisbon bookshop and the even more hazy Diego. Whether these brothers followed the instructions of Columbus, or whether they disobeyed him—or whether their power was helpless against the influx of unprincipled and vicious conquistadors—has never been satisfactorily determined. The fact is that although Roldán would seem to have been a rebel against Spanish government as represented by Christopher Columbus, Columbus did little to hinder Roldán after Columbus arrived in August 1498. Columbus did nothing about Roldán's curious little independent state for two years. By the year 1500, some elements of Santo Domingo's population complained about Columbus, and Roldán, to Ferdinand and Isabella.

Their Majesties sent Francisco de Bobadilla to Santo Domingo with letters of credence that superceded the *Titulo* Columbus had been granted in Santa Fé in 1492. Conventional history says that Bobadilla was so horrified at Columbus's mismanagement and summary justice that he ordered Columbus to be put in irons. But perhaps it is significant that Bobadilla could at first find no one in Santo Domingo willing to touch Columbus; "Respect and compassion prevented those present from acting,"[16] wrote Las Cases. Finally, one man was found who was willing to fetter the Admiral of the Ocean Sea. He was a former cook on board one of Columbus's previous expeditions.

The chained Columbus left Santo Domingo in early October 1500 aboard the caravel *La Gorda*.

Once out at sea, the ship's commander, with great respect, offered to release Columbus from his fetters. Columbus refused: "I have been placed in chains by the order of the sovereigns... and I shall wear them until the sovereigns themselves order them removed."[17]

After a very fast and uneventful passage, the *La Gorda* anchored in Cadiz in late October 1500.

At Cadiz, and then Seville, where Columbus requested to go right after his arrival, the admiral in chains was a painful sight. Yet he walked through the streets impassive, pride in his eyes, dragging his chains behind him with such a clamor that all who passed turned around to look.[18]

He shamed Their Majesties into freeing him for, of course, to most Spaniards he was a hero. Some sort of deal seems to have been cut between the Crown and Columbus. He was stripped of all his titles and prerogatives granted under the *Titulo*, and yet he was permitted to mount one more expedition across the Atlantic. We will recall that the *Titulo* had been written in the past tense, and it was in "perpetuity," and could not be legally revoked (even by a monarch's whim) without causing an outcry of public opinion. Yet, Columbus still had some sort of power and it was enough to buy him one last chance to find the true "Indies" and thus consolidate his "past tense" and perpetual rights.

Columbus weighed anchor on May 9, 1502, leaving Cadiz with a small fleet of four caravels: a flagship whose name is not recorded; the *Santiago*, the *Gallega* and the *Vizcaina*. They sailed again to the Canaries for their transatlantic departure—

This time Columbus steered clear of Gomera, whose lady governor was now advanced a bit in years and was now remarried.[19]

This is, of course, a reference to Doña Beatriz, Columbus's lover of former years. Columbus may have avoided her, not so much because she had aged (as he had) since 1492 and was married again, but because both Doña Beatriz and Don Francisco de Bobadilla came from the same powerful and noble Spanish family. Since Don

Francisco had been sent to Santo Domingo in 1500 with powers usurping Columbus's own, and had ordered Columbus chained, perhaps Columbus thought it best to avoid all relations with this particular family, even his former mistress.

The fleet reprovisioned on Grand Canary, sailed the short distance to Maspalomas, and crossed the Atlantic to Martinique in the very short time of only 20 days. This was the fastest transatlantic passage made by Columbus, and a passage that few modern yachts could equal. From Martinique he sailed for Santo Domingo to take on supplies, but en route perceived the unmistakable signs of an impending hurricane. He was denied entry into Santo Domingo either for reprovisioning or for seeking shelter. Even so, Columbus warned a Spain-bound fleet of 20 vessels of the coming storm, advising the captains to stay in port. Columbus himself sought shelter at a small inlet called Puerto Hermoso.

The hurricane hit, just as Columbus had predicted. On August 30 all 20 vessels of the fleet were lost as they set sail in spite of Columbus's warning. In less than half an hour all the ships and men were destroyed in the Mona Passage within sight of Santo Domingo. When the storm had passed, Columbus set out on his last, desperate gamble:

> ...Thus he decided to sail directly into the still unfamiliar western zone of the Caribbean, in the hope, which he believed to be well-founded, of finding terra firma in that direction as well... And then by hugging the coast he could set out in search of the passage leading to the Indies.[20]

In short, this time Columbus headed straight for the continental shore of Central America. He coasted the present countries of Belize, Honduras, Nicaragua and Costa Rica. Now, it cannot be denied that this peninsular-like isthmus of Central America does more or less resemble the Malay Peninsula or archipelago, the so-called "Golden Cheronese," as it was known in Columbus's time. This Golden Cheronese was depicted at the eastern extremity of Asia on all ordinary maps of the time, but somewhat vaguely depicted. Conventional history maintains that Columbus thought he was coasting this Malay Peninsula and that he was but the width of Italy from the realm of the Great Khan—"no more than the distance from

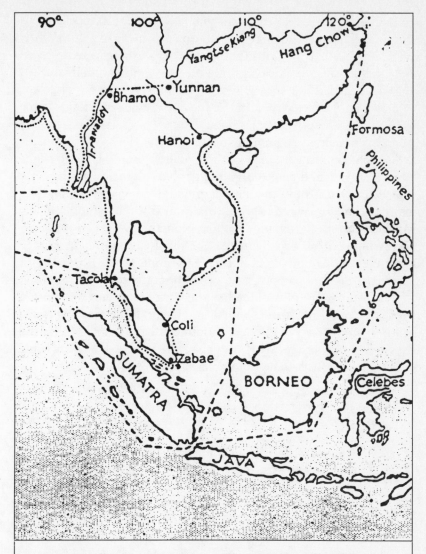

The Malay Peninsula and associated islands of Sumatra and Java were called "The Golden Cheronese" in Columbus's day and were considered to possess wealth and civilization second only to China itself. This was, in fact, true during the 15th century and the dotted lines indicate pre-European trade routes already established by Far Eastern peoples before and during the medieval period.

Courtesy: Harper & Brothers, New York. From *Conquest by Man* by Paul Hermann.

Pisa to Venice,"[21] as Columbus succinctly put it. Yet, as he sailed this wild and almost uninhabited "Moskito Coast"—now more often mistakenly called the Mosquito Coast (mosquitoes were named after the Moskito Indians who are the only human inhabitants of this coast with its hordes of insects)—Columbus must have known, whatever he chose to write, that he was not on the eastern side of the Golden Cheronese.

In his time it was common knowledge that the Malay Peninsula and its neighboring islands of Java and Sumatra boasted some fabulously rich and civilized Hindu-Arabic sultanates. In the early 16th century this Golden Cheronese had a very large population, many coastal cities and a grand tradition of ocean shipping. The Moskito Coast offered none of this. Nonetheless, it *was* a rapidly narrowing peninsula as the maps like Piri Re'is and Hadji Ahmed show clearly. Columbus could at least hope to find a strait, or passage, at its very narrowest point—if he could reach that point.

Unfortunately for Columbus, the winds and currents on the Moskito Coast flow strongly north and Columbus was trying to sail south in ships that could not tack into the wind very well. For 28 days the four caravels battled against the contrary elements and made good barely two hundred miles:

> . . . the caravels were subjected to constant punishment, their sails torn and their anchors, shrouds, hawsers, launches and a good portion of their provisions lost. The men were exhausted and desperate, continually making vows to go on pilgrimages. They even acted as each other's confessors! I have seen many storms, but never one so terrible that lasted so long. What wrung my heart the most were the sufferings of my son. I was sick, at death's doorstep on several occasions, but I still gave orders from a little cabin that the sailors had built for me on the poop deck.[22]

There are four things about this passage from Columbus's Log of his last voyage that are worthy of note. For the first time he seems to have had a loyal and willing crew: the sailors may have been "exhausted and desperate," but they did not mutiny or disobey orders. Secondly, there seems to have been no priests on this expedition because the men acted as "confessors" to each other in the Cathar and Protestant fashion. Third, Columbus's son, Fernando, was on this voyage and, fourth, Columbus was very ill. Did Columbus take Fernando on this all-important last attempt to find the passage to the "Indies" so that Fernando could claim the "perpetual" titles and prerogatives even if Columbus himself died in the attempt?

By sheer determination and a dying man's still-indomitable will, the caravels managed to reach the location of today's Panama Canal. Columbus sailed into Chiriqui Lagoon, and the natives told him that another ocean was only nine days away overland. But there was no immediate passage through the isthmus for Columbus's ships—no reserve of strength, will and health to march across the narrow spit of land, build a ship on the other side, and reach the Indies. A ship's route through Central America to Asia wasn't made possible until 1914 with the construction of the Panama Canal.

In the long view of history, Columbus and the conspiracy of which he may have been a part, lost their momentous gamble by just 26 miles.

Thwarted at the very entrance to a canal that would be dug 412 years later, all of Columbus's luck rapidly deserted him. His four ships had been riddled by toredo worms and were leaking badly. He made it to Jamaica, but a storm drove the *Santiago* into Columbus's flagship and both vessels were lost. The other two were not sufficiently sea-worthy to continue. They became stranded barracks for the crews of all four vessels. Christopher Columbus, defeated and dying, faced the prospect of ending his days as a castaway on unknown Jamaica.

> Thus the last fleet ever commanded by Columbus met its end, and his last voyage, by far the most trying, also came to an end, although an inconclusive one, with the admiral facing the prospect of living out his last days cut off from the rest of the world, where no one would know what had happened to him until years, even decades, after his death. This did not happen. Nonetheless, in Jamaica Columbus lived through an adventure that would have broken the spirit of just about any man who did not possess his power of will.[23]

The hero of this dark hour was Diego Mendez. Although he did not think it was possible himself, Mendez volunteered to try to reach Santo Domingo in a native dugout canoe. Mendez wanted some volunteers to make the hazardous voyage with him, but told Columbus:

"If they all refuse, I shall risk my life in your service, as I have done before." No volunteers stepped forward and Mendez, with six local Indians, set out across the 100-mile passage to Hispaniola. This first attempt failed when Mendez's canoe was attacked by hostile natives and was forced to turn back. Mendez had set an example, however, and finally two canoes set out, the second under the command of Bartolomé Fieschi. This doubled the odds of reaching Hispaniola. And, in the end, both canoes made it in what Samuel Eliot Morison called "one of the most daring adventures in the history of the sea."[24]

Naturally, no one in Santo Domingo was particularly anxious to rescue Christopher Columbus. Mendez and Fieschi pleaded in vain with the authorities for a ship. Four months passed. Columbus gave in to despair:

> Until now I have always taken pity on my fellow man; today may Heaven have mercy on me, may the earth cry for me, as I wait for death alone, sick and racked with pain. I am so far away from the Holy Sacraments that if my soul should here leave my body, not even God would remember it. Those who love charity, truth and justice, let them cry for me now.[25]

Help arrived when it was no longer expected. A personal friend of Columbus, Diego de Salcedo, chartered a caravel at his own expense. On June 28, 1504, Columbus and his hundred surviving companions were rescued and taken back to Santo Domingo.

On September 12, 1504, Columbus took ship for Spain on his last transatlantic crossing. He died on May 20, 1506, in Vallodolid Spain, in a house, still preserved, on a street now called "Calle de Cristobal Colón." From his symptoms, described both in his own Log and from other sources, modern medical experts are inclined to believe that Columbus had diabetes, syphilis or both.

If the entire Columbus epic was a noble conspiracy to create a New Jerusalem for religious refugees, then it must be judged to have been a magnificent attempt, a daring gamble. It failed, yes, but nothing can dim the valor of those men who accompanied Columbus on that last 1502–1504 voyage to find the all-important strait. Nothing can denigrate the constant effort that had been maintained on behalf of a humanistic goal for several centuries.

Litigation to claim Columbus's legacy was pursued by verified descendants up until the mid-1700s. But the Crown had its iron-clad defence: Columbus had not reached the "Indies," and all of his concessions rested upon his doing so.

Chapter 10

The New Jerusalem

The purely legal case of Columbus's heirs could not have been argued successfully after Amerigo Vespucci's 1502 realization that the 1492 discoveries were a "new World", and certainly not after the return of Magellan's decimated expedition in 1521.

But purely legal considerations are of little concern to anyone except lawyers, and of much less concern to people fighting for their lives. What happened between, say, 1493 and about 1520 when the identity of Columbus's discoveries remained in "reasonable doubt"? These 27 years or so represent a kind of "mini-Dark Age" in European and American history. The men-on-the-spot, the "conquistadors" were too busy to write because they were conquering. When some finally did sit down to write in their middle and later years (which few reached), memories were conveniently clouded by both religious and political considerations. In short, the very first years of "The Conquest" are obscured. The first colonizing generation left fewer records than history would like and, in any case, the documentation leaves a lot unsaid.

The situation is complicated by the fact that Queen Isabella ordered monthly crossings of the Atlantic in 1494 in order to populate and establish Spain's claims to the New World. Many, or even most, of these people were not literate, and very naturally, because most of these emigrants were not from favored classes with access to education. Only those with no strong ties to Spain's economics and culture left. In fact, only Spain's religious and cultural detritus consigned themselves to the Atlantic crossing. They had nothing to lose in Spain, they could perhaps carve out a life in Columbus's "Indies." Even with Columbus's first epic voyage in 1492 the only requirements for sailors willing to sign on was that they provide a given name and a place of birth and/or current residence. No family name was required. Thus, in the roster of Columbus's 1492 crew we find "Pedro de Sevilla" which means nothing less, but nothing more, than "Peter of Seville." Rodrigo de Triana, the man who first sighted indisputable land, is a case in point: he was simply "Roger of Triana" and we know *nothing* more about him.

This constituted the identification required for the first, and all-important, 1492 voyage of discovery. Nothing more was expected for the monthly voyages of colonists that Isabella decreed in 1494.

With lax emigration requirements like this, anyone could ship out so long as they could pronounce, in Spanish, a given name and some recognizable place of birth or residence in Spain. Since much of "Spain" had but recently been taken from the Moors, the customs inspectors (if there were any) would likely accept any town name as a place of birth or former residence. Then, if it were tacitly known that Moors, Jews and "heretics" were leaving Spain, and a blind eye was to be turned to their departure, it becomes clear that anyone could have sailed across the Atlantic between the decreed monthly crossings in 1494 and about 1520 when official Spanish organization began to get a handle on things under the watchful eye of the Church.

If our conspiracy theory is at all valid, we would expect some whispers from these first-generation years (1494–1520) that colonists from Spain were not orthodox Roman Catholics, but heretics. And, in fact, such rumored complaints have come down to history from this period.

In 1506, the Bishop of Puerto Rico complained to Their Majesties and the Vatican that ships were bringing "mostly Jews" as colonists.[1] Four years later, in 1510, the Bishop of Cuba made exactly the same complaint to the same authorities; the ships brought mostly Jews and he adds, "secret heretics."[2] The official Royal census for 1545 noted that 25 percent of Mexico City's population were admitted and openly practising Jews; and this figure *did not include* "secret Jews," heretics, *conversos* or secret Muslims.[3] If this was truly the case, then the majority of Mexico City's population must have been non-Catholic. This seems to have been true because, in 1527, Francisco Fernandez de Castillo wrote: "there are more Jews than Catholics in Mexico City."[4]

Pinto de Lima, writing in 1552 from South America, confirmed the same situation there when he noted that "three-quarters of the Spaniards in South America are of Jewish blood."[5] And Laerte de Ferreira, writing three years later, simply comments that "Jewish blood is common among the conquistadors."[6]

According to official Spanish records, by 1650 there were 15 synagogues in Mexico City alone, three in Puebla, two each in Vera Cruz and Guadalajara, and one each in Zacatecas, Campeche, Merida and Monterey.[7] These are truly amazing figures considering that we are speaking of a period just 150 years at most after the first discovery. Colonists came by caravel in the early days and, aside from the fact that many of these little ships were lost, they could not carry very many people. Later, of course, larger galleons were used which were safer and had more carrying capacity. Still, these ships were nothing compared to the vessels that carried immigrants to North America in the 1700s and 1800s. Spaniards represented but a thin veneer over a substratum of native Amerindians (who were, admittedly, being rapidly wiped out) and a replacement labor population of hundreds of thousands of African slaves. For a synagogue to exist in places like Merida (in the middle of Yucatan), Zacatecas and Monterey meant that even these small and dusty frontier settlements had a significant "Jewish" population.

The contemporary Spanish historian, Salvador de Madariaga, summed up the situation when he wrote: "When the Inquisition expelled the Jews from Spain, they left behind a deeply judaized Spain and went abroad no less hispanified."[8]

Complaints of bishops and the other comments quoted refer mostly of Jews but also mention heretics and even Muslims. Indeed, it is a minor mystery of history why Columbus, in preparation for his third voyage, in 1498, which was a mixed exploratory and colonizing expedition, requested and received three Arab-speaking interpreters![9] Did he expect to encounter Arab traders and ships in the vicinity of the "Great Cam's" realm? Possibly. But if this construct has any claim to validity, he may have needed them in order to ease communications between mixed Spanish and Moorish colonists.

There can be little doubt that the majority of dissidents emigrating to escape the Inquisition were Jews. A great many unconverted Jews had lived in Moorish Spain enjoying religious toleration. When Granada surrendered, however, "Moorish Spain" ceased to exist and so did religious toleration. Tens of thousands of known, practising Jews had to get out of Spain, somehow, by August 3, 1492, or profess outwardly credible Roman Catholic orthodoxy until some opportunity to leave presented itself. This large population of Jews from Moorish Spain doubtless greatly outnumbered the surviving Cathar heretics of Jewish, Islamic and Christian origin. But that does not necessarily mean that the conspiratorial planning and negotiations which made the exodus of dissidents possible was primarily a Jewish achievement. If the data presented in the previous pages are judged to be at least credible, and worthy of consideration, then the conspiracy of which Columbus may have been a part had its origins in the Cathar heresy of the Pyrenees and had essentially been initiated by the fall of Montségur in 1244. Although Jews were to become the dominant category of refugee fleeing Spain, the conspiracy itself was not primarily a Jewish one but Cathar-initiated one.

Although the edict of August 3, 1492, expelled the Jews from Spain, it did not prevent them from settling in Spanish territories. This may have been merely an oversight on the part of the Church because Spain at that time had no territory outside of Iberia: Columbus had not yet discovered it. Yet it also may have been a deliberate oversight and, one might say, the Roman Church more or less expected religious dissidents to colonize the New World once it had been discovered. We cannot know what the official attitude may have been in 1492, but we do know that it changed around 1550. Spain exported the Inquisition along with colonists, and the Inquisition immediately set about the extermination of all Jews and heretics who would not convert.

This had surprising historical repercussions. Many dissidents converted and avoided the stake, but many refused and were burned alive. This happened in all the major cities of the New World. Some dissidents, however, rather than be burned or recant their faith, fled into the hinterland beyond the easy reach of the Inquisitors. And it is interesting to note that whatever skills these people had practised before in Spain and Mexico, they reverted to their original ancient occupation. The Cathar Christians, Muslims originally from North Africa and Jews originally from Palestine had all been herdsmen of cattle, horses and sheep. Their methods of herding were also similar or identical. They used long poles to prod cattle in the desired direction, just as Berbers do today and as horsemen in France's *comargue* do today.

As strange and as ironic as it may seem, then, these mixed religious refugees from the transplanted New World Inquisition became "cowpokes" and started the cowboy tradition of northern Mexico and the southwest United States. The first known European cattlemen in what is now Texas was Don Luis de Carvajal y de la Cueva, of the same Carvajal family that once helped finance Columbus's 1492 voyage. Don Luis started his Texas ranch in 1591 as a practising and unrepentent Jew. Unfortunately for Don Luis and his family, Texas wasn't far enough from the Inquisition. Almost all of the Carvajals were tracked down and burned alive in Mexico City between 1594 and 1597.[10]

All of the refugee cowpokes, and there were hundreds of Jewish and heretic and even Muslim families of them, did not perish in the flames of the Inquisition. Many, or even most, went further afield than Don Luis and found safety: to extreme northern Mexico, and especially into the Sierra Orientale; further north into present-day New Mexico, Arizona, California, Colorado and elsewhere. Eventually, they adopted the American Indian lariat, which was more efficient than their traditional poles, and they seem to have gradually become more or less orthodox Catholics. But they were still called "cowpokes" when newcomers from the Northeast English colonies trickled southwest to adopt the trade and the name lingered even when now-independent Americans settled the west.

But the ancient Berber-Islamic, Jewish and Cathar heritage survives to this day, although it is well disguised. The cowboy's musical instrument is the guitar, a word deriving from *al qu'tar*, Arabic for a kind of lute. Although the lyrics of traditional cowboy songs gradually changed to English, the melodies of some have survived for over a thousand years, now, and were originally Moorish or Jewish or Provençal tunes from the Pyrenees. A rodeo is an exhibition of herdsman skills and one event is a demonstration of virtuoso horsemanship around a complicated course. This is called *a la jineta* in Spanish, and the term is still used even in some American rodeos. Yet, this event is named after the *Zeneta* tribe of Berbers, who were in the army of Tariq Ibn Zayid when he invaded Spain in 711 A.D. Zeneta horsemen were Tariq's best light cavalry and they rode in a hell-for-leather style that is still demonstrated in 20th-century rodeos.[11]

One might go even a bit further and say that the Hollywood phenomenon of the "singing cowboy," with his well-known respect for, and protection of, women, reflects a kernel of historical reality beneath celluloid exaggeration. It is the chivalry of Provençal troubadours expressed by Gene Autry and Roy Rogers.

If some wisps of a romantic legacy survive from the culture of these refugee Jews and heretics, a legacy that originally derives from the Provençal civilization and the belief-complex centered on the Holy Grail, we must also honestly acknowledge the fact that there is a brutal and inhumane legacy as well. The conquistadors practised torture, enslavement of innocent people and genocide on a scale not rivalled until Hitler's Holocaust.

The native population of the Americas before Columbus has been estimated by various experts, with widely divergent figures, to be from 3–10 million people.[12] It is reasonable to suggest that the majority of these native Americans lived in the tropics where high civilizations based on an extensive and sophisticated agriculture flourished. Indeed, there can be no argument that the Western World today largely feeds on vegetables domesticated by native Americans, and domesticated by the tropical civilizations of Mexico and the Andeas. Corn (maize), potatoes (both "sweet" and "Irish"), tomatoes, all squashes, all beans came from America. Some of these foods stimulated the increase of some European populations once the vegetables had been introduced into Europe. An example is provided by Ireland, which proved to be so favorable for potatoes that they became a staple food that allowed a rapid increase in population over just three to four generations. When a combination of unusual climatic conditions, plus (apparently) some sort of disease, resulted in a few years of poor potato harvests, the terrible Irish "Potato Famine" occurred. Thousands of Irish people faced the grim choice of starving or emigrating, and this accounts for the huge influx of Irish into North America during the mid-1800s.

The point of this is that agriculture in Mexico and western South America was fully capable of supporting millions of people. By contrast the more primitive hunting-gathering cultures of North America and some parts of South America must have represented a very small percentage of pre-Columbian Amerindian population. The vast majority of native Americans must have lived, therefore, in the very region that Spain's conquistadors exploited so ruthlessly. European diseases, plus brutal enslavement very quickly decimated this "Meso-American" native population. How many human beings died of smallpox and measles; under the lash of Spanish over-seers? History will never know. But the victims can be counted in the millions. That much is certain. And, when the native Amerindian labor force started to become insufficient for Spanish needs, and in some places this happened within just a century or less, hundreds of thousands of imported black Africans were subjected to the same sort of slavery and genocide. Since the Spaniards bred slaves from those originally imported from Africa, history can never know the number of these victims, either, but again the figure must be in the millions. The brutality was sometimes unbelievable by modern standards, and probably only possible because Europe itself was so accustomed to cruelty as an everyday fact of life. On the Spanish cane plantations, a recalcitrant slave was boiled alive in molten sugar as an example to others. In forestry operations, a recalcitrant slave was strapped between two planks and sawn in half lengthwise. Starvation rations were the gnawing reality of a slave's every day, and any slave who dropped from sickness or malnutrition was flogged to death on the spot. Naturally, any remotely attractive girl or woman was a sexual toy for as many conquistadors as cared to amuse themselves with her, and the racially mixed population of Latin America today derives originally from countless rapes.

Clothing the sheer greed and cruelty that made life a living hell for millions was the threadbare justification of crocodile piety: only through slavery could the heathen Indians and blacks become exposed to Christianity, become converted, be saved. Their reward was, obviously, awaiting them in the "next world" not in this one, a convenient situation for both God and the conquistador. Through slavery the victims could perhaps attain salvation in the hereafter, just like signs at the entrances to Hitler's concentration camps smirked: "Work will make you free."

If, as I have argued, immigration to the New World was at least partly an escape from the Spanish Inquisition negotiated by a conspiracy that seems to have included Christopher Columbus, then we must face the fact that the fortunate Jews, heretics and Muslims who left Europe did not extend much compassion to Indians and Africans. If the bishops' complaints about the flood of Jews and heretics are at all factual, and if most of the conquistadors were, indeed, of Jewish blood or heretics, then the much-vaunted traditional humanity of Jews and Cathars lapsed into ignoble inhumanity in the New World. The fact cannot be avoided that at least some Jewish or heretical conquistadors revealed themselves to have been among the most cruel and callous people that the world has ever produced. Their crimes of torture and genocide fully matched the achievements of the Inquisition and the Nazis. That cannot be reasonably denied. At least some of the Jew and Cathar immigrants left their chivalry behind along with most of their other belongings.

But, in spite of the documentation about the prevalence of Jews and heretics among New World colonists and conquistadors, and in spite of the fact that some Jews and Cathar heretics undoubtedly perpetrated monstrous crimes against humanity, I cannot believe that Jews and Cathar heretics were responsible for most of the slavery and carnage in the Americas even if they represented a majority of the early European colonists. Recall Columbus's Log. He spoke highly of the Haitian "King" who helped salvage the *Santa Maria* and assisted with sheltering the ship's crew. Genuine respect and admiration were communicated in what Columbus wrote of this chief and these Taino Indians. In fact, he dares to hint that Taino morality was superior to that of Castile:

> Tuesday, 25 December 1492
> . . . I certify to Your Highness that in no part of Castile could things be so secure; not even a shoestring was lost!

It was Columbus who travelled slowly along the coasts of Cuba, Haiti and the Dominican Republic recording his interest in the people, their customs, their domesticated plants and their helpfulness; it was Martín Alonso Pinzón who sped ahead looking only for gold. If Columbus truly represented a conspiracy to create a New Jerusalem in some sort of association with the Grail Complex, then it would seem probable that most, at least, of the Cathar heretics and hunted Jews would have shared a Columbus-like view of the new lands and not the view of Martín Pinzón. They sought a home where they realized that they would be few in number among native people with whom they must coexist. They did not come for conquest and gold so that they could return to Spain and buy noble titles, which was the motivation of the worst conquistador exploiters. The Cathar heretics and Jews could not return to Spain at all. So, although participants or beneficiaries of "the Columbus conspiracy" may indeed have represented the majority of immigrants in the early days of New World colonization, and although some of them doubtless joined in the conquistador orgy of greed and cruelty, most of them did not. They came as colonists, not conquerors. This supposition is at least partly supported by the behavior of heretics and Jews once the Inquisition became established in "New Spain." Very few recanted their faith, and they were burned for it. But many of them fled into the unknown and unexplored interior of North America, and again colonization and coexistence was both their motive and their necessity. They did not push into the hinterland to conquer the people already there. On the contrary, as a mere sprinkling of Europeans among more numerous Indians, they established ranches among Apaches, Comanches, Payute and other native tribes and nations. And, somehow, for roughly 250–300 years this scattered population of European Jews and heretics managed to survive among the very same Indians who *had to be wiped out* in fierce wars when the U.S. cavalry came to conquer in the 1800s.

It would seem self-evident, therefore, that these Jews and heretics carried with them, wherever they went, human values that differed greatly from the values of the Inquisition, Spaniards who came as conquerors and later Anglo-American settlers who also came as no-nonsense conquerors.

In becoming ranchers in the unknown interior they adopted a way of life that could not include slavery. A hired Indian *vaquero*, and there were plenty of them, was no slave. His job was to look after cattle and horses on remote ranges where grazing was available and, in the arid southwest, this might mean travelling many miles from the *hacienda*. There was nothing to stop a slave from riding off into the sunset. *Vaqueros* were free men by definition, at once independent from, but loyal to, the rancher who paid and sheltered them. Indeed, from that curious mix of independence and utter loyalty remains, in our romanticized traditions, the ideal cowboy. It is worth noting that these inland ranchers also hired runaway African slaves, and there were plenty of black *vaqueros* as well as Amerindian ones, in the 1500s and 1600s in the southwest.

From the *vaquero* evolved all those "frontier virtues" that Americans today exaggerate, romanticize, embellish, betray and yet still profess to emulate: independence combined with loyalty; a basic self-reliance tempered with the commonsense realization that co-operation is frequently necessary for survival; cocky self-confidence, not arrogance, softened by the recognition that tolerance is also necessary for self-preservation; honesty forged by the necessity of directly confronting a harsh environment.

When the "west was won" and there was no longer any geographical frontier, the notion grew in the Unites States that these same *vaquero* virtues, if applied to politics, could create a progressive society. True, these virtues were more often professed than manifested, more often betrayed than honored, but in crisis situations the latent seed of "frontier virtues" sometimes sprouted in surprising ways. That kernel of Cathar humanism from medieval Provence proved to have astonishing vitality even though very few people today are aware of its origins.

America's most beloved president, Franklin Delano Roosevelt, seems to have reflected these "frontier virtues" at a time when the United States urgently needed them. This was ironic since FDR himself sprang from the sophisticated "eastern establishment." Stranger still, there are hints that Roosevelt not only knew about the conspiracy in which Columbus seems to have been an operative, but may have been a 20th-century expression of it himself. Is the Grail Complex alive and well? Can the Holy Grail still motivate people who have molded society in our own time? Perhaps.

FDR won the election of 1932 and was destined to reside in the White House for almost four full terms of office, popularity unmatched in U.S. political history. It was the darkest time of the Great Depression; Nazis were emerging in Germany; and human agricultural ignorance conspired with a few years of anomalous weather conditions to create the Dustbowl Tragedy—farmers had plowed the topsoil incorrectly for decades and then a drought dried this topsoil to dust which the wind blew away. Crops failed, farmers went bankrupt; waterholes dried up and cattle perished so that ranchers were ruined too. A pathetic cavalcade of hopeless people in broken-down jalopies set out from the midwest and southwest, headed for someplace, anyplace, where they might be able to earn a living again; most headed for California. Called "Okies" because Oklahoma was the center of the Dustbowl, some of these people reached California where they were able to establish farms again, while others ended up in the Pacific Northwest and generally found a new livelihood.

FDR had campaigned on his recovery and reconstruction strategy which he called the "New Deal." Although he was a scion of the eastern establishment and came from a wealthy family, his New Deal was a departure from pure "free enterprise" (as some conveniently called it) and his own eastern establishment elite of industrialists repudiated it. But the people in the midwest and southwest supported his strategy, while more intelligent people elsewhere realized that it was the only solution to the crisis. Basically, FDR's strategy was to use government funding to create jobs and to preserve farms and ranches with subsidies so that their owners would not have to abandon their land. This got people out of breadlines and soup kitchens and back to work; it alleviated the worst suffering of the Dustbowl and encouraged farmers and ranchers to hang on and try to regenerate the land. FDR's make-work projects were carefully chosen. There were dozens of them, but two major ones were to have far-reaching implications: he created a web of highways over all of the United States to facilitate the transport of people and goods; he undertook a massive project to tame the Tennessee River with a system of dams that not only prevented flooding of southern farmland but also produced huge amounts of electricity.

All this was criticized as being "socialist" by the eastern power elite in particular and by political conservatives everywhere in America. But it worked, people could see that it was working, and the people voted for him time and again. Aside from his material strategy, FDR had a psychological strategy. He frequently used network radio for a series of "Fireside Chats" with the American people. These broadcasts were not political propaganda, they were *explanations* of the various New Deal projects and the president's delivery was always calm and confident. He conveyed the unmistakable impression that he had no doubt whatsoever that the country would recover, was recovering, and he told Americans that "the only thing you have to fear is fear itself."

During World War II, Roosevelt's make-work programs of the 1930s had a direct effect on the military defeat of Germany and Japan. The system of highways allowed American-produced war material to move swiftly across the country to seaports on the Atlantic and Pacific. As for the electricity of the TVA ("Tennessee Valley Authority") it possibly won the war. In the desperate race to develop the Atomic Bomb, both the Nazis and the Allies had brilliant scientists. What Germany did not have was the huge surplus of electricity required to separate fissionable Uranium-235 atoms from non-fissionable Uranium-238. America's massive "Manhattan Project" workshop had to be located at Oak Ridge, Tennessee, because only the TVA-tamed river could supply sufficient electricity for the uranium refining process.

It must be said here that Franklin Roosevelt had two rather curious friends and personal advisors who cannot be considered "mainstream" by American standards then or now. One was the Jewish financial wizard, Bernard Baruch. He was more than a financier; he had also been a student of the neo-Cathar mystic, George Gurdjieff, in the 1920s. Perhaps understandably, Baruch chose to ignore this episode of his life in his autobiography intended for American readers, *Bernard Baruch: My Story*, but his study under Gurdjieff is documented by another of the mystic's students, Louis Pauwels in *The Morning of the Magicians*.[13]

The other friend and advisor was the modern, iconoclastic architect, Frank Lloyd Wright. Wright was a student of ancient lore, and particularly of legends relating to the Holy Grail. Wright was so fascinated by the de Bouillon legend that he named his estate "Taliesin" in honor of the Arthurian bard who stumped Maelgwn Gwynedd's 26 learned *ollaves* with his riddle. This is our little Gwion of the burned finger. I have already suggested that the answer to Gwion/Taliesin's riddle was "Holy Grail." Why would Frank Lloyd Wright name his estate after this obscure 6th-century Welsh bard?

It may be that FDR appreciated these friends because he himself had some interest in, or direct connection with, the Holy Grail story. In 1909, when still a young man, FDR bought shares in the "Old Gold Salvage and Wrecking Company,"[14] a company of adventurers bent on excavating the mysterious construction on Nova Scotia's Oak Island that's commonly called "the money pit" (though no money has ever been found in it). There have been dozens of theories, naturally, about the purpose of the man-made "well" that descends hundreds of feet into this small island on the Atlantic coast of Nova Scotia. Any of these theories may prove to be correct, or none, but most have concentrated on the "pit" alone with the obvious notion that something of value must be buried at the bottom of it: pirate treasure (Captains Kidd and Drake are the most popular candidates); Francis Bacon's original manuscripts proving that he "wrote Shakespeare"; the famous golden chain of Cuzco, which escaped Spanish greed, buried for safety by wandering Incas—and so on. In 1982, I visited Oak Island for the Nova Scotia Ministry of Culture, ignored "the money pit" and concentrated on the so-called "pirate walls" that are also on the island. These walls seemed to be exactly the same sort of rubblework type of construction as the castle ruin in the middle of the province. The Nova Scotia peninsula's narrowest point just happens to be where the castle ruin is in the middle and where the Oak Island constructions are on the Atlantic Coast. Oak Island is only 17 airline miles from the castle. Offering yet another theory, I suggested that the walls on Oak Island were the remains of an Atlantic Coast lookout post intended to warn the inland castle of any unwanted transatlantic visitors. As for the pit, I thought it had been intended as a decoy to keep unwanted visitors busy until the castle-dwellers could evacuate or prepare a suitable defence. If the money pit was just a decoy it has done its job very well because treasure hunters have been obsessed by it to the exclusion of looking beyond their noses for 190 years! An estimated $2 million has been poured into the pit by various excavating companies, but not one cent has come out!

Is it just coincidence that FDR was interested in this Nova Scotia mystery? Did he want to keep informed about these excavations that were so close to a castle just 17 miles away that may have been established by Henry Saint-Clair on behalf of the Grail Dynasty? Only FDR could answer these questions, but it is known that even during World War II he wrote to the salvage company enquiring about the progress of excavations. There's an intriguing thing that should be mentioned here, even though it may be unimportant. *De Bouillon* means "Golden" and the de Bouillon Dynasty of the 12th century would certainly be "Old Gold." FDR bought shares in the "Old Gold Salvage and Wrecking Company." Perhaps one is entitled to ask what evidence of the de Bouillon story may have been salvaged without publicity—and, equally, what may have been wrecked in an effort to suppress the story?

Even during World War II, Franklin Roosevelt conceived the idea of the Marshall Plan to rebuild war-torn Europe, *even enemy countries*. FDR thought that the endless cycle of European wars might be stopped if Germany and Austria were assisted to rebuild their cities and economies along with allied nations. This notion was, of course, quite contrary to the European practice of trampling and raping a defeated country. FDR sent Bernard Baruch abroad to sell this novel idea, but it met with just as much ridicule as FDR had experienced from his own eastern establishment in the Dirty Thirties. One British Peer, an industrialist, was particularly scornful of the Marshall Plan at a high-level dinner-meeting in London. As Baruch tells it:

> One gentleman decided to amuse the company by asking me the riddle—why were Roosevelt and Columbus alike? His answer was that, like Columbus, Roosevelt did not know where he was going or where he was when he got there, or where he had been when he got back.
>
> Rising, I replied, "Perhaps it is true that Roosevelt and Columbus were alike, since both explored new frontiers and new horizons and both brought a new world into existence to redress the troubles of the Old World." Churchill banged the table in approval, crying "Hear, hear!"[15]

Although Franklin Roosevelt died before the 1945 defeat of Nazi Germany, his successor, Harry Truman, carried on with FDR's policies, including the Marshall Plan. Truman also retained FDR's personal negotiators, Bernard Baruch and Frank Lloyd Wright, who went to Geneva to thrash out the details. There, according to an article in the French magazine *Le Charivari*, they met with a most remarkable man whom we have met before: Pierre Plantard de Saint-Clair, leader of the Order of Sion.[16] This Order had been created by Godfroi de Bouillon when he was *de facto* King of Jerusalem in 1100 A.D., and surfaced again under Plantard's leadership in 1956. Plantard de Saint-Claire had been a French Resistance hero, had been publisher of the Resistance journal *Vaincre* ("Vanquish") and had been tortured by the Gestapo. According to *Le Charivari* Pierre Plantard de Saint-Clair's lineage reached back to the 12th-century Provençal civilization and he embodied both the secret bloodline of the "Ardently Sprouting plant" and that of the noble Saint-Clairs. The magazine described him as "one from whom the great of this world take counsel." And there is no doubt that French President Charles de Gaulle called upon Pierre Plantard de Saint-Clair to calm the French people in a series of broadcasts during the Algerian crisis of 1958.[17] Who is this Pierre Plantard de Saint-Clair? Few apparently know who he is, but it seems obvious that he still has some sort of connection with the Holy Grail. . .

I brushed against the same mysterious Grail Complex by accident. During the 1960s I worked with T.C. "Tommy" Douglas, leader of Canada's New Democratic Party. Although Tommy Douglas's name is a household word in Canada, he is probably unknown to most Americans, so I should describe his career very briefly. He was sort of Canadian version of Franklin Delano Roosevelt and came to prominence at about the same time, the Depression and Canada's "Dustbowl Tragedy." Unlike Roosevelt, though, Douglas actually came from the west because his Scottish family had emigrated to the Canadian province of Manitoba. And, unlike Roosevelt, Douglas was forced to form his own political party called (first) the Co-operative Commonwealth Foundation, or CCF, and later called the New Democratic Party, or NDP, which still exists. This party was led by Christian ministers, not Marxists, seeking a world of simple, genuine Christian ideals. It attracted prairie farmers and urban unemployed during the Depression. Douglas adopted, or copied, many programs of the New Deal and was feared and ridiculed by Canada's own eastern establishment. Douglas's

party came out of the west, straight out of "frontier virtue" values
and it proved immediately popular. It was popular enough to scare
the two Canadian traditional parties the Liberals and the Conservatives, all through the 1930s and 1940s although it actually came to
power only in western provinces. Now, however, it is a national
party represented in all Canadian provinces. Liberal and Conservative governments survived only by "borrowing" NDP programs
which Douglas had "borrowed" from the New Deal. This is why,
although Douglas never came to power as a "President" in Canada
(i.e. a "Prime Minister"), the country nevertheless kept pace with
U.S. economic recovery and war-readiness, given its much smaller
population and much larger land area.

In her biography of T.C. Douglas, author Doris French Shackleton tells us that Tommy's Scottish father had long been a Freemason
and that Tommy decided to join the junior order of the Masons, the
Order of Jacques de Molay. In a ceremony, Tommy Douglas took the
part of Jacques de Molay. As Doris French Shackleton tells it:

> The play concerned the life and death of the patron of the junior
> order, Jacques De Molay, the fourteenth century knight-at-
> arms who led expeditions against the Saracens and was put to
> death as a heretic by Philip the Fair of France. Tommy took the
> title role and threw himself into the part.
>
> "My father was there and he was sparing in praise as in most
> things. When we came out he said 'Let's walk' which we did, for
> a distance of about four miles. I knew he had been deeply
> moved. We walked in silence. Going up the front steps he
> tapped me on the shoulder and said, 'you did no bad'."
>
> Douglas is reluctant to talk about experiencing a "call," he is
> more apt to joke about impromptu prayers at De Molay meet-
> ings.[18]

This was just not a "play" to entertain Masonic dads. It was a
ceremony in which Tommy Douglas at age 17 pledged to *become*
Jacques de Molay. This compelled him to become a minister in the
drought-blasted province of Saskatchewan, compelled him to help
form a new political party to alleviate Canada's Great Depression
with a Canadian version of FDR's New Deal and later, I think,

helped him to tolerate the Marxists who climbed on his bandwagon. Millions of Canadians came to love him even if they didn't vote for him. A political critic, Jack Scott of the *Vancouver Sun*, wrote:

> To call him a politician, as you'd call Bennett or Diefenbaker a politician, is to insult him. He was and is a dreamer and a humanitarian, incorruptible, genuine and intellectually honest. . . He's a good deed in a naughty world.[19]

Tommy Douglas died in 1986, and I spoke briefly with him during his last illness. He confirmed that the Order of Jacques de Molay was the most formative aspect of his political life. Naturally, he never openly admitted this while he was an active politician, but only "joked" about impromptu prayers at de Molay meetings. The reason that he dared not admit to the Order's importance in his life is that most modern people could not have understood the truth: *Tommy Douglas had sworn to preserve, protect and represent the Holy Grail.*

Tommy's favorite campaign song baffled the Marxists in his entourage. It was a British Labour Party hymn that had been adapted from Blake's poem "Jerusalem." Tommy changed the lyrics for Canadian application. And, at whistlestops on the prairies and even at urban fund-raising barbecues in cities like Toronto, he would sing out and lead his supporters with these words:

> I shall not cease from mental fight,
> Nor shall my sword sleep in my hand,
> Till we have built Jerusalem
> In this our green and pleasant land.[20]

Separated from Christopher Columbus by five hundred years in time, and by thousands of miles in distance, but part of the same ongoing conspiracy, Tommy Douglas would echo the obsession of Columbus. Jerusalem was not a specific place to be taken by force, it is an ideal to be achieved with compassion. A society of individual freedoms tempered with individual responsibility. The crusade goes on.

Columbus seems to have been part of an ancient conspiracy whose long-term goal is the progress and humanization of humanity. Although his key to the barrier of the Ocean Sea was snatched from Columbus's hand so that his New Jerusalem perished in the flames of the Inquisition five hundred years ago, it was but a temporary defeat in the continuing conflict. His great contribution was, and is, that his key has taken the conspiracy's momentous secret struggle to every shore washed by the Ocean Sea. The contest is not against any specific Church. It is essentially only against ignorance and intolerance. If the chance for a New Jerusalem perished in Columbus's time in the tropical New World that he discovered, it did not quite perish in other places. Because of his key to the barrier of the Ocean Sea, it is possible that seeds of New Jerusalem, already planted all over the earth, may one day embrace the whole world.

Epilogue

If there was a conspiracy to create a New Jerusalem in the New World, and if Columbus was an operative in this noble cause, then we must judge that both he and the conspiracy of the Holy Grail failed in Latin America. It had been a magnificent attempt, a momentous gamble, but the forces ranged against the conspiracy's limited resources were too powerful. Within half a century or so, Spain and the Church began to regain control of Latin America. The Inquisition was established; Jews and heretics fled, converted or died at the stake.

Was there a conspiracy? Is there a conspiracy that is still going on? Is this conspiracy and its long-term human goals known to living people now?

Aside from the evidence that has already been offered in the previous pages which, I think, argues forcefully for the existence of a secret conspiracy dedicated to human development under the aegis of the Holy Blood, we must consider additional evidence that does not directly relate to Columbus but does relate to later events in the Americas.

First, in Latin America itself, the conspiracy apparently did what it could to strike back at Spanish and Roman Catholic domination and inhumanity. Bold captains like Frobisher, Hawkins—but above all Francis Drake, "The Dragon"—attacked Spanish settlements in the Caribbean and preyed upon the convoys of galleons carrying plundered riches of America back to Spain. There can be no doubt that these earliest "pirates" were not mere robbers and cutthroats, but operated with chivalry for some noble cause. Yes, they were remarkable fighting men, and they sank many Spanish ships. And yes, the gold they carried back to England was welcome, but

Hawkins and Drake also always extended quarter to a battered Spanish vessel. They became as famous for their chivalry as for their apparent invincibility. No woman was ever raped by Drake or his crew, for instance, although not a few Spanish ladies attempted to seduce Drake. When Drake advanced on Portobello in Panama, the garrison of Spanish officers and men fled . . . but many of their wives remained behind to meet "The Dragon" in person. It is recorded that Drake and his officers treated the highest-ranking ladies of Portobello to a sumptuous feast in the captured town.[1] None of the women ever complained of ill-treatment, to say no more.

There can also be no doubt that theirs was a Cathar-like religious perspective among these earliest pirates. They abhorred the symbol of the Crucifix, as the Cathars had rejected it, as an appropriate focus for worship of Jesus. In his journal Drake described a captured jewel-encrusted Crucifix as "a depiction of a god nailed upon a cross,"[2] and regarded it as a primitive idol.

Another group of pirates, about a century after the generation of the Armada, retained the same chivalrous outlook while preying upon Portuguese shipping in the Indian Ocean, Portugal by that time having accepted the Inquisition within its borders under pressure from now-powerful Spain. These pirates, a mixture of French, English and American colonials, established the remarkable republic of Libertatia on the island of Madagascar. More than a century ahead of their time, these pirates outlawed all forms of slavery and instituted democracy in one of the most astonishing and little-known episodes of history. In addition to relieving Portuguese and Mogul ships of their gold and jewels and spices, they attacked slavers and freed their victims—and by this action earned the enmity of "official" France, England, Holland and the vested financial interests of these countries. Libertatia was finally wiped out by a combined French, English and Dutch fleet under pressure of slaver lobbying in these countries.[3]

It appears certain that some Libertatia pirates were associated with the Holy Grail complex because one such pirate, just before he was hanged on the Indian Ocean island of Réunion, threw a coded message into the crowd. This message was preserved and has recently been deciphered by a Russian expert. It said that the real treasure of Libertatia resided in Nova Scotia! Was this a reference to Henry Saint-Clair's castle settlement? Is it possible that Libertatia was another attempt to create another religious and political haven? Unfortunately, not enough documentation survives about the remarkable republic of Libertatia to offer a definitive answer to these questions. History is merely confronted with the anomalous fact that a few freebooters and pirates developed a social and political system more progressive than anything that then existed in Europe.

After the capture of a slave ship off the coast of West Africa in 1699, one of the Libertatia pirates, Captain Mission, a renegade priest, gave this speech to his crew before freeing the slaves:

> The trading for men can never be agreeable to the eyes of divine justice. No man has the power of the liberty of another, and while those who profess a more enlightened knowledge of the Deity sold men like beasts, they proved that their religion was no more than grimace. . .I have not exempted my own men from the galling yoke of slavery and asserted my own liberty, to enslave others. Although these men are distinguished from Europeans by their color, customs or religious rites, they are the work of the same Omnipotent Being and imbued with equal reason. Wherefore I desire that they be treated like free men— for I would banish even the name of slavery from among them. [4]

As Hamilton Cochrane, author of *Freebooters of the Red Sea*, comments:

> It is indeed noteworthy that such antislavery sentiments, including the idea of equality, were voiced by a humane pirate 150 years before Abraham Lincoln declared that all men were created free and equal. [5]

Of course, after these very first 16th-century "pirates", who seem to have been the Holy Grail's navy, the quality of piracy declined as common riff-raff and vicious psychopaths took up the practice: L'Ollonais, Edward Teach, William Kidd.

In addition to sending a handful of anomalously chivalrous pirates against the might of Spain and Portugal, and against slavers of all nations; and in addition to possibly establishing the anomalously progressive brief settlement of Libertatia, the Grail Conspiracy apparently concentrated on securing the religious haven that it did have in Nova Scotia. This was the mid-peninsular castle settlement that, according to *The Zeno Narrative*, had been founded by Henry Sinclair of 1398.

As explained previously, the Treaty of Tordesillas of 1494 effectively prevented the Spanish Inquisition from encroaching on this secret refuge in Portuguese territory.

However, by about 1590 or so, even this Nova Scotian haven began to be less secure. First, the Inquisition had by that time been established in Portugal and might eventually ferret out the secret of the Nova Scotia haven because a considerable number of Portuguese nobility and common mariners must have known of it. Second, the ordinary colonial expansion of European nation-states threatened the Holy Blood's refuge. France, Britain and Holland were considering colonies in North America, in the "Portuguese" possessions that Portugal did not assert. True, many of the early colonists would likely be Protestants seeking religious freedom themselves, but this did not necessarily mean that such Protestants would be any more tolerant of the Grail secret than the Vatican. Protestantism had evolved far from its Cathar origins, and had forgotten its origins. By the very nature of human institutions, and also probably because of hideous experiences in the religious wars that were ravaging Europe, Protestants had become, very frequently, just as intolerant and bigoted as Roman Catholics.

Nova Scotia, being almost a peninsula surrounded by the Atlantic Ocean, was extremely vulnerable to attack by almost anyone. According to *The Holy Blood and The Holy Grail*, the Grail Conspiracy resolved to create a new haven within the heart of French society, a kind of institutionalized haven disguised as a new religious Order. This was the Order of Saint-Sulpice, founded by Jean-Jacques Olier. It is interesting to note that this Saint-Sulpice, in whose honor the new Order was named, was a 6th-century *British* hermit who, according to a number of troubadour-composed Grail Romances, gave Galahad advice about how to find the Grail.[6] This is as far as the authors of *The Holy Blood and the Holy Grail* went: they presented evidence arguing that the Grail Conspiracy determined to create this sort of institutionalized refuge disguised as an orthodox Order within French society.

In *Holy Grail Across The Atlantic* I argued that the Grail Conspiracy went one step further. It founded a new refuge to replace the increasingly threatened Nova Scotia one, and it was not solely "institutional" although the Seminary of Saint-Sulpice protected it, but a new settlement buried in the heart of New France—Montreal. The authors of *The Holy Blood and the Holy Grail* either ignored the fact, or were ignorant of it, that Jean-Jacques Olier was one of several people who were instrumental in planning and planting the Montreal colony and that the Seminary of Saint-Sulpice orchestrated all the fund-raising and personnel-recruitment for Montreal.

It would take some time to establish a new refuge, however, and in the meantime ordinary explorers and would-be colonists had to be led away from the vulnerable Nova Scotian one. In *Holy Grail Across The Atlantic*, I presented evidence that Samuel de Champlain was apparently the prime operative assigned to this "disinformation" mission. Just like Columbus, we do not know who Samuel Champlain was. His youth and family background are utterly unknown. Then, as with Columbus, his name may have been an alias for someone else. Florian de la Horbe in his book, *The Incredible Secret of Champlain*, presents evidence that the man history knows as Champlain was actually Guy Eder de la Fontanelle, a pirate. In order to gain credence as an explorer so that he could become New France's official explorer and map-maker, Champlain went on a voyage to New Spain in 1599 and wrote a comprehensive account of it along with maps and illustrations that would later serve as a kind of personal presentation to Henry IV, King of France. It is strange that Champlain, who is thought to have been a Protestant according to some historians, was able to get a place in a Spanish expedition to the New World, but he did. He had help from the commander of the expedition "a nobleman named Don Fransisco Coloma, a knight of Malta," as Champlain described him. Is it only coincidence that Coloma is the Spanish analog for "Dove"? Only coincidence that the Knights of Malta (i.e. the Knights of St. John of Jerusalem) were founded by Baudoin de Bouillon at the same time that he founded the Knights Templar? Champlain wrote in his journal:

> . . . we sought out General Coloma, to know if it would suit him that I should make the voyage. This he freely granted me, with evidence of being well pleased thereat, promising me his favour, which he has not since denied me upon occasion.[7]

Thus did Champlain gain a place in the expedition that made his name as an explorer. King Henry IV of France hired him, in 1603, to explore and map New France, a job that required about 13 years.

Champlain explored New England's coast, and sent Etienne Brulé as far south as Chesapeake Bay and as far west as Lake Erie. Champlain explored Nova Scotia and New Brunswick, the St. Lawrence and parts of Ontario. I demonstrate in *Holy Grail Across The Atlantic* that many of Champlain's maps and descriptions are *purposefully inaccurate* where the region of Sinclair's haven in Nova Scotia is concerned. Champlain was able to play a double game: on the one hand, he was supposedly mapping and exploring for potential colonists, but on the other he provided inaccurate maps and descriptions. He eventually became governor of New France and was able to hinder colonization so that only 18 colonists came to Canada in the 20 years of his rule.

Anomalous facts swirl around Champlain as thickly as around Columbus. Although supposedly "an ardent Catholic," according to Canada's conventional historians, his life-long friend and business associate was the Sieur de Monts, a Protestant or Huguenot. Champlain was behind the scheme to cede Canada to the Knights of Malta, while de Monts may have been the son of Pietro del Monte, Grand Master of the Knights of Malta from 1568 to 1572. In any event, Champlain's friend, the Sieur de Monts, was able to buy the Castle of Ardennes as a retirement home although he was frequently bankrupt. This castle had belonged to the Templars, had been later turned over to the Knights of Malta, and there de Monts died in 1628.

Around the year 1635 during the last days of Champlain's term as governor:

> . . . in Paris the Hundred Associates, under the guidance of Cardinal Richelieu, were meeting to choose a new governor. The reason is not clear—whether Champlain was regarded merely as too old, whether his policy had crossed that of the cardinal, or whether some intrigue was at work. There was indeed a plan afoot to turn Canada over to the Knights of Malta; and for all we know Champlain may have approved the project. . .[8]

As with Columbus, we cannot avoid the fact that Champlain, too, had curious and tenuous connections with "Doves," Knights of Malta and a complex of inter-related personalities and organizations that lead back, eventually, to the Kingdom of Jerusalem. His covert role seems to have been to delay colonization of New France, and especially of Nova Scotia, until Montreal could be established under the protection of the Saint-Sulpicians. As Florian de la Horbe observed:

> . . . Champlain always pretended that he wanted to establish a French population in Canada and to double trade by agriculture. But there is an absolute contradiction between the efforts that he made in this design . . . and the results.[9]

Montreal was eventually established in 1642 and was called Ville Marie, the "City of Mary" and it was officially dedicated to the "Holy Family." The inhabitants of Sinclair's haven were transferred to Montreal immediately and placed under the care of Jeanne Mance, "the angel of the colonies," or so I conjectured from the evidence in *Holy Grail Across The Atlantic*. Another group came in 1653, and the Nova Scotian haven, which had served its purpose since 1398, was destroyed in 1654 to become the ruins visible today.

The Seminary of Saint-Sulpice spread out from Montreal and founded priories in major cities of the American colonies: Boston, New York and Philadelphia. This may be of significance. We will recall that the Sinclairs were the hereditary heads of Scottish Freemasonry, a "neo-Templar" order that was established at Rosslyn after surviving Templar knights fled there. It seems at least possible that Freemasonry came into the American colonies with the assistance of the Seminary of Saint-Sulpice which, after all, protected the secret inhabitants of Henry Sinclair's Nova Scotia settlement.

Freemasonry played a crucial part in the American Revolution, and, although no surviving document asserts it, it is possible if not probable that American patriots met secretly in priories of the Saint-Sulpician Order. Certainly, the last place that British authorities would search for Masonic revolutionaries would be within the walls of a supposedly orthodox Roman Catholic religious order! But there is much evidence that the Saint-Sulpicians were not so orthodox and, in fact, represented the Holy Grail complex and the Knights of Malta and Knights Templar that de Bouillon's dynasty established long before.

Is it mere coincidence that George Washington and the next three presidents of the United States were Masons? Coincidence that *all* of

the generals in America's Continental Army were Masons? Coincidence that fifteen hundred other officers beneath the rank of general
were also Masons? Coincidence that the city of Washington, D.C.,
was designed by a Mason, as was the Washington Monument? Is it
mere coincidence that the Washington Monument was opened with
Masonic ceremonies?[10]

No, there can be no reasonable doubt that there was, has been
and is, a conspiracy dedicated to the preservation of the Holy Grail
and, at the same time, dedicated to the evolution of social progress.
Indeed, in the West, it might not be too much of an exaggeration to
say that most social progress has been molded by the Holy Grail and
its operatives. This seems to have been true from the time of Jesus
himself, to the days of King Arthur, to the ill-fated Kingdom of
Jerusalem of the de Bouillons, to the time of Christopher Columbus
and his betrayed New Jerusalem, to the time of the anomalous
pirates who struck back at slavery and religious intolerance, to the
time of Champlain and the dedication of Montreal to the "Holy
Family," to the time of George Washington and the American
Revolution to establish "A New Order of the Ages" (the message on
the Great Seal of the United States). The secret conspiracy to
promote compassion and social progress extends up to the time of
Franklin Delano Roosevelt who was involved in "salvaging and
wrecking" a site connected with Henry Sinclair's Nova Scotian
haven, and whose two special representatives, Bernard Baruch and
Frank Lloyd Wright, were anything but mainstream personalities. It
extends to the last days of Tommy Douglas, who died in 1986, and
who was inspired by the Jacques de Molay junior order of the
Freemasons. The conspiracy must still exist today because we know
that the leader of the Order of Sion since 1956, Pierre Plantard de
Saint-Clair, is alive and well and living in Paris.

In our time the word "conspiracy" has acquired evil and deroga-
tory connotations, but these negative accretions are the result of
modern usage and contemporary political corruption. A conspiracy
need not have anti-social or criminal purposes or motivations. A
conspiracy can equally be a more or less clandestine group of men
and women dedicated to positive and progressive social ideals, and
the conspiracy of the Holy Grail seems always to have been precisely
this. A conspiracy can be highly organized, but it need not be so.

With respect to the Holy Grail conspiracy, it seems to be rather highly organized at the very top levels, but much more informal at lower levels. The actual leaders of it may be "card carrying" members who know each other and have strict security procedures, but many of the conspiracy's most efficient operatives seem merely to have been exceptional men and women to whom a unique perspective of human development and purpose was presented. It was a perspective that made sense to them, that held out the hope of a better world, and they committed their lives to it. It seems to have been a view that cut across major religious dogmas of all sorts, and that cut across political and social dogmas and stagnation of all sorts. We have seen that the Cathar philosophy of Provence was able to attract Jews, Christians and Moslems and inspire them with a deep faith, a sense of purpose and also with great courage. Pirates like Captain Mission were inspired by a vision of humanity that transcended the bigotry, politics and economics of his own time. Both Franklin Delano Roosevelt and Tommy Douglas disregarded the socio-political labels of their time, labels which were actually meaningless and irrelevant but which were used to polarize people who found it easier to react than to think, and borrowed economic principles from both "communal" and "capitalist" economic philosophy. Only a marriage of both economic philosophies could solve North America's Great Depression, and neither FDR nor Douglas hesitated to perform the rites. Both were distrusted by the Far Left and the Far Right with equal passion. But, in each case, their unfettered, undogmatic and unorthodox meld of economic and social measures worked to ensure greater human compassion and greater human productivity and social commitment.

There's a conspiracy, or seems to be, built around the secret of the Holy Grail and it has been responsible for much of our progress. But only at the highest level is it a super-organized card-carrying affair. Anyone can join this conspiracy who has succeeded in freeing himself or herself from the religious, political and social dogmas and labels which act to separate people and put them in conflict.

In *The Columbus Conspiracy*, which necessarily takes place in the medieval period on the very threshold of the Renaissance, the Roman Catholic Church has been presented as the prime enemy of the Holy Grail complex and the prime enemy of humanism in

Europe. I have made no attempt to duck this issue, because the medieval Church *was* all that and more. It has been estimated that its Inquisition wiped out from three to six million people between 1209 and 1750—and all in the name of the love of God. The medieval Church's intolerance, pomp, wealth, cruelty and dogma were a travesty of the teachings of that gentle Rabbi-carpenter from Nazareth. That is a fact, and it must be faced.

But the Roman Catholic Church was not the first enemy of the Holy Grail's conspiracy to enhance the knowledge, dignity and freedom of humanity. During the lifetime of Jesus, the corruption of Rome and the jealousy of the Pharisees were the enemy.

So, in fairness, it must be noted that even during the medieval period and the Renaissance many supposedly "orthodox" Roman Catholics aided the Grail Conspiracy covertly. Naturally, only a few names have surfaced for historians because these operatives, above all, played a dangerous game. Saint Bernard seems to have been a convert to Catharism, and there is evidence that Saint Francis was as well. Father Lallemant, a Jesuit, was entrusted with assessing the personnel recruited for Montreal—and he worked for highly unorthodox Jean-Jacques Olier on behalf of highly unorthodox operatives and heretic refugees. Captain Mission of Libertatia had formerly been a priest, but then took to piracy and freeing slaves in the 1690s. There were doubtless many more who dared not let even a whisper of their names inform the ear of history.

And today? What are the enemies of the Grail Conspiracy? Capitalism? Communism? Protestantism? The Vatican still?

All and none. These philosophies, religions and organizations are composed of *people*. People can be surprising. Although most people may be wholly committed to the narrow orthodox view of their country, political philosophy, religion or corruption because of successful propaganda, there are always some who may profess to tow the line but who secretly cherish a larger perspective of human life and purpose. Some of these few people, in turn, might find themselves secretly assisting the conspiracy. Or, at the least, they might not betray it. *Among people* the conspiracy of the Holy Grail has only ever had two enemies.

Ignorance and intolerance.

Notes

Chapter One
Landfall

1. Morison, Samuel E., *Admiral of the Ocean Sea*, Vol. 1, Boston: Little, Brown & Co., 1942, p. 23.
2. Ibid.
3. Las Cases, Bartholme de, *Historia de las indias*, Vol. 1, Mexico City: Fondo de Cultura Economico, 1951, p. 123.

Chapter Two
Key to Discovery, Key of Bondage

1. But quoted here as the extract appears in Barry Fell's *America B.C.*, New York: New York Times Book Company, 1976, p. 239.
2. Fell, *America B.C.*, p. 240.
3. But quoted here from Arthur Poznanski's *Precursores de Colón, Las Perlas Agri Nosotros*, 1933, p. 322. Seneca also predicted in his book (usually translated as his "Natural History") that someday a mariner would discover land further from Europe than Thule, and this was a favorite quotation of Columbus's—see Frederick Pohl's *The Lost Discovery*, New York: W.W. Norton & Co. Inc., 1952, p. 231
4. Heyerdahl, Thor, *The Ra Expedition*, New York: Doubleday, 1971, pp. 77–79 for a discussion of the Lixus ruins.
5. Hermann, Paul, *Conquest By Man*, New York: Harper & Brothers, 1954, pp. 82–83.
6. Ramos, Bernardo, *Inscripcões e Tradicões da America prehistoria*, Rio de Janeiro, 1932.
7. Private correspondence.

8. Severin, Tim, *The Brendan Voyage*, London: Hutchinson, 1978. Severin's replica leather-hulled (over an ash frame) medieval Irish curragh succeeded in crossing the Atlantic from Ireland to Newfoundland in two sailing seasons with a stop in Iceland. Traditions of medieval Irish seafaring on the Atlantic are compiled in the *Navigatio Sancti Brandani Abbatis* (roughly "voyages of Saint Brendan, Abbot") a book written in the 10th or 11th century but thought to refer to voyages of the 6th century.

9. Basil Davidson almost singlehandedly brought lost African cultures to popular knowledge in a series of books including *The Lost Cities of Africa* (Boston: Little, Brown, 1959), *The African Genius* (Boston: Little, Brown, 1969) and *A History of West Africa* (Garden City: Doubleday, 1963) which are the sources for this discussion.

10. From Ibn Battuta's *Travels in Asia and Africa* originally published in Morocco in 1356 and translated into English by H.A.R. Gibb in 1929 and quoted here from Davidson's *Lost Cities*, p. 79.

11. Davidson, *Lost Cities*, pp. 79–80.

12. al-Omari, Ibn Fadl Allah, *Masalik al Absar fi Mamalik al Absar*, Cairo circa 1342; (French translation, Paris: Gaudefroi-Demembynes, 1927); English translation quoted here by Davidson, *Lost Cities*, pp. 74–75.

13. Wittmack, *Die Nutzpflantzen der Alter Peruaner*, Berlin: 1932, p. 340; and also A Rochebrun's *Recherches d'ethnographie botanique su les flore des sépultures peruviennes d'Ancon*, pp. 346 and 348.

14. From Fernando Colón's *The Life of Colón*, London: 1981, but quoted here from Frederick Pohl's *The Lost Discovery*, p. 250.

15. Pohl, *The Lost Discovery*, p. 251.

16. Hermann, *Conquest By Man*, p. 290.

17. Hermann, *Conquest By Man*, pp. 112–124 and also pp. 136–7 concerning debate about a searoute around Africa. The belief that Africa curved away toward the east and approached Indonesia is "supported" not only by the existence of crocodiles in both the Nile and Indus rivers, but by a very curious circumstance that has puzzled and disturbed modern scholars. The large island of Madagascar off the east coast of Africa *is* populated by Malays from Indonesia and not by Africans, yet there is no historical record of what must have been a large migration across the Indian Ocean by these Malays—see Eberhard Stechow's famous paper *Wann kamen die Malaien zuerst nach Madagaskar?* (roughly "When Did The Malayans First Come to Madagascar?") as printed in *Forschungen und Fortschritte*, Nr (o). 18, Berlin, 1944. Stechow wrote another paper on the same subject: *"Kannte des*

Altertum die Insel Madagaskar?" (roughly "Can we know Madagascar's Ancient History?") *Petermanns Geographische Mitteilungen*, Gotha, 1944. The curious geographic fact is that the Persian Gulf and the Red Sea look as if they were once river valleys that were suddenly widened by some cataclysmic event, perhaps the same event that formed Africa's "Rift Valley," which is a huge scar in the earth's crust. Now, if the Persian Gulf and Red Sea were mentally "closed up" to the proportions of rivers, then Africa's southern portions *would* extend across the Indian Ocean and almost meet Indonesia. The Malays now in Madagascar could have gotten there by a relatively short ocean voyage, or perhaps by island-hopping on land masses that disappeared in the cataclysm. Yet, the cataclysm that opened the Persian Gulf and the Red Sea, and which placed Africa in its present position, must have happened more than a million years ago (it is thought). Were modern people in existence then? Could such a memory have been preserved for so long? It is certain that something more than the coincidence of crocodiles in the Nile and Indus sustained the ancient belief that Africa once (and might still in the medieval period) curve toward Indonesia.

18. This chart is mentioned in Davidson's *Lost Cities*, p. 178.
19. Levi-Strauss, Claude, *Tristes Tropiques*, New York: Atheneum, 1974, p. 109.
20. Montagu, Ashley, *Man's Most Dangerous Myth: The Fallacy of Race*, New York: Oxford University Press, 1974, p. 96.
21. Ibid.
22. Davidson, *A History of West Africa*, p. 232.
23. Bacon, R.H., *Benin, The City of Blood*, London: 1887, p. 46, but quoted here from Davidson's *Lost Cities*, p. 134.
24. Davidson, *Lost Cities*, p. 198.
25. It is interesting that the first Mendaña expedition *followed Inca sailing directions* in an attempt to reach the Polynesian Islands but made a navigational error and thus passed too far away from the Tuamotu group to sight these low-lying islands. Mendaña later "discovered" the Kiroshiwo Current and a route from the Philippines to Mexico. See Thor Heyerdahl's *American Indians in the Pacific*, London: George Allen and Unwin, 1952, for a full discussion of these voyages, pp. 480–493.
26. Severin, Tim, *The Sindbad Voyage*, London: Hutchinson, 1982. The account of a voyage from Oman to Canton, China, aboard a replica medieval Arabic "boom." The sailing qualities of the replica ship, *Sohar*, are fully described in this fascinating book.
27. Some experts made it 92 crewmen. See *The Log of Christopher Columbus*, trans. Robert H. Fuson, Camden (Maine): International Marine Publishing Company, 1987, "Appendix C", pp. 223–228.

Chapter Three
Blood Royal

1. It seems as though this story will finally be told. Niven Sinclair of Timon Films, London, plans to produce a television mini-series about the Saint Clair saga. This presentation will focus on the little-known story of "Prince" Henry Sinclair's voyage to Nova Scotia in A.D. 1398 almost one hundred years before Columbus's voyage, and Prince Henry's establishment of a settlement in the New World. Aside from Niven and Andrew Sinclair's original research, the television and book presentation is also based on: *Holy Blood, Holy Grail* by Michael Baigent, Richard Leigh and Henry Lincoln (London: Jonathan Cape, 1982) and these authors' sequel, *The Temple and the Lodge*; *Prince Henry Sinclair* by Frederick Pohl (New York: Clarkson N. Potter, 1974); and my own *Holy Grail Across The Atlantic* (Toronto: Hounslow Press, 1988). It is to be hoped that the televised presentation and book, of *A Sword on a Stone* will redress a 600-year injustice in the understanding of European discoveries. All of the evidence indisputably places "Prince" Henry Sinclair (1345–1400?) in the very first rank of European transatlantic discoverers and explorers, with achievements that rivalled, or surpassed, those of Christopher Columbus. Indeed, as the argument of *The Columbus Conspiracy* unfolds, and if it is valid, Henry Sinclair must objectively be judged to have "surpassed" Columbus in that he successfully established a refuge for "Templar-related" religious heretics when Columbus failed to do so. It is most fitting that this television and book presentation will be made by two members of the Sinclair clan, since the concealed history is that of their own lineage.
2. Baigent et al., *Holy Blood, Holy Grail*, pp. 110–113.
3. Baigent et al., *Holy Blood, Holy Grail*, pp. 79–94.
4. Baigent et al., *Holy Blood, Holy Grail*, pp. 174–177.
5. Baigent et al., *Holy Blood, Holy Grail*, pp. 35–57.
6. Ibid.
7. Hermann, *Conquest by Man*, pp. 67–70.
8. See Edward Burman's *The Templars, Knights of God*, London: Thorson's Publishing Group, 1986; also Malcolm Barber's *Origins of the Knights of the Temple, Studia Monastica*, XII, 1970, pp. 219–240; and Baigent et al., *Holy Blood, Holy Grail*, pp. 35–57.
9. Lubicz, R.A. Schwaller de, *The Temple In Man*, Brookline (Mass.): Autumn Press, 1977, pp. 35–37, discusses the idea that Solomon's temple, known to have been constructed with the help of imported Egyptian masons, incorporated the Ancient Egyptian canon of sacred architecture—which was, apparently, the stylized proportions of a woman giving birth so that worshippers could pass through her pubis and thus be "reborn." When European Gothic cathedrals were built

during the time of Templar power, all of them reflected (more or less) the sacred architecture of the Temple of Solomon, which went directly back to Egyptian prototypes such as the Temple of Dendera. So, all who passed out of Gothic cathedrals after Mass were symbolically "reborn." Therefore, all Gothic cathedrals accommodated many thousands of "rebirths," and they were all dedicated to "Our Lady," Mary, presumably the mother of Jesus. Yet, strictly speaking, the Virgin Mary experienced but *one* birth, and that by Divine Conception. Mary Magdalene/Bethany (they seem to have been the same person), *if she was the wife of Jesus*, may have had more than one child and thus be a better candidate for being the "Our Lady" of the Cathar-Templar-inspired cathedrals. That is possibly what the so-called Templar-Cathar "heresy" may have been trying to convey (secretly) to those with the wit to understand. Yet, there's an even deeper level here.

"Mary" means "of the sea"—so, did this originally Ancient Egyptian "blueprint" for sacred architecture preserve the very old racial memory that human life was "upgraded" or "reborn" *from the sea*? If so, Gothic cathedrals not only resonate with Mary Magdalene/Bethany, *but with much older* Egyptian and Sumerian "myths" of some (female) sea creature who upgraded humanity in most ancient times. One of these "creatures" was the Egyptian goddess Isis, whose oceanic origin is always shown in Ancient Egyptian art by her fish tail. Another fish-tailed deity is the Assyrian *god* (whose sex may have been changed by Indo-European speaking invaders) Dagon, also always shown with a fish tail. The earlier Sumerians, cultural ancestors of the Assyrians *before* the invasion of Indo-European-speaking invaders into Mesopotamia, remember these "sea creatures" as "Oannes" and these creatures were either regarded *as female or as of no sex*. The Dogon tribe of Africa remember the same "sea creatures" who set them on their road toward truly human development, and called them "Nommo". . .*feminine*. Therefore, the "Mary" of Gothic cathedrals may hark back to (1) Mary, the wife of Jesus, and (2) the "of the sea" creature (mostly feminine) who first upgraded humanity.

This *very ancient* "sea mother" antedated the slightly less ancient "earth mother"—and both mothers were much later (2000–1500 B.C.) denigrated by incoming, invading Indo-European language-speakers who had "sky gods" and a patriarchal social structure. The "sea mothers" and "earth mothers" of the ancient Mediterranean and Mesopotamian worlds were either "raped" (displaced from their shrines), forced to become "wives" (like Hera of the Olympian pantheon) or were made "sisters" of more important gods—like Diana/Artemis gradually became regarded as the insignificant "huntress" (and lesbian) sister of the great god Apollo. But, did the Templars and Cathars remember something more ancient, more "real" and more balanced than the prevailing Roman Catholic Church? Was this the reason that women in Provençal culture enjoyed a much higher status than in the rest of 13th-century Europe? Perhaps. I tend to think so and, in my correspondence with the late Joseph Campbell, I think that he realized this too. . . and, I think, we were both initiated into this view by the poetic *intuitions* of Robert Graves, author of *The White Goddess*, London: Faber and Faber, 1948, who really said it all, and long before it became fashionable: our weapons and our destruction of the environment through industrial pollution *are a direct result* of Western humanity's "rape" of the sea/earth "mother" goddess. And, according to Robert Graves, we won't cease from this activity until we let ourselves be once again embraced by the "sea/earth mother."

10. Most modern scholars accept that Wolfram von Eschenbach's "Mun-salvaesch" was "Montségur."

11. See a full discussion of this in *The Quest for Arthur's Britain*, edited by Geoffrey Ashe, London: Granada Publishing Limited, 1968. See also *The White Goddess*, chapter "The Lion With the Steady Hand" (i.e. Llew Llaw Griffes).

12. Angebert, Jean-Marie, *The Occult and the Third Reich*, Toronto: McGraw-Hill, 1975, pp. 66–93.

13. Delno West, armed with a previously unknown and untranslated (supposed) text authored by Christopher Columbus himself, allegedly discovered in Spanish archives, argues that Columbus actually wanted to acquire gold in the New World in order to finance a real, new "Crusade" in the Middle East. As I hint in the text of this book, something of this sort may have been penned by Columbus, but only to flatter the pretensions of Ferdinand and (less certainly) of Isabella. As I suggest in this book, the "newly united Spain" (i.e. the united thrones of Aragon and Castile) were together insufficient to take by force the Moorish outpost of Granada, let alone launch a new Crusade in the Middle East. All of the gold in Europe (and the New World), and all of the available knights/soldiers were unequal to any such task. . . and Columbus would have known this. . . as did everyone else in Europe.

As I make clear in this book, Columbus's goal was a "crusade," but one to establish a "New Jerusalem" in this "New World" and he may well have worded these sentiments in a way acceptable to Ferdinand which would certainly have flattered and (perhaps) confused him as to Columbus's own goals and motivation. It may have bought Columbus some valuable time for the 1502 voyage, which was of extreme legal importance. As of the year 1500 A.D., *no* combination of European powers could have retaken Palestine by force. The "Ottoman Turks" were firmly in the saddle in that year, but themselves were only vassals of an incomparably greater sovereign in Central Asia known to history as "Tamerlane" (i.e. "Timur-i-leng", "The Iron Who Limps"), the Caucasian heir of Genghis Khan's polity by virtue of a momentous victory somewhere in Central Asia. The lord of the Middle East in

Columbus's time was Bayazit II, a hapless vassal of "Tamerlane's", whose grandfather was caged by this central Asian monarch. Europe vaguely knew of "Tamerlane", the awesome power behind the already-formidable power of the Middle East. Henry VIII of England wrote to "Tamerlane" of "Asia" pleading that, if Tamerlane invaded Europe, he would spare Britain! Around the time of Elizabeth I, Marlowe wrote the play "Tamburlane The Great," with a similar entreaty (not necessary, since "Tamerlane" had perished in 1405 near Peking).

The point of all this is that a new crusade was out of the question in Columbus's time as a matter of brutal fact. Europeans could not confront the power of "Bayazit The Great" (see Shakespeare), much less the vague and terrible power behind *him*. Everybody knew all this, and more. It was hoped that this "Tamerlane" might be the "Prester John," a Christian super-power in Central Asia with whom the popes in Rome were trying (without much enthusiasm) to establish contact.

This hope/belief/fear and body of thought grew out of the fact that a few of "Tamerlane's" generals *were* Christian (Nestorian Christians) and this knowledge percolated back to Europe in much-garbled form. And, although some of these generals did possess more military might than all of Europe combined, they were still a religious minority within "Tamerlane's" Caucasian-Mongol-Chinese world view. Tamerlane's real (and imagined) presence terrorized about six generations of Europeans, from roughly 1350 until 1580. The *real* "Tamerlane" was born in Samarkand about A.D. 1336, but he left a long shadow over European thought and affairs, as has been demonstrated. Timur-i-lang's son, Jehangir ("World Gripper") invaded India and started the "Mogul" dynasty there (i.e. Mongol," though he was no more "Mongol" than anyone from London). This was the power that first the French, and then the English, confronted in their 18th-century bid to add India to their world empires.

In short, in Columbus's lifetime there was absolutely no possibility for a successful "crusade" in the Middle East, and everyone of any acumen knew it.

Chapter Four
Echoes of Ancient Truth?

1. Muck, Otto, *Atlantis*, New York: New York Times Book Co., 1978, pp. 148–153. Sometimes entitled *"The Secret of Atlantis"*, this most valuable book on the subject has suffered because (1) its author was probably Nazi and undoubtedly worked on the guided missiles developed at Peenemünde, and (2) after Muck's death in 1956, English-language editors of his work tried to "improve" upon Muck's original arguments with "updated" material. Whatever one wishes to think of

him in political respects, his handling of the "Atlantis" problem has never been equalled *scientifically*. The existence and uniqueness of the Basque language is a factor that Otto Muck deals with more honestly than subsequent scholars who have swept the "Basque problem" under the carpet.

2. Bogin, Meg, *The Women Troubadours*, New York: W.W. Norton, 1976, pp. 22–24 and 35–61 are particularly relevant here, but her whole book is fascinating.
3. Baigent, et al., *Holy Blood, Holy Grail*, p. 23
4. Runciman, Steven A., *A History of the Crusades*, London: Harmondsworth, 1978, p. 88.
5. Shah, Idries, *The Sufis*, New York: Anchor Books, 1971, p. 122.
6. Baigent, et al., *Holy Blood, Holy Grail*, p. 39.
7. Birks and Gilbert, *The Treasure of Montségur*, London: Thorson's Publishing Group, 1987, pp. 113–120.
8. Baigent, et al., *Holy Blood, Holy Grail*, p. 56, quoted from Rougemont's *Love In the Western World*.
9. Such as Pierre Plantard de Saint-Clair and Alan Poher; see *Holy Grail Across The Atlantic*, pp. 339–347.
10. Esty, Katherine, *Gypsies, Wanderers In Time*, London: Victor Gollancz, 1962, p. 124.
11. Hermann, Paul, *Conquest By Man*, pp. 44 (map) and 25–48 traces the ancient Rhone–Rhine route from its first apparent use during the Hallstatt salt trade of circa 2500 B.C., through the Bronze Age trade in amber and bronze (1500 B.C.) right up to Late Roman and Dark Ages times when the route was still in use. "Holy Refugees" from Palestine would certainly have used this well-travelled route if going north and then west from Marseilles, and would probably have stopped for a while at the lower Rhine city of Asciburgium (modern Eschenberg) before crossing to England. Although river-side paths made this route feasible for land traffic, most people would have preferred the established barge services that operated as early as 1000 B.C.
12. Sanderson, Ivan T., "Yesu of the Druids," *Pursuit*, Vol. 6, No. 1, January 1973, pp. 18–19. A discussion of the botany of the Glastonbury Thorn.
13. *The White Goddess* is relevant because it is an attempt to answer the riddle of the "Hanes Taliesin."
14. From Geoffrey of Monmouth's *Historia Regnum Britanniae* ("History of the Kings of Britain"), but quoted here from *The Quest for Arthur's Britain*, Geoffrey Ashe, ed., London: Granada Publishing Limited, 1968, p. 73.
15. Baigent, et al., *Holy Blood, Holy Grail*, pp. 361–364.
16. Bradley, *Holy Grail Across The Atlantic*, pp. 180–181.
17. Baigent, et al., *Holy Blood, Holy Grail*, p. 246 refers to Roger Peyefitte's 1965 work.

18. Baigent, et al., *Holy Blood, Holy Grail*, p. 331–342.
19. Ibid., pp. 222–232.
20. Davis, Charles, in *The London Observer*, March 28, 1971, p. 25.
21. Ibid.
22. Baigent, et al., *Holy Blood, Holy Grail*, pp.304–306.
23. Baigent, et al., *Holy Blood, Holy Grail*, pp. 306–308.
24. "The Holy Koran Exhibition" in Toronto, 1970, included an information pamphlet showing the parallel genealogies of Abraham-Christ/ Abraham-Mohammed springing from Sarah and Hagar respectively.

Chapter Five
Two Columbuses! One Master Mariner

1. Fuson, *The Log of Christopher Columbus*, pp. 13–35 for a full discussion. "Columbus, The Man."
2. Ibid.
3. Granzotto, Gianni, *Christopher Columbus, The Dream and the Obsession*, New York: Doubleday, 1986, pp. 124–129 for a full discussion.
4. Ibid.
5. Eschenbach, Wolfram von, *Parzival*, trans. Helen M. Mustard and Charles E. Passage, New York: Vintage Books edition, 1961, p. 2 of Parzival text.
6. Davidson, *Lost Cities*, pp. 232–241.
7. Heyerdahl, *American Indians in the Pacific*, pp. 133–167 for a full discussion of Japanese and Chinese influences among the Northwest Coast Indians.
8. Severin, *The Sindbad Voyage*. The whole book is relevant here because Severin shows that the "Sindbad the Sailor" tales really amount to a chronicle of all the places visited by medieval Arabic shipping. Also, Severin and Villiers *(Sons of Sindbad)* usefully differentiate the various types of Arab sailing ships of the medieval period—mostly called "dhows" by Western readers. But there were "baggalas," "sambuks," "dhows" and "booms" and many more types that were very different in hull form and rig.
9. I designed a 32-foot "kit" fishing boat (for export to the southwest Caribbean) based on the "stitch-and-glue" method, and this proved to be satisfactory. In 1986–87 I constructed the bow of an expedition barge using the same technology.
10. Heyerdahl, *American Indians in the Pacific*, pp. 480–562 for a very complete account of Andean rafts.
11. Heyerdahl, *American Indians in the Pacific*, pp. 632-856.
12. Dr. David Lewis, particularly, studied Polynesian navigation and replicated some of their methods for sailing around the world in his

catamaran *Rehu Moana* (see *Daughters of the Wind* and *Ice Bird* for some references to this).

13. Clocks capable of keeping time to the second at sea, called "chronometers" to distinguish them from less accurate ordinary clocks, were first made by John Harrison, a Yorkshire carpenter in the mid-1700s. In 1714, the British Admiralty had instituted a prize of £20,000 for the solution to finding longitude at sea and Harrison's chronometers were a response to this incentive. After years of litigation and frustration, Harrison was awarded part of the prize. Four of Harrison's original chronometers still survive in the Greenwich Maritime Museum, restored in 1920 by Commander Rupert T. Gould who also published, in 1923, *The Marine Chronometer* which makes fascinating reading for those truly interested in minutae of nautical history.

14. Fuson, *The Log of Christopher Columbus*, p. 134.
15. Fuson, *The Log of Christopher Columbus*, p. 42.
16. Fuson, *The Log of Christopher Columbus*, p. 44.
17. Fuson, *The Log of Christopher Columbus*, p. 16.
18. Pohl, *The Lost Discovery*, pp. 241–242.
19. Ibid.
20. From Fernando's *Life of Colón*, but quoted here from Pohl's *The Lost Discovery*, p. 234.

Chapter Six
Lapsus Calami

1. Fuson, *The Log of Christopher Columbus*, p. 14.
2. Ibid.
3. But quoted here from Hermann's *Conquest By Man*, pp. 108–111, which gives a very full description of the "Thule problem."
4. Ibid.
5. Granzotto, *Christopher Columbus . . .*, p. 143.
6. Fuson, *The Log of Christopher Columbus*, p. 16.
7. Personal correspondence with Michael Baigent 1988.
8. Tompkins, Peter, *The Romance of Obelisks*, pp. 152–173.
9. Baigent, et al., *Holy Blood, Holy Grail*, pp. 156–158.
10. Baigent, et al., *Holy Blood, Holy Grail*, pp. 51.
11. Hermann, *Conquest By Man*, p. 290.
12. Baigent, et al., *Holy Blood, Holy Grail*, p. 51.
13. Pohl, *Prince Henry Sinclair*, pp. 113–114, quoting from the so-called "Zeno Narrative" published in Venice in 1558.
14. Pohl, *Prince Henry Sinclair*, pp. 156–164.
15. Hapgood, Charles, *Maps of the Ancient Sea-Kings*, Radner: Chilton Books, pp. 12–26 for a full discussion of A.E. Nordenskiöld's work.
16. Hapgood, *Maps of the Ancient Sea Kings*, p. 170.

17. "Has Canadian Archeologist Found Part of Atlantis?", *Toronto Star*, February 18, 1988, p. M4.
18. Hapgood, *Maps of the Ancient Sea-Kings* reproduces some of Stimson's letters in an appendix.
19. I.F. Pigafetta, *Report on the Kingdom of Congo...*, London 1881, p. 137.
20. But quoted here from Pohl's *The Lost Discovery*, pp. 231-232.
21. Granzotto, *Christopher Columbus...*, p. 197.

Chapter Seven
The Portuguese Connection

1. Pohl, *The Lost Discovery*, p. 233.
2. Hermann, *Conquest By Man*, pp. 292–296.
3. Fuson, *The Log of Christopher Columbus*, pp. 195–196.
4. Fuson, *The Log of Christopher Columbus*, p. 194.

Chapter Eight
Capitulations

1. Granzotto, *Christopher Columbus...*, p. 189.
2. She was most probably the sister of Diego de Harana, one of Columbus's financial backers.
3. Fuson, *The Log of Christopher Columbus*, p. 14.
4. Pohl, *The Lost Discovery*, pp. 240–241.
5. Ibid.
6. From Fernando's *Life of Colón*, but quoted here from Pohl's *The Lost Discovery*, pp. 239–240.
7. Ibid.
8. Fuson, *The Log of Christopher Columbus*, page 37.
9. I have not been able to find any actual historical source to explain when, or why this was done, but *all* representations of the *Santa Maria* from 16th-century woodcuts to modern plastic models agree on showing Templar crosses on her mainsail (at least). "Saint Mary", of course, could refer to either the Virgin or the Magdalene, and it may be significant that Columbus bothered to change the name of his flagship from its original name, *La Gallega*.
10. Fuson, *The Log of Christopher Columbus*, p. 228.
11. Estimate from Robin Moore's *The Treasure Hunter*, New York: Doubleday, 1961, p. 29.

Chapter Nine
The Best Laid Plans

1. Fuson, *The Log of Christopher Columbus*, p. 57.
2. Ibid.
3. Ibid.
4. Fuson, *The Log of Christopher Columbus*, p. 61.
5. Fuson, *The Log of Christopher Columbus*, p. 58.
6. Fuson, *The Log of Christopher Columbus*, p. 60.
7. Fuson, *The Log of Christopher Columbus*, p. 61.
8. Fuson, *The Log of Christopher Columbus*, "Appendix B," pages 209–221.
9. Fuson, *The Log of Christopher Columbus*, p. 153.
10. Fuson, *The Log of Christopher Columbus*, p. 167.
11. Fuson, *The Log of Christopher Columbus*, p. 151.
12. Ibid.
13. *Toronto Star*, June 15, 1988, p. M6, "Canadian Researcher Reveals Tales of Columbus's Crew."
14. This "Prester John" may have been a garbled idea of Tamerlane. See note 13 for Chapter three. When Bayazit I was storming Christian Constantinople in 1402, Tamerlane appeared and put an end to the attack, thus saving this Christian city. But Tamerlane's arrival was purely coincidental and his goal was to settle a score with Bayazit, not save Christians.
15. Granzotto, *Christopher Columbus . . .*, p. 289.
16. Las Cases, *Historia*, Vol. 1., p. 188.
17. Granzotto, *Christopher Columbus . . .*, p. 256.
18. Ibid.
19. Granzotto, *Christopher Columbus . . .*, p. 261.
20. Ibid.
21. Colón, Fernando, *Life of Colón*, p. 282.
22. Ibid.
23. Granzotto, *Christopher Columbus . . .*, p. 280.
24. Morison, *Admiral*, p. 223.
25. Granzotto, *Christopher Columbus . . .*, p. 282, but paraphrased from Fernando's *Life of Colón*.

Chapter Ten
The New Jerusalem

1. Rogers, Stan, *Dark and Dashing Horsemen*, New York: Doubleday, 1974, p. 73.
2. Ibid.
3. Ibid.

4. Ibid.
5. Ibid.
6. Ibid.
7. Rogers, *Dark and Dashing Horsemen*, p. 75.
8. Madariaga, Salvador de, *Christopher Columbus*, New York: Unger, 1967, p. 286.
9. Colón, Fernando, *Life of Colón*.
10. Rogers, *Dark and Dashing Horsemen*, p. 79.
11. Rogers, *Dark and Dashing Horsemen*, p. 61.
12. Means, Philip Ainsworth, "Population in the Precolumbian Americas," *History*, Vol 39, No. 3, March 1948, pp. 56–79.
13. Pauwels, who himself was a student of Gurdjieff, asserts that Baruch was also a student (along with Katherine Mansfield) in 1926.
14. O'Connor, D'Arcy, *The Money Pit*, New York: Coward, McCann and Geoghegan, 1976, pp. 229–231.
15. Baruch, Bernard, *My Story*, New York: Pocket Books, 1958, p. 286.
16. Baigent, et al., *Holy Blood, Holy Grail*, p. 194.
17. Ibid.
18. Shackleton, Doris French, *Tommy Douglas*, Toronto: McClelland & Stewart, 1975, pp. 28–30.
19. But quoted here from Shackleton's *Tommy Douglas*, pp. 290–291.
20. Ibid.

Epilogue

1. Ashton, Niven, *Queen's Dragon*, London, 1892, p. 267.
2. Ashton, *Queen's Dragon*, p. 169.
3. Cochran, Hamilton, *Freebooters of the Red Sea*, New York: Bobs-Merrill, 1965, pp. 83–108.
4. Cochran, *Freebooters of the Red Sea*, p. 91.
5. Ibid.
6. Goodrich, Norma Lorre, *King Arthur*, Danbury (Conn.): Franklin Watts, 1986, p. 184.
7. Champlain, Samuel de, *The Works of Samuel de Champlain*, (ed. H.P. Biggar), Toronto: University of Toronto Press, 1971, Vol. 1., p. 10.
8. Adair, E.R., "Evolution of Montreal Under the French Regime," *Canadian Historical Review*, January 1948, p. 26.
9. de la Horbe, Florian, *L'Incroyable Secret de Champlain*, Editions du Mont Pagnotte, Paris, 1958, p. 83. Author's translation.
10. Tompkins, *The Romance of Obelisks*, pp. 152–158 includes photographs of these Masonic ceremonies that opened the Washington Monument. The other "Masonic statistics" of this paragraph also derive from Tompkins.

Annotated Selected Bibliography

Bibliography

The following titles are by no means all of the sources consulted while researching *The Columbus Conspiracy*, but they will lead the interested reader more deeply into the "Columbus enigma" and into fascinating byways of history.

Baigent, Michael; Leigh, Richard; and Lincoln, Henry. *The Holy Blood and The Holy Grail*. London: Jonathan Cape, 1982. Also the sequels by these authors: *The Messianic Legacy* and *The Temple and the Lodge*.

Bradley, Michael. *Holy Grail Across the Atlantic*. Toronto: Hounslow Press, 1988.

Colón, Fernando. *Life of Colón*. London, 1881. The basic biography of Columbus upon which all later biographers and commentators have had to depend (unfortunately) because of the lack of other direct data.

Fuson, Robert H. (translator). *The Log of Christopher Columbus*. Camden (Maine): International Marine Publishing Company, 1987. A new and modern translation of the 1492 log (original lost) based mostly on the Las Cases copy and incorporating new "re-thinks" about Columbus, expert data concerning his ships and navigation, and fascinating "Appendices" pertaining to relevant aspects/enigmas of the 1492 voyage.

Hapgood, Charles. *Maps of the Ancient Sea-Kings*. Radnor:

Chilton Books, 1968. A scientific analysis of the portolan maps—including maps such as Columbus and Henry Sinclair apparently had, and used. There's a real mystery here.

Hermann, Paul. *Conquest By Man*. New York: Harper and Brothers, 1954. A still valuable presentation of human exploration from the earliest times until Columbus.

Madariaga, Salvador de. *Christopher Columbus*. New York: Unger, 1967. This immensely scholarly work may well rank as *the* modern biography of Columbus, the one that first questioned the "traditional" views of Samuel Eliot Morison with uncomfortable facts.

Pohl, Frederick J. *The New Columbus*. Rochester: Security-Dupont Press, 1986. A very modern new look at Columbus based partly on Madariaga's "re-think" of 21 years earlier.

—*Prince Henry Sinclair*. New York: Clarkson N. Potter, 1974. The story of Henry Sinclair and his 1398 voyage to Nova Scotia, an expedition inspired by the transatlantic adventures of a Shetland or Orkney fishing boat that must have taken place circa 1350–1370. One of the fishermen/castaways spent almost 13 years in the "New World," travelling from Nova Scotia to Mexico and back, before building a small boat to return to Scotland.

—*The Lost Discovery*. New York: W.W. Norton & Co., 1952. An early Pohl work about Irish, Viking, Welsh and "Celtiberian" voyages across the Atlantic before Columbus.

Wiesenthal, Simon. *Sails of Hope: The Secret Mission of Christopher Columbus*. New York: Christopher Columbus Publishing, 1979. A (naturally) "Jewish-oriented" interpretation of the once-hidden facts about Columbus, by the indefatigable Vienna Nazi-hunter. Based on Madariaga, a highly readable and probably distorted picture of the historical truth!

Michael Bradley was born in the southern United States and immigrated to Canada with his family in 1959. He was educated at Dalhousie University in Halifax, Nova Scotia where he won the Dennis and De Mille writing awards. His field of study was history and he was the only Dalhousie undergraduate ever to be offered a Doctorate study programme bypassing the Master's prerequisite. Bradley declined this offer to become a professional writer, but lectured at Dalhousie University's Centre for African studies on the subject of primitive and non-western navigation.

Bradley's eight non-fiction books have all dealt with history in its broadest sense, and have all offered provocative and controversial interpretations of known data: *The Cronos Complex* (1973); *The Iceman Inheritance* (1978); *The Black Discovery of America* (1981); *Crisis of Clarity* (1985); *Dawn Voyage* (1987); *Holy Grail Across The Atlantic* (1988); *More Than A Myth* (1989); and *The Columbus Conspiracy* (1991). His two novels *Imprint* and *The Mantouche Factor*, were reprinted in U.S. mass market paperback editions and were optioned for film adaptation.

Michael Bradley now lives in Toronto, continuing his research and writing on historical subjects, as well as writing screenplays and film treatments. His hobbies are sailing, boat design and navigation.